Fair Future

*Resource Conflicts, Security
and Global Justice*

A REPORT OF THE WUPPERTAL INSTITUTE
FOR CLIMATE, ENVIRONMENT AND ENERGY

EDITED BY
Wolfgang Sachs and Tilman Santarius

TRANSLATED BY
Patrick Camiller

Zed Books
LONDON & NEW YORK

Fernwood Publishing
HALIFAX& WINNIPEG

Originally published in 2005 as *Fair Future: Begrenzte Ressourcen und Globale Gerechtigkeit* by C. H. Beck, Munich
This English edition, *Fair Future: Resource Conflicts, Security and Global Justice* was first published in 2007

in Canada by Fernwood Publishing Co., Ltd
32 Oceanvista Lane, Site 2A, Box 5
Black Point, Nova Scotia, B0J 1B0
www.fernwoodpublishing.ca

and in the rest of the world by
Zed Books Ltd, 7 Cynthia Street, London N1 9JF, UK and
Room 400, 175 Fifth Avenue, New York, NY 10010, USA
www.zedbooks.co.uk

Cover designed by Andrew Corbett
Set in 10/13 pt Bembo by Long House, Cumbria, UK
Printed and bound Malta by Gutenberg Press Ltd

Distributed in the USA exclusively by Palgrave Macmillan, a division of
St Martin's Press, LLC,175 Fifth Avenue, New York, NY 10010

A catalogue record for this book is available from the British Library

US Cataloging-in-Publication Data is available from the Library of Congress

Library and Archives Canada Cataloguing in Publication
Sachs, Wolfgang
Fair future: resource conflicts, security and global justice / Wolfgang
Sachs, Tilman Santarius.
Includes bibliographical references and index.
ISBN 978-1-55266-231-1
1. Sustainable development. 2. Social justice. 3. Equality.
4. Globalization—Social aspects. 5. Globalization—Economic aspects.
I. Santarius, Tilman II. Title.
HN18.3.S33 2007 333.7 C2007-900431-8

ISBN 978-1-84277-728-2 hb (Zed Books)
ISBN 978-1-84277-729-9 pb (Zed Books)
ISBN 978-1-55266-231-1 pb (Fernwood Publishing)

Contents

Tables and Figures

Tables

Preface

Three years ago, when a group of researchers from the Wuppertal Institute began the preparatory work for this book, the initial question was: 'What kind of globalization is sustainable?' Globalization is not a new development, so much was clear. But how are the current phenomena and trends to be explained and evaluated? Globalization was and remains capable of being shaped for the future, but where should a start be made? There is much to suggest that the globalization of ecological crises and the conflicts over strategic raw materials such as oil, gas, water and precious metals have long been the driving force and harbinger of an 'age of resource wars' (Michael T. Klare). Is it therefore not amazing that so many critics of globalization 'forget' about ecology? Is the globalization of ecology not all the more pressing because a long-term transgression of the global limits of nature is possible only at the price of ecological crises and disasters?

When the German edition of this book was already at the printers, the greatest natural disaster in living memory – the tsunami in South-East Asia at the end of 2004 – took the lives of thousands upon thousands and caused untold suffering for millions more. Never before had the world been so tightly bound together in a common fate as in those days when the scale of the disaster was evident on everyone's television screen. It was also the greatest tourist tragedy of all time. Perhaps this was what made people in the affluent North feel not only humbled by the violence of nature but also responsive to the sufferings of the poor. For mixed in with the grief and the donations was a bitter realization that the mind-boggling scale of this natural worst-case scenario, if not its actual causes, was man-made. It is hard to live with the thought that there could have been tens of thousands fewer deaths if the poor in the Indian Ocean had had a tsunami early-warning system similar to the one available to the rich in the Pacific. It became clear to us that we rich, through our exaggerated use of resources, will bring about other man-made crises, and that the effects on the poor, though perhaps more insidious, may be no less terrible than those of a naturally caused tsunami.

This book deals with questions that have again and again succumbed to collective repression: global justice and the fate of the biosphere. We are immediately affected by budget deficits or unemployment rates, but climate change, poverty and struggles over resources appear much more remote. Are these global challenges too great? This book sets in relief what everyone suspects but no one feels responsible for. How, in future, will a much larger number of people be able to make a dignified living in a world of limited natural resources? This is the key issue of the twenty-first century.

Nor is it only an ethical issue: it also concerns our self-interest as citizens of this 'one world'. Resource conflicts are fuel for minor and major confrontations, which may set villages or whole countries ablaze. We need no reminding how saturated with oil is the recent history of the Middle East, the crisis region *par excellence*; close examination soon reveals how often a shortage of land or water has spurred religious and ethnic conflicts; and economic news reports inform us how strongly a populous country like China (and soon India) pushes beyond its frontiers for oil or copper, soya or wood. In short, resource hunger makes for a troubled world. No global security order can be constructed unless the goods of nature are handled sparingly. Therefore, strategies to increase resource productivity are also a policy of peace.

Nevertheless, it would be wrong to consider resource conflicts only as a security issue. In the end, it is a question of justice or injustice, power and powerlessness – and hence of fairness in the transnational space. The current trend to yoke together environmental and security issues is actually dangerous, for those who talk of security usually have in mind their own and not that of others. What matters, instead, is to understand conflict situations around the world not only as a security problem but also as a result of injustice. Not for nothing does the saying 'Peace is the work of justice' belong to the age-old fount of political wisdom.

But more justice in the world cannot be achieved by globalizing the Western model of prosperity: that costs too much money and too many resources, and it would completely ruin the biosphere. So, development stands at a crossroads: either most of the world remains excluded from prosperity, or the prosperity model is constructed in such a way that everyone can participate in it without making the planet inhospitable. It is a choice between global apartheid and global democracy. This book takes a stand for a democratic, cosmopolitan ecology. It shows that the transition to ecological models of prosperity is indispensable from the point of view of world democracy, and that it is both feasible and often economically useful. It is high time that the models of production and consumption which established the wealthy societies are made resource-light and naturally sustainable. For this purpose, a multitude of effective technologies, close-to-nature processes, shrewd organizational forms and quality-conscious lifestyles have been developed over the past thirty years – even if power interests and market pressures have up to now prevented a breakthrough. In the poorer countries, on the other hand, what counts is a start in the right direction. In this respect China is an ambivalent example, since its much-admired economic successes have more the character of a disaster in ecological terms. Ecological and technological 'leapfrogging' over resource-intensive forms of production could offer the chance to bring work and bread to more people, in both the South and the North, and at the same time to cultivate natural capital.

With *Fair Future*, the Wuppertal Institute would like to bring to public attention the issue of global resource justice. It has published a series of research reports on the Internet (www.wupperinst.org/globalisation), which come to a provisional conclusion with the present book. More than twenty people were involved for more than three years in the cross-disciplinary group ('What Kind of Globalization Is Sustainable?') and its discussions were the soil in which this book grew.

Chapter 1 introduces the reader to the problem of global justice today. Is it necessary to sacrifice ecology to have greater justice, or to sacrifice justice to have more ecology? What ways are there of escaping this tension?

Chapter 2 documents who corners how much of the world's finite environmental space. Where does all the oil, copper and grain actually go? A first glance at the geography of material flows makes it clear that the industrial countries use the lion's share of natural resources. But a second glance reveals some movement: newly emergent countries and classes in the South are making a strong push to increase their share.

Unequal appropriation of natural wealth is not a given. Chapter 3 looks at the instruments of power and illustrates how asymmetrical distribution of resources is guaranteed through geopolitics, trade distortions, investment power and governmental agreements. Inequality is not reprehensible in and of itself. But when does it turn into injustice?

Reflections about justice have traditionally focused on national societies. Chapter 4 investigates what might be called fairness in global society. It asks what is so disturbing about an unjust world and outlines four guiding principles of transnational resource justice: human rights, distributive justice, fair trade and compensation for harm done.

These lead in Chapter 5 to a first conclusion: namely, that the achievement of resource-light styles of prosperity is the first important contribution to greater resource justice. It begins to emerge that the industrial countries (and the North in the South) will have to make vigorous reductions in their claim on resources so that countries in the South can improve their position. Thus, both the North and the South are required to venture a leap into a solar economy, involving radical changes in energy use, transport and agriculture.

Chapter 6 shows that different models of production and consumption will require an architecture of global cooperation. So, the second major conclusion is that no sustainable globalization can be expected without a political shaping of transnational markets. Multilateral Environmental Agreements, the World Trade Organization and a legal framework for the activity of transnational corporations will have to ensure that, in the rising global society, human rights and the principles of fairness and environmental sustainability no longer yield precedence to the principle of economic growth.

Chapter 7 argues that Europe's mission in world politics lies precisely in the project of sustainable globalization. In view of its altogether fortunate recent history, it is now up to the old continent to enter the world arena on behalf of legality, cooperation and the common good, in alliance with other, especially developing countries. Europe will have a cosmopolitan vocation – or none at all.

A book can be unfashionable yet still explosive. The effort will have been worthwhile if this book manages to sharpen the reader's eye for the global in the local and to counter the collective repression of transnational responsibility.

I would like to express my heartfelt thanks to the Wuppertal team of authors under Wolfgang Sachs and Tilman Santarius for the work they put into this book.

Peter Hennicke
President of the Wuppertal Institute

1
Justice for Realists

What matters is not to predict the future but to prepare for it.

Pericles, fifth century BC

Unless all the signs are wrong, a circle that opened more than five hundred years ago is now closing. The Great Departure began on 3 August 1492, from the port of Palos on the Spanish Atlantic coast, when Christopher Columbus set sail with three ships and ninety men on a westward voyage to reach the continent that Marco Polo had crossed long before by an eastward land route. Turning his back on the inhabited world, he tackled the watery wastes; the prospect of gold and divine favour led him into the unknown. Columbus's voyage was the opening act in Europe's thrust outward into the world: it introduced, as we can now see, the linking-up of the planet in accordance with the model of the West. In the next few centuries, hosts of missionaries, soldiers, settlers and merchants followed in Columbus's wake, to convert, subjugate and civilize alien peoples – and to bring the modern world to them. The sailing ships eventually gave way to freighters and aircraft as vehicles of interconnection, and these in turn were compounded by telephones, TV programmes and electronic infrastructure. Now an arc stretches all the way from Columbus to CNN: the expansion of Euro-Atlantic civilization across all five continents. The Great Departure from Palos was the distant inauguration of a trans-epochal process which, by the end of the twentieth century, was being called 'globalization'.

But what was true for five hundred years is true no longer. Through all the ups and downs of history, a distributive law was at work whose operation is now suspended: the positive yield usually went to the North, and the pain and suffering to the South. Profits and power were concentrated in the Euro-Atlantic core, while exploitation and cultural erosion prevailed in the periphery. To be sure, benefits such as schools, hospitals and trade emerged in the South too, and even the North was not completely immune from the invasion of unsuitable plants or from economic decline as a result of colonial entanglements. But, on the whole, a secret magnetism ensured that the bitter fruits clustered at one pole and the positive results at the other. The North was scarcely ever plagued with the harsher consequences of global interconnectedness.

Now, however, the tide appears to be changing. For a decade or two the adverse results of interconnectedness have also been reaching the North. It is as if the old magnetism has lost its power to hold things in order: the negative effects are beginning to wander around, and the North can no longer protect itself from painful dislocations. It began with the economy: rising countries like Mexico or Malaysia, Korea or China have been blossoming into veritable rivals, luring jobs and investments away from the formerly unchallenged industrial heartlands; employment and growth – the key promises of prosperity – have come under pressure there. Next, human flows of refugees and economic migrants from the South and East have been pushing semi-legally, semi-illegally into the prosperity fortresses of the Euro-Atlantic zone. Nor can environmental threats be scared off by frontiers: if the rainforest in the South is cleared, if the diversity of plant and animal life disappears or the release of climate-altering gases grows, then this does damage to the biosphere, in the North as well. And, finally, dictatorships of various hues continually develop into a military threat even to the strongest of the rich countries. Megaweapons and missile systems can sometimes turn political dwarfs in the South into military giants, which may even inspire fear in the well-armed North. At the beginning was Columbus's Great Departure, and at the end are the threats returning from without. The circle that first opened with Europe's expansion is now closing.

Interconnected world

The threats arising from global integration are nothing new for the countries of Africa, Asia and Latin America. All too often they have had to watch themselves become poorer and more dependent with each new spurt of integration. In recent years, however, the North has been discovering its own vulnerability – an experience it had previously been spared. Profits can no longer be had at zero cost, as the societies of the North begin to be affected by the collateral damage of globalization.

The new vulnerability

In an analogy with 8 August 1942, we may think of 11 September 2001 as a symbolic date marking the end of the epoch of immunity: not because no threats had previously forced their way from outside into the fortified Euro-Atlantic space, but because the destruction of the World Trade Center may be read as a portent of the new vulnerability. Magnified by the truly hard-to-beat act of flying civil aircraft into skyscrapers, the attacks demonstrated that the American superpower could not defend itself against weak but determined enemies, even within its own frontiers. For the first time in its history – leaving aside Pearl Harbor – the United States came under attack from an external enemy on its own territory. This unparalleled offence should probably be seen as the source of the fear and grim determination that subsequently marked the American response.

The injury was further aggravated by the David versus Goliath constellation. All the attackers came from the Arab world, and so the attacks were seen by many observers as acts of the South against the North. Of course, it would be wrong to regard the terror in Manhattan as a torch wielded by the poor against the rich. But the terrorists did have roots in a milieu of impotence,[1] which binds together a considerable part of humanity through a sense of inferiority, or indeed abasement. This is based on a long history of humiliations – from the arrogant division of Arabia between Britain and France after the fall of the Ottoman empire, through the inability of Islam to find its way around in modernity, to the lasting wound of Palestine – and has produced a culture of rage and resentment from which terrorists draw their impetus and resonance. It is not so much poverty as outrage at the division of power in the world which is the fuel sustaining terrorism.

The one-sided vulnerability of the South has thus been replaced by a mutual vulnerability of all countries on earth. Of course, Washington may have the means to deploy its armed forces everywhere in the world and even to fight several wars at once, but it was not in a position to defend its own country, 'because interdependence permits the weak to use the forces of the strong jujitsu style to overcome them'.[2] So, in a quite precise sense, 9/11 has also become a symbol for the darker aspects of globalization. The cancellation of geographical remoteness means that not only good deeds but also threats to the world are bound more closely together. For globalization, in our contemporary experience, causes the world to shrink – indeed, its core dynamic is that spatial distance between different locations is reduced and even abolished by means of transport and communications systems. The list of those who benefit from this shrinking of space is not confined to the tourist who sets off for distant shores, the businessman who opens up far-flung markets, or the bank customer who can draw cash from a machine far from home. There is also the smuggler who can obtain air tickets, the economic criminal who shifts dirty money, or the terrorist who organizes simultaneous attacks. The world is becoming smaller, even for those who make life a misery. The new vulnerability of the powerful derives from this change in spatial conditions.

The zones of profit and loss are therefore moving closer together. The division of the world between rich and poor is becoming a threat, because disasters have recently been forcing their way into living rooms via the television screen, because the victims are standing outside the front door, and because economic differences across the world are moving jobs from one country to another. No ocean is distant enough, no wall high enough, to seal off even strong countries from economic crises, epidemics, ecological threats and stateless violence. The road joining the world together is no longer one-way, as it was for so long in the past, but increasingly triggers a contraflow of goods, people and emissions that disturbs the peace of the North. At the beginning of the twenty-first century, Western civilization is faced with the bitter realization that its enormous power over the world and nature by no means gives it comprehensive control. On the contrary, through spatial and temporal displacement, it generates effects that may destabilize even the core.

Levels of interdependence
In previous centuries, too, international links left their mark on humanity. One need only think of the spread to Europe of South American plants such as the potato or maize, or the slave trade in the triangle formed by Africa, England and the Caribbean/Americas, or the change in consumption habits in imperial Britain resulting from the imports of sugar, coffee and cocoa. Nevertheless, the last three decades have driven this process to new heights. In the period of globalization, networking has become not only spatially more extensive but also more intensive; it has accelerated and, at the same time, sown the effects associated with it more widely than in the past. Reciprocal contacts have given rise to a compact world, at three levels of interdependence: technical, political and symbolic.

At a technical level, the last few decades have witnessed the emergence of a spatially and temporally denser globe. Like every phase in the development of an interconnected world, globalization is marked by a distinctive system of conveyance. Whereas the colonial phase rested upon caravels, the imperial phase on steamships and the development phase on air transport, the basis of globalization is the digital infrastructure. Without the global network of glass-fibre cables, mobile radio aerials, relay stations and communications satellites, there would be no joining up of the world in real time and with zero distance. Electronic data flows make geographical distance inconsequential. Kilometres shrink in cyberspace to a mere mouse click, as the resistance of space itself is broken. And, since the costs of data transfer and processing have also plummeted, worldwide interaction has become the stuff of everyday life for the transnational middle class. Developers in various parts of the planet work simultaneously via the Internet on the construction of a new car model, while a mail-order customer in England may be put through to someone working at a call centre in India. In the constant, intensive and ultra-rapid flow of information bits around the earth is realized the abolition of distance and the assimilation of different times.

At a political level, the passage to transnational globality has shaken the organization of social coexistence on the basis of the national state. Globalization has brought with it the end of what has been called the 'Westphalian constellation'.[3] The European national state took shape in the wake of the Treaty of Westphalia of 1648, which established the principle of territorially related sovereignty. In its idealized version, the nation-state encompassed a territory in which there was one overarching system of government, one economy, one nation and one culture. Like a container, the nation-state held society in all its aspects within a clearly demarcated space.[4] At an international level, this unit then entered into friendly or hostile relations with other units of the same kind. Both dimensions – the sole responsibility of the national state for both internal order and external representation – were unified in the concept of sovereignty, even if it never completely corresponded to the reality. But, with globalization, these containers have broken open. Goods, money, information, images and people now flow across frontiers and lead to the formation of a great transnational space in which interactions occur as if national spaces did not exist. The earlier (never complete) integration of economy, government system and culture within a single territory has fallen apart, so that states are now one actor among others in the midst of transnational networks. Corporations or non-governmental organizations operate beyond the control of states and with scant regard for frontiers. States which once solemnly declared their independence are today better advised to proclaim their mutual dependence. Without supranational cooperation, they can have only a more and more limited influence in a transnational world.

At a symbolic level, on the other hand, a self-reflexive idea of the globe has taken shape, in which more and more people see their existence as linked to the totality. To be sure, there would be only a sketchy awareness of global interdependence if, in the years since the Apollo mission to the moon, the image of Earth as the blue planet had not been available. For the first time in history, the earth as a whole has become visible to human perception – albeit through the medium of photography.[5] The image has synoptic power: it allows us to survey oceans and continents and reveals wide fields of reciprocal relations previously hidden from our eyes. This photo of Earth from the cosmos is an indelible part of contemporary imagery; it adorns reports on the environment and television news programmes, T-shirts and commercials. Without it, the meaning of 'one earth' or 'one world' would scarcely be clear. Moreover, it produces a perception that places local action within a global framework. Does it not suggest to everyone that, with sufficiently fine resolution, he or she could be found somewhere in the picture? This visual blending of global and individual existence is in the course of shifting the cognitive and moral coordinates of self-perception. It suggests that the consequences of what we do may stretch to the other end of the planet, and that everyone is responsible in some degree. So, the use of a car on one occasion may be bound up with the greenhouse effect, and an aerosol can or plane trip may similarly participate in the global crossing of frontiers.

This allows us to draw a provisional balance sheet of globalization. The outline of a world society is emerging out of a multitude of national societies. Since communication links, division of labour and images of the world are now without frontiers, since mutual dependence has increased on the surface of the globe, the world is slowly, and certainly not everywhere, assuming the character of a society. Indeed, the emergence of a global society may count as the distinguishing feature of our times. It is by no means agreed, of course, what shape this global society will have. Its present situation is comparable to that of national societies a couple of centuries ago. Just as national states, having incorporated smaller entities such as cities or principalities, developed into kingdoms, democracies or dictatorships, so may global society assume very different shapes as it brings smaller entities such as transnational corporations, states and organizations of international civil society into a new constellation. It is still uncertain what its ideals and institutions will be, and who will be the winners and losers. That will be the outcome of ever new debates, competing utopias and lengthy power struggles. Such names as Seattle, Porto Alegre and Davos have become symbols for a trial of strength between different perspectives for global society. What kind of globalization do we want? That is the key question.

Preventive justice
Justice, as the Church Father Augustine once said, is what distinguishes a society from a band of robbers. In the age of globalization, the world is moving closer together; whether the result is global democracy or global despotism will be decided by the measure of justice. In the former case, the mutual dependence of states and nations will be taken into account through an order of transnational law and respect. In the latter, despite the fact of interdependence, stability will be produced through the supremacy of certain power groups. In other words, the shape of the world ahead depends on whether the rule of law or the law of the ruthless gains the upper hand. In the spring of 2003, quite a few observers feared that the United States, in waging war against Iraq without the cover of international law, had made a world-historical decision to switch the points in favour of the second alternative. In any event, global interconnections have made such a qualitative leap that nothing less than the future shape of the world order is at stake in the international disputes of the early twenty-first century.

Now, since the time of the Greek polis, there has been a succinct answer to the key question of what constitutes a successful society: namely, the rule of justice. For an unjust society does not correspond to human aspirations, nor is it able to survive for long. How much each person should have of the goods of society, how great should be his or her share of respect and rights: these questions must be settled equitably. However controversial the actual shape of justice has been throughout history, few have doubted the validity of the principle. Justice, it may be said, has the same significance for the social world as the ecosystem has for the natural and language for the cultural world: it is the backbone of a lasting order. Why should this be any different in global society?

The promoters of globalization certainly had in mind income from profits, increased power or even engineering achievements – but not exactly justice. Nevertheless, with its success, they have produced a world of reciprocal dependence in which the question of justice is unavoidable. For in a big wide world the question of justice is posed nationally, whereas in a world grown smaller it is posed transnationally. So long as people see themselves as mainly dependent on powers in their local or national area, they have no incentive to direct their demands for justice to targets beyond their own society. And, similarly, so long as people exercise power and influence only in their local or national arena, they have no special reason to gear their actions to the well-being of distant nations. But, if a mutual dependence without frontiers develops, both the demand and the responsibility for justice spread more widely. Then it is not surprising that, for example, the Ogoni of the Niger Delta accuse the Anglo-Dutch Shell corporation of human rights violations, that the island of Palau claims reparations from faraway Germany for the pillage of resources in colonial times, or that countries in the South are taking legal action to force an end to the dumping of agricultural products from the North on to their markets. It is also logical enough that the UN Secretary-General expects rich countries to make a stronger commitment to the war on want in the South. The struggle for justice takes place to a considerable extent on the global stage.

So long as one-sided relations of dependence were the rule on earth, justice was a matter for philanthropists; powerful societies did not have to fear any negative feedback if they failed to concern themselves with it. But, since mutual dependence has come on to the agenda, justice has been a matter for realists. As the attack on the World Trade Center made abundantly clear, the powerful are also affected by the sufferings that result from their actions in distant places. Unless all the evidence is deceptive, the threatening aspects of dependence mean that the world stands at a junction: one fork leads to a just order and the other to an order based on hegemonic domination. To put it more sharply, the powerful societies can opt either for preventive warfare or for preventive justice. In the years since 9/11, under the leadership of the United States, the military-cum-secret-service alternative has been to the fore. It is therefore to be feared that the infrastructure of electronic surveillance, preventive erosion of legality and international troop deployment, which has been built up as the answer to terrorism, will mutate into a trans-national defensive ring against crises of any kind. To counter this drift, it is necessary to develop the idea of preventive justice and to formulate a policy in accordance with it. The present book is intended as a contribution to this endeavour.

Divided world

Not much more than sixty years ago, in 1939, Colin Clark first compiled figures on the national income of a series of countries.[6] Since then, gross national product has established itself as an indicator that allows us to assign each nation a ranking in the Olympic tables of economic performance. This statistical operation has the undeniable advantage of producing a clear picture out of an unclear world. When looked at more closely, however, it rests upon the prejudiced view that a single yardstick can be applied to all cultures, and that the quality of a civilization is discernible in the level of its national income. Each country's degree of development can then be expressed in terms of whether it is rising or falling on the scale. Only the triumph of the economic world-view made possible this now conventional mode of classification. Once the very different ways of life from Réunion to Rajasthan had been reduced to a hierarchy of aggregated income figures, the enormous gap between 'rich' and 'poor' countries suddenly appeared before our eyes. Unequal economic strength has ever since been what divides the world into champions and also-rans, just as income growth now counts as the gilded route along which a society can flourish and prosper.

This global model of development gave rise to a monumental historical promise that, sooner or later, every nation would be able to close the gap with the rich and to share in the fruits of economic civilization.[7] This promise united two underlying interests: the interest of the North in extending its economic arena, and the interest of the South in finally gaining recognition and justice. The North wagered on expansion, the South on the race to catch up. Within a few decades the baneful division of the world inherited from colonialism was supposed to be reduced, if not completely overcome. Greater equality among nations: this was the horizon that drove the history of North–South relations in the second half of the twentieth century.

The gap between nations
But the hope was not fulfilled. This becomes clear if we measure the field of inequality today. A common method of representing inequality

within a society establishes the extent to which a given distribution of income deviates from the condition of perfect equality. In the so-called Gini coefficient, the degree of inequality in a society is measured on a scale from 0 (everyone has the same income) to 1 (one person has all the income). The higher the coefficient, then, the more marked is the polarization between rich and poor. If this is applied to global society, with the help of *per capita* gross national product, we get the trend represented in Figure 1.1 for the period from 1950 to 1998.

The spread of inequality between countries was lowest at the beginning of the years in question. Then came a period of slight and uneven increase until approximately 1978, when the gap between rich and poor began to widen strongly and constantly – altogether by nearly 20 per cent. The reason for this almost continual growth of inequality is not hard to identify. Contrary to the expectation in the countries of the South that they would finally close the gap, the rich countries grew faster than Latin America and Africa (though not Asia) throughout the half-century; both continents experienced the trend more as the rich drawing further ahead than the poor catching up. The hope that integration into the world economy would bring superior growth to poor countries thus turned out to be wishful thinking. Moreover – again contrary to a widespread expectation – growth rates during the period of globalization from the end of the 1970s were lower than during the previous twenty years for every region of the world.[8] All in all, if we compare the two periods, globalization halved the growth rate, with the relative lag especially pronounced in Latin America and Africa. Hence the field of runners in the world economic arena grew further apart during the globalization years.

To measure the ensuing inequality, it is revealing to compare conditions at global and national level. For the world, understood as a collection of states, exhibits a degree of inequality similar to that experienced internally by nations occupying the highest rung of wealth. Thus, in 1998 the Gini coefficient for the worldwide community of states was just under 0.54,[9] which clearly distinguishes it from individual countries such as Italy (0.36) or South Korea (0.32) but places it almost in the same league as Brazil (0.59) and South Africa (0.59).[10] Anyone who finds conditions in Brazil or South Africa unacceptable can feel no different about the world as a whole. In the stark spread of power and privileges, the fact is that the economic division of the world is a decisive hurdle in the way of global society.

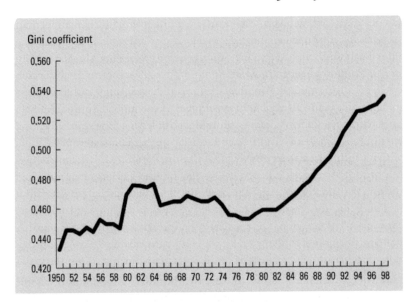

Figure 1.1 Unweighted international inequality by Gini coefficients (1950–98). Gini coefficients are a way of measuring inequality within a society. Especially since the mid-1980s, inequality among the countries of the world, measured by the relationship between their *per capita* incomes, has sharply increased. Source: Milanovic 2002: 27.

Nevertheless, these figures do not tell the whole truth, as the statistical representation of inequality is full of snares. The rising polarization between rich and poor countries is only one aspect of the inequality dynamic at world level; the other is that all kinds of things are moving within the polarized field. A focus on inequality between nations easily leads to an optical illusion, since it is not appropriate to consider nations as individual entities of the same value. So, in the calculation of international Gini coefficients, population size is not a relevant factor – which means that billion-plus China and India are treated in exactly the same way as Sri Lanka or Nepal. Yet, in the last two decades, China and to a lesser extent India have made great leaps forward in terms of economic growth, with the former's *per capita* income growing at an average of 8 to 10 per cent and the latter's at an average of 5 to 7 per cent. In fact, if one gives the same weight to populations of the same size, rather than to all nations as such, the trend towards greater inequality disappears.[11] Or rather, if GNP is weighted by population size, the trend is actually reversed: inequality between national populations has been decreasing since roughly 1980 and reached its lowest point for half a century in the 1990s (Figure 1.2).

We seem to be faced with the bewildering conclusion that whether global inequality is rising or falling depends on the statistical spectacles one wears. There are good grounds for both ways of looking at things: the unweighted GNP values give information about the relations among nations, and the weighted ones about the relations among national populations. The hopeful tendency in the latter is due above all to China: no other country has registered such a degree of simultaneous growth in both population and income. No wonder that friends and critics of globalization continually get bogged down in arguments about inequality, for statistically there is evidence for both a negative and a positive result. Whereas its critics complain of a widening income divide between countries, its friends point to the fact that hundreds of millions of people with rising incomes in China and India will soon be drawing several more hundreds of millions along with them.

But, even if one keeps in view the inequality among nations, there can be no doubt that South Korea and Taiwan, and also Mexico, China and India, are narrowing the gap with the rich countries. A group of 10–15 countries is in the throes of 'catching-up' development – even if it remains true that China and India, for example, despite their progress in growth, would have to keep it up for another hundred years or so to reach even the existing income level of the United States.[12] The situation looks different, however, for the great majority of countries. The gap with the industrial countries has increased a little in the case of Latin America, but has shot up for sub-Saharan Africa and the least-developed countries in general.[13] Africa and parts of Asia are a very long way from catching up – on the contrary, they are falling further and further behind. In other words, since approximately 1970, when all the countries in the South were in roughly the same *per capita* income bracket, the field has been redrawn through both upward and downward movements. The once relatively homogeneous group of countries has undergone dramatic polarization, as some have spurted ahead and left the others standing.

So, the globalization era has had a Janus face: looking hopefully to the future as many countries have joined the global growth economy, looking back despairingly as many others have been excluded from it. It is therefore mistaken to speak without qualification of world economic

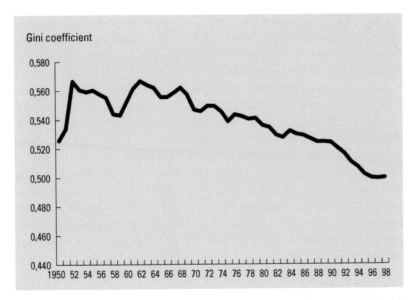

Figure 1.2 International inequality by Gini coefficients, weighted according to size of population (1950–98). Such weighting shows a marked rise in international inequality since the 1970s. Source: Milanovic 2002: 69.

integration in the wake of globalization; the truth is that a process of global fragmentation can be observed.[14] Alongside the industrial countries, where the control centres of the world economy are located, a number of strongly rising economies have become production areas for hardware and software, while a peripheral zone contains the majority of the world, excluded from the global economy. This includes both whole countries, especially in Africa but also in Latin America and Asia, and many regions within the emergent economies, too. Looking back at the high hopes of the post-war decades, one is forced to conclude that the expectations of convergence in the development of nations have been proved wrong. The world is developing, but in two opposite directions.

Internal inequality
As statisticians see it, overall economic inequality among people in the world depends on two factors: the scale of inequality among countries and within countries. If, to use a thought experiment, all nations were similarly situated in terms of income, there would still be inequality

among people, but its scale would be determined only by the structures of distribution within individual countries. Conversely, if all nations had achieved income equality within their borders, the scale of inequality in the world would depend purely on the inequality among nations. What would follow if all countries had the same average income? A lot would follow – for statisticians explain a good three-quarters of the variation among people by the variation among nations.[15] The population-weighted income gap between, say, the United States and India is considerably larger than that between Manhattan and the Bronx, or between Bombay's Malabar Hill and the Dharavi Slum. Greater equality of income among countries is therefore still the royal road to global justice in relation to incomes. Yet inequality within societies does still play an important role, because the comparative framework in people's experience continues to be provided first and foremost by their own society.

Clearly some societies are more unequal than others. Someone living in South Africa is exposed to a much greater discrepancy between rich and poor than is a resident of South Korea. One useful typology of societies classifies them according to the shares of total income taken by the richest 20 per cent, the middle 40 per cent and the poorest 40 per cent of the population.[16] At one end of the scale are the extremely polarized countries, where this ratio is around 60:30:10 – that is, where the richest 20 per cent draw roughly 60 per cent, the middle classes roughly 30 per cent, and the poorest 40 per cent roughly 10 per cent of the total income. Countries such as Brazil, Chile, Mexico, South Africa, Botswana, Zimbabwe, Kenya and Thailand fall into this category. At the other end of the scale are the least polarized societies, where the typical ratio is 40:40:20. These include most industrial countries with the exception of the United States, but also Ghana, India, Indonesia, Taiwan, South Korea and Egypt. In between, the moderately polarized countries have an inequality ratio in the region of 50:35:15; these include, apart from the USA, the majority of countries in the South, from Honduras to Vietnam, and from Peru to Nigeria. Roughly speaking, the extremely polarized group is mainly in South America and Africa, while the least polarized is to be found more in Europe and Asia.

Looking back over the last few decades, one is struck more by the stability of income relations than by the changes within them. Like cliffs in the surf, the relations of inequality have defied the recurrent waves of development, growth and globalization. A lessening of inequality has been the exception. If there have been changes at all, they have tended more to involve a sharpening of inequality. Thus, in the period from 1980 to 2000, out of a total of 73 countries, inequality increased in 48 and decreased in only nine.[17] This means that the globalization of markets has been associated with both negative and positive changes in the structure of inequality, even if increased polarization has been visible far more often. Above all in the countries of the South (apart from Taiwan), there has been no lasting diminution of inequality during the last two decades. In countries such as China, Chile, Colombia or Mexico, the spread of inequality (expressed in Gini coefficients) has increased, whereas it has remained the same in South Korea, Indonesia, the Philippines, India and Brazil.[18] Where it has really exploded is in the former Communist countries: the societies in Russia, Poland and Bulgaria (though not Hungary since 1994) split apart at a breathtaking rate in the course of the 1990s. In sum, we may say that economic globalization scarcely correlates with a decline in international inequality, but rather with its deepening or, in the best of cases, with stagnation.

Harder to grasp are the mental shifts that have accompanied the globalization of economics and culture. The horizon of wishes and hopes has been growing wider. For the awareness of inequality mainly depends on the reference group against which people measure their own situation. If no other group carries any weight – which is the case in many cultures – then even the poor see no reason to classify themselves as underprivileged. But, if the comparative horizon shifts to reference groups living in distant parts or much further up the social ladder, then the perception of one's own deficit grows sharper and triggers either pressing desires or a strong sense of frustration. Earlier theorists of development called this the 'revolution of rising expectations'. Only with globalization does it really break through worldwide and among all groups, both masses and elites. More and more people compare themselves no longer with their neighbours but with the possessions and lifestyles of distant groups. Elites, too, rebuild their expectations, comparing themselves no longer with the small privileged layers in their own country but with those in rich countries who are still more favoured. This widening of the comparative horizon to all levels of the social hierarchy works in two ways: as a fuel for hopes and demands, by encouraging people to place the crossbar higher; and as an explosive, if rising expectations diverge too much from the limited possibilities of realization and create a chronic sense of getting less than one's fair share.

The fate of many a society in the coming decades will depend on the direction in which this dynamic of inequality develops.

Drift of world poverty

Fundamental issues often bring about sharp controversies. This is also true of the question as to how world poverty will develop. Few questions go so close to the nerve of the prevailing world order; few have unleashed such persistent debates in the international public. Quite opposite answers can be heard, and it has become difficult to find clarity amid the jungle of different assumptions, investigative methods and interests. For example, a pamphlet published by the International Forum on Globalization asks: 'Does globalization help the poor?' – and ends with a confident 'No'.[19] The *Economist*, considering in detail the issue of who gains from globalization, gives an equally confident answer: the poor.[20] Some complain about globalization while others praise it, but the surprising thing is that the two sides dispute even the evidence about poverty. There is no agreement as to whether global poverty is increasing or decreasing, quite apart from the role played in it by globalization.[21] So, to use a more cautious formulation, has the lot of the poor improved during the period of globalization?

The answer is a cautious 'yes', followed by a salvo of 'buts'. If we take the World Bank's definition of poverty as a life with an income below US$360 a year (one dollar or less per day), then we can say that between 1980 and 2001 the number of people living below this threshold fell by 390 million – from 1,481 million to 1,092 million.[22] In view of the rising population throughout the period, this should be seen as a huge success. Moreover, the proportion of the poor in the global population has also declined: whereas in 1981 it still stood at 40.4 per cent, it had fallen by 2001 to 21.1 per cent.[23] If we raise the poverty line to two dollars a day, then the proportion of the world's population earning less than that sum declined over the same period from 66.7 per cent to 52.9 per cent. However, these reported successes rest mainly on the integration of several hundred million people into China's and, to a lesser extent, India's growth economy. Outside China, the number of extremely poor people rose during this period from 840 million to 890 million.[24] The number of income-poor scarcely changed proportionately in Latin America and actually increased in sub-Saharan Africa as well as Eastern Europe and Central Asia. Outside China and India, then, more people live in extreme poverty today than twenty years ago – and certainly more than ever in the past. Yet the World Bank and other champions of progress see things in the rosy morning light of economic globalization; their optimism that open markets and growth have set the world on the right path is rooted in the belief that a third of the world's population (in China and India) has started to move and that in principle the same model can be repeated in other regions.

Sceptics pour water into the wine of the optimists. Casting doubt on the definition of the poverty threshold, they argue that it is wrong to believe that people classified as poor are those who in their own country have the daily equivalent of one dollar at their disposal. For the counterpart is defined not by the rate of currency exchange but by purchasing power. In other words, in the case of Bangladesh or Paraguay someone is counted as absolutely poor only if their situation is like that of a poor person in the United States who earns one dollar a day there. And that, to put it bluntly, is brutally poor. Furthermore, the method by which purchasing power parity is ascertained results in the inclusion of too few people in the category of extreme poverty;[25] the poverty threshold of one dollar of purchasing power equivalent therefore plays down the extent of poverty. It also contradicts the general agreement to omit any component of relative disadvantage in favour of the absolute dollar threshold in the calculation of poverty, since the one-dollar poor are distinctly worse off in a developing economy than in a country with a low total income. If one takes this into account and sets the poverty threshold at a third of average spending in a society, then the proportion of the extremely poor increases by 8 to 10 per cent – that is, to 50.1 per cent in 1981 and 28.1 per cent in 2001.[26] A statistical representation of poverty in accordance with World Bank conventions therefore underestimates the true extent of poverty in the world.

Highly aggregated numerical sequences and the vagaries of global poverty data may also conceal qualitatively opposite realities: the fact that some are falling while others may be rising, or that there may be a loss of prosperity along with monetary gain. If income statistics show successful figures, this makes it tempting to assume that everything else remains unchanged. For the balance sheet contains only profits and no losses. What must those give up who now earn more than one dollar a day? It is by no means the case that the hidden costs of income growth among the poor are unknown, only that they cannot be incorporated into a cost curve projection. The blind spot includes the fact that monetary income usually favours men and leaves women worse off; or that whole occupational groups such as weavers or fishermen may lose their livelihood; or that someone earning one dollar a day often migrates to the city and can no longer rely on family networks or the free goods of nature. Poverty statistics also mould themselves to a tacit watchword: anything that cannot be put in monetary terms does not happen. Critics of globalization therefore like to bring up particular cases of qualitative impoverishment to counter the overall statistics – and they are right to do so. The contradiction is thus to some extent dispelled: the champions of globalization and the sceptics are each right in their way; they cultivate two different aspects of the truth.

The focus on poverty easily directs our attention away from inequality. The two dimensions certainly do not coincide with each other. Poverty is an absolute concept and contains that part of the population which lives below a defined threshold. Inequality, on the other hand, is a relative concept and refers to the spread in the distribution of income. If poverty declines thanks to economic growth, it is by no means agreed what this means for inequality within a society. It all depends on how the growth is distributed. Accordingly, a fall in poverty may go together with less inequality but also with the same or higher levels of inequality. If the profits of growth are mainly siphoned off by the upper and middle classes, the fall in poverty is not as great as it might have been if the opportunities resulting from growth had been taken up. This is precisely what is happening in the two showpiece countries: China and India. Protracted economic growth has reduced poverty at the same time that it has increased inequality.[27] It has created a less impoverished but more hierarchical society. In both countries, the differences in income between social classes and between the rural and urban population have been increasing. What is more, the difference between regions has widened considerably. In China a gulf has been opening between the eastern coastal and the western mountainous regions, as has the gulf between India's southwestern and northeastern states. It would seem from the evidence that, in both China and India, growth has primarily strengthened the economic power of already privileged classes and regions, while in the process raising many people above the poverty threshold. China and India are supposed to be examples for the struggle against poverty in the twentieth-first century, but they do not herald a very bright future for distributive justice. The signs are more that a 'world without poverty' – to quote the World Bank slogan – can still be a thoroughly unequal world.

Finite world

If there was one book in the twentieth century that marked a new era, it was the bestseller *Limits to Growth* which first appeared in 1972.[28] All at once the post-war faith in progress was hit by the suspicion that the finite character of the biosphere might impose limits to economic growth. Mutually reinforcing changes thus occurred at the levels of experience, public attitudes and scientific theory, eventually producing a sudden leap in the social learning process. The earth, contrary to the basic assumptions of economic thinking at the time, was recognized as a finite system.

What are limits?

In the first few years after *Limits to Growth*, the finite natural basis for human economic activity was seen mainly as a question of finite resources. Like some earlier figures in classical political economy – from Thomas Malthus through John Stuart Mill to William S. Jevons – the authors of *Limits to Growth* focused on how, within just a few decades, the depletion of mineral, energy and agricultural resources could undermine the foundations of the economy. In other words, they conceived of nature as a storehouse of means of production, which was visibly shrinking as more and more was taken from it at an ever-faster rate. This view of things had an initial impact because it was clear that non-renewable resources, as the name suggests, would come to an end sooner or later under conditions of high demand; the only question was: when? It is precisely this which has given rise to repeated controversy in the last few decades, since no firm predictions are available. When oil or mineral supplies run out will also depend on the reaction of the economy to likely shortages ahead, even if – as the 'father' of ecological economics, Nicholas Georgescu-Roegen, never tired of emphasizing[29] – there can be no doubting the long-term entropic character of the conversion of fossil reserves. Greater elasticity of the economic system may postpone the time of exhaustion – new technologies may to some extent replace resources, higher prices may dampen demand, and a shift to services may reduce the consumption of raw materials per unit of value creation – but it will not be able to eliminate the prospect altogether. Thus, the invention of chemical agriculture has shaken Malthus's predictions, and the development of the service economy has toned down the gloomiest forecasts of the limits to growth. Unfortunately, however, those warning of ecological disaster repeatedly fall into the trap of taking the present state or trends of technology and the economic structure and projecting them into the future. If the predicted collapse then fails to take place, the economic smooth-talkers feel in a stronger position and a relieved public honours them as 'eco-optimists'. This debate has recurred at regular intervals in the last few decades – from the dispute between Paul Ehrlich and Julian Simon in the United States to the recent controversies in Europe regarding Björn Lomborg. The main conclusion seems to be that it is easy to say that limits will be reached, but difficult to say *when*. It might be possible to get by with this dilemma – if nature were no more than a stock of materials for human economic activity. But nature is by no means only a store of raw materials: it is a basis for life, or rather *the* basis for life. Limits to growth may thus appear not only from the side of resource availability but also from that of the sustainability of life. The silent effect of nature on the progress of people and societies (including their economy) is all too easy to overlook. However, the biosphere and the worldwide flora and fauna are nothing other than the relatively thin cover of the globe, which in the interplay of ecosystems and organisms creates the preconditions of life. The supply of water, foodstuffs and other substances necessary for human and other life is only one part of this; the other is the maintenance of bio-geo-chemical cycles, both global and local, which assure the web of life. Whether through photosynthesis for the nourishment of plants or insects for the pollination of flowers, through ocean currents for the fertility of expanses of land or air pressure for the conveyance of huge masses of water, nature time and time again, at no cost, looks after the founts of all biological existence.[30] A forest, for example, holds in stock cubic metres of timber that can be sold for the production of paper. Loss of the forest would entail costs both for its owner and for the timber clients, and so excessive use of the resource becomes an economic problem. Already before financial costs become evident, however, the forest begins to lose its ability to play a part in reproducing the tissue of life. Less water is filtered and retained, streams become scantier during drought and more violent during rain, the soil erodes more easily, game and then birds disappear, and one fewer means is available to purify the air. Life-supporting ecosystems thin out if they are overused or so loaded with harmful chemicals that they are unable to regenerate. This kind of limit is especially applicable to biological resources; the economy is not damaged at first, but large or small areas of nature are rendered less hospitable to the diversity of life – including human beings.

The distinction between limits to resource availability and limits to the strain on ecosystems allows us to see more clearly what is at stake in the dispute between those who stand for 'weak' and those who stand for 'strong' sustainability.[31] The former argue that there is no objection to the using up of nature so long as what is lost is turned into greater technical, human or financial capital. The latter maintain that there are limits to the replacement of nature by capital, and that we are sawing off the branch on which we sit. In relation to dwindling resources, one might think that the natural loss will be offset by a gain in prosperity; it makes some sense there to speak of 'weak sustainability', as environmental economists do. But, with regard to the dwindling conditions for life, no gain in prosperity can make up for that kind of loss. Here it is a question of 'strong sustainability', which means that the limits to growth can in no way be replaced by the growth of limits.

It is therefore misleading to think of limits to growth as a clear line beyond which there is suddenly disaster, as in the familiar image of a train hurtling towards the precipice, or of an organism suddenly breaking down under ever-greater strain. Both metaphors assume that catastrophic changes affecting everyone will suddenly occur in the near future – which would be the case in only a few scenarios, such as the diversion of the Gulf Stream. More often, however, unpleasant changes take place more slowly, with medium intensity and socially uneven effects. Their course is more linear, as in the 60 per cent melting of the Alpine glacier mass over the last one hundred and fifty years. An appropriate metaphor might be that of a fabric that is gradually worn down: first a couple of threads come loose almost without being noticed, but then the function and beauty of the cloth is gradually impaired, until it shows holes and tears or even starts to come apart.[32] It is advisable to picture the transgression of the limits to growth as first such a series of cumulative processes and only then sudden moments of change.

Natural systems are thought of as being in constant change. For this reason, too, limits are hard to define. In modern ecological theory, the solidity of the fabric of life is called the 'resilience of ecosystems' – that is, their capacity for resistance. In this perspective the normal state of ecosystems, in all orders of magnitude, is not a stable equilibrium. Rather, they are in a state of motion and automatically adapt to changing conditions, especially to shocks and disturbances coming from outside. The resilience of ecosystems therefore consists in their ability to handle such shocks, to recover and return to a balanced flow.[33] Where such a mobile equilibrium prevails, it is difficult to set firm limits to the resilience of ecosystems; there are no clear-cut breaks. Load limits on nature are therefore better thought of as corridors of elasticity. Still, if the disturbances become too great, the ability to handle them breaks down and the ecosystem is transformed into an unchanging state.

Limits are thus dynamic and cannot be defined with any assurance – but they are none the less real for that. The load-bearing capacities of ecosystems – and by extension of the biosphere – are not static or marked by simple causal relations. They are dependent on two constantly changing conditions: on the one hand, the stress and strain bound up with production and consumption and their associated technologies; on the other hand, the elasticity of the interplay between a-biotic and biotic factors within an ecosystem.[34] Since, however, neither the effects of human innovation nor those of biological evolution can be laid down in advance, the limits of carrying capacity cannot be determined with any assurance either. In the nature of things, they are unknowable. But the uncertainty of knowledge does not do away with the reality of the limits. Here, above all, the truism holds that absence of proof is not to be confused with proof of absence. A political strategy for handling environmental limits already follows from this insight. Where knowledge is absent, the rational strategy is not to wait for proof but to take precautions.

Warning signs of overload
Some developments on the planet permit no other conclusion than that humanity, for the past two centuries, has been overstretching the elasticity of global ecosystems. Even a brief glance at the stock of certain resources illustrates the depth of the trail etched into the biosphere by human economic activity.

Global resource and environment trends

Environmental indicator	Trend
Atmosphere	In the last hundred years the global climate has warmed by 0.6 to 0.7 degrees Celsius. Depending on developments, scenarios point to an increase of 1.4 to 5.8 degrees in average global

temperature by the end of this century. In the twentieth century, the temperature of the northern hemisphere rose more steeply than at any time in the past thousand years; the 1990s were probably the warmest decade of the millennium. True, the average temperature is subject to natural oscillations; but there is strong evidence that global warming in the past fifty years has been due mainly to human activities.[35]

Wetlands

Wetlands are extremely important for the preservation of biological diversity and the hydrologic balance. Since 1900 more than a half of the world's wetlands have been lost.[36]

Biological diversity

Biological diversity is not only important because of the inherent value of each species; it is also a basic prerequisite for the stability of the ecosystems on which human beings depend. But on both sea and land, species loss has sharply increased throughout the world; the earth is currently in the sixth-largest extinction period in its history, but the first actually brought about by one biological species: homo sapiens.[37] The reasons for this are the annihilation and ecological degradation of biotopes, the overuse and pollution of ecosystems, the introduction of species that drive out existing ones, and global warming.

Soil and land

It is estimated that 50 per cent of the global land surface has been directly changed by human influence, with consequences especially for species diversity, soil structure, nutrient cycles and climate.[38] Some 23 per cent of usable land surface has undergone such extensive degradation that its productivity is declining. One important factor is soil erosion; human activity has caused erosion affecting 15 per cent of the world's soil (an area larger than the USA and Mexico combined).[39]

Water

More than half of accessible freshwater is used for human purposes, 70 per cent of it for agriculture (mostly irrigation).[40] Huge underground freshwater deposits formed over thousands of years are being whittled down. In the United States, for example, the Ogallala acquifer has been so overused for the irrigation of cornfields that 40 per cent of the irrigated areas might become wasteland over the next 20 years. Similar situations exist in Nigeria and the Middle East.

Forest

In the course of human history, the area of forest has fallen from 6 billion to 3.9 billion hectares. In 29 countries, more than 90 per cent of forest has been lost since the sixteenth century. In the 1990s the world's forest declined by 4.2 per cent, mainly in the South, not counting reforestation.[41] Apart from the felling of trees, the death of forest is also a factor. In European forests, in 2001, one fifth of the tree crowns under investigation had suffered medium to severe damage.[42]

Fishing grounds

Overuse of fish stocks is endangering the ecological equilibrium of coastal ecosystems and oceans. According to the UN Food and Agriculture Organization, more than one quarter of all fish stocks are currently exhausted or threatened with exhaustion as a result of overfishing, and a further 50 per cent are being fished to the biological limit.[43] It is estimated that global fish stocks nearly halved between the beginning of the 1970s and the end of the 1990s.

At a very general level, the effects of material flows due to human activity are already greater in scale than some of the cycles sustained by

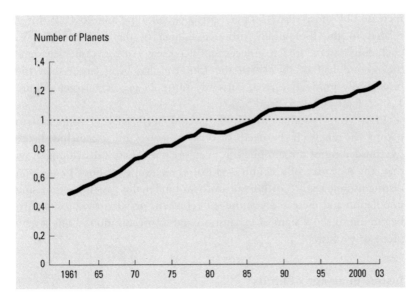

Figure 1.3 Global ecological footprint (1961–2003). The ecological footprint of humanity was two and a half times larger in 2003 than in 1961. Currently, each year it exceeds the earth's biological capacity by approximately 20 per cent. This constant overburdening of the planet is possible only for a limited time. Source: WWF 2006

nature. In other words, the activities of the technosphere already exceed those of the ecosphere; human activities affect the face of the earth at the same time as, and already more than, natural forces do. Furthermore, changes caused by man occur at a speed that is often greater than changes in nature. Especially in the twentieth century, pressure on the fossil and the biotic stock increased in a way never before seen in history.[44]

One attempt to express overuse of the biosphere in a single indicator is the so-called 'ecological footprint'.[45] Each country has its own footprint, which describes the total area required to build its infrastructure, to produce food and other goods and services, and to absorb emissions from the consumption of fossil fuels. If all the strains on the biosphere — apart from environmental pollution — are added up and converted into area magnitudes, it is possible to quantify the ecological footprint that humans leave on the planet. In the past forty years this indicator has changed dramatically: the global ecological footprint increased by more than 150 per cent between 1960 and 2000. If this is related to the biologically productive area of the world – that is, excluding deserts, frozen surfaces and deep seas – it turns out that since the second half of the 1980s the footprint has been larger than the biologically productive area, currently some 25 per cent larger (Figure 1.3; cf. Figures 2.4, 5.2 and 5.3).[46]

Each year, in other words, the world needs more resources than nature can renew. If the needs of other creatures are also included, the overburdening of the biosphere is even greater. These calculations show that, for a quarter of a century, global ecological overshoot has been a distinguishing feature of human history. Under the pressure of a rising population and increased volumes of economic activity, the biosphere is beginning to show signs of exhaustion and disorganization. Truly a new phase of evolution!

Justice in an age of limits

It was in October 1926 that Mohandas Gandhi formulated one of the insights which make his thought carry into the twenty-first century. In one of his columns for *Young India*, the mouthpiece of the Indian independence movement, he wrote: 'God forbid that India should ever take to industrialization after the manner of the West. The economic imperialism of a single tiny island kingdom (England) is today keeping the world in chains. If an entire nation of 300 million took to similar economic exploitation, it would strip the world bare like locusts.' Some eighty years later this statement has lost none of its relevance. Indeed, its importance has increased, since today there are no longer 300 million but 1,000 million setting out to imitate Britain. Gandhi suspected that it would not be possible for India, let alone China or Indonesia, to emulate the level of economic exploitation imposed by the British model. A multiplication of Britain would be a multiplication of colonial pillage directed inwards, to such an extent that the planet's protective cover would be affected. The bio-physical limits to the spread of industrial civilization, which became recognizable in the late 1930s, have impressively confirmed Gandhi's intuition.

Threefold ecological justice
It is now apparent that ecology concerns itself with bio-physical limits. But what it has to do with justice is not so clear. In what sense can

environmentalism be thought of as a question of justice? After all, conservationists and environmental researchers get by often enough without pausing to think about justice. Although there is a growing awareness that ecological limits pose new issues of justice, until now the emphasis has mainly been on justice between creatures or generations, and very little on justice between countries or social classes.

Biosphere justice may be regarded as the first form of environmental justice. Every living thing is part of the biosphere. Life is not strewn here and there, but exists as a coherent whole. All that crawls and flies, all that walks on earth and passes away, whether in Patagonia or Pennsylvania, is joined up in the common production of the thin cover of life which encircles the planet. This is the basis for our use of concepts such as justice to refer to relations between humans and other living creatures. For life proves to be a jointly organized event including the amoeba and the baobab tree, the worm and the whale. Human creatures behave no differently: even if they dispose of language and culture, they do not stand in opposition to nature; they are part of the community of life on earth. Nature is not so much an environment, a surrounding world, as a world shared with others.[47] In this perspective, trees and rivers, insects and mammals, the whole circle of earth's creatures have their rights.[48] These rights are not absolute for any creature, nor are they the prerogative of human beings. People have the right to nourishment, to clothing, to a space in which to live, to culture. But they have no right to destroy the living space of other creatures, to bring a lake to the point of biological collapse, or to wreak havoc with the climate. Within the community of the biosphere, human claims to property and power are restricted by the rights of other living things. From the point of view of biosphere justice, then, it is a question of (to quote the first principle of the Earth Charter) recognizing 'that all beings are interdependent and every form of life has value regardless of its worth to human beings'.[49]

The concept of inter-generational justice, on the other hand, focuses on the relationship between people living today and future generations. It extends the principle of fairness along the temporal axis and thereby widens the circle of the human community. To meet present needs without threatening the satisfaction of future generations' needs: this was the credo of the Brundtland Commission, which laid the foundation stone for the period in the 1990s when 'sustainable development' was on everyone's lips.[50] Whereas posterity had previously been regarded as undeserving beneficiaries of inexorable progress, they were now seen as its potential victims. Nuclear power, climate change, species loss and population increase may be cited as examples of potential colonization of the future by the present. But to what extent do those who come before have the right to fix the opportunities available to those who come after? The answer is: reciprocity. Those born now owe to posterity what they themselves have received from previous generations. Just as parents are expected to pass on free to their children what they owed to their own parents, so are generations under an obligation to observe the rule of reciprocity. For this reason, people alive today cannot be considered in the full sense as owners of the earth's natural assets; rather, they are trustees of a legacy and have to hand it over undiminished to those who come after them, as it was left to them by those who had come before.[51]

Nevertheless, the above two concepts of ecological justice have a blind spot: namely, human institutions and the relations among them. Human society and the relations within it are treated as a 'black box'. This is easy to understand if we bear in mind that conservationists tend to break up reality into two separate spheres: the natural and the human. Impressed by the conflict between the two, they often disregard the fact that 'man' is a fiction. Issues of justice within generations alive in the present escape their attention. Their picture is so uniformly dark that it is impossible to see any details: no one stands out by virtue of wealth or poverty, power or powerlessness. It is this conceptual indifference to questions of power and distribution which smoothed the way for the Brundtland definition to enter prime ministers' offices and company boardrooms.

But consumption of the environment marks not only the relationship between humans and nature, but also relations among human beings. Changes to the environment are usually good for some and bad for others. Who will take how much from the ecosphere? Who can make what use of natural resources? Who has to bear which burdens and cope with which of the many costs? These are the key issues of environmental justice among people living at the same time, that is, of intra-generational or resource justice. They are posed because the advantages of consuming the environment (property, prestige, profit, power, etcetera) as well as the disadvantages (pollution, privation, poverty, etcetera) do not usually affect the same people in the same place and at the same time, but are distributed in an uneven manner. Both advantages and disadvantages are concentrated in different social groups, in different places and perhaps also at different times (see Chapter 2).[52]

The pattern of resource appropriation often follows the lines of force of money and power. Certain groups, regions and countries take the lion's share of natural resources. And what economic theorists like to call the 'externalization of negative consequences' has not only a bio-physical but also a social profile: the externalization of advantages and disadvantages is a mechanism structuring societies into winners and losers. In this context, power may be defined as an ability to internalize the benefits of environmental consumption, and to externalize the costs in marginal areas, among socially weak classes or at a later point in time.

All three dimensions of ecological justice endeavour to preserve the hospitability of the planet. In each one it is a matter of securing the rights to existence and development of a group of earth-dwellers: in the first variant, non-human living things; in the second, later generations; and, in the third, disadvantaged people and countries. To whom do the oil reserves, the rivers, forests and atmosphere belong? Who has what right to the life-serving accomplishments of the biosphere? How much should each take for their own well-being, without restricting the rights of others? These are the issues of ecological justice in general and – in relation to present-day global society – of resource justice in particular. And these issues become all the more acute as the bio-physical limits to the use of nature become more clearly visible.

When it is no longer possible to expand the use of nature, the rights of weaker people and nations to life and liberty can be preserved only through a different use and distribution of natural resources. The more that the carrying capacity of ecosystems reaches its limits, the greater is the threat to the freedom of the less strong – for ecological limits cast their social-economic shadows long before they are finally crossed. Petrol in the pumps becomes more expensive, regions become arid as water reserves dry up, the price of imported grain skyrockets, and fishermen return home with empty nets. Shortages make themselves felt through intensified competition, higher prices and legal exclusions, as well as through declining quality and loss of natural resources. Social peace often breaks down even before environmental peace, in the ecological sense, is seriously disturbed. In the century ahead, the growing shortage of resources and environmental goods will be the background for numerous major and minor conflicts (see Chapter 3).

The dilemma of catching up

Especially with regard to the struggle for justice, the bio-physical limits to conventional growth are incomparably more visible than in the past, now that the postulated synergy between the demand for justice and the policy of economic growth no longer operates. For a long time it has been a core political certainty that justice is created through growth, both nationally and internationally, and it has been accordingly assumed that the desire for greater equality will drive growth forward. Economic take-off, according to this common view, will in the long run automatically solve the problem of justice. After the Second World War, this coupling of justice and economic growth became the conceptual cornerstone of the development age. In the last few decades, however, since the finite nature of the biosphere became evident, this cornerstone has been standing on shaky ground. For in a limited environmental space, conventional growth can no longer create justice – except at the price of a ruined biosphere.

In the development age, justice was understood as a greater share for more and more people in a growing social product. The social contract between North and South envisaged that growth and social policy would start a process whereby the disadvantaged countries and peoples would be able to 'catch up' with the rich nations.[53] This was the tacit assumption behind the United Nations system and bilateral development cooperation. Two interests converged here: the North hoped that expanded markets would bring it new scope for profits, and thereby political stability; while the South hoped to achieve greater equality and recognition.[54] Subsequently, the demand of countries in the South for a fairer world was translated into a demand on them to integrate their national economies into the growing world economy. At this level nothing changed (on the contrary) with the arrival of the age of globalization, or when the Washington Consensus of 1986 made stable currencies the priority and turned its back on the social state as a new basis for development policy. As before, official policy makers and the great majority of economists continued to see growth and world market integration as the royal road to greater equality among nations and the eradication of poverty within nations.

However, throughout the history of colonial domination, Southern nations had to recognize their weakness *vis-à-vis* the industrial countries, and this resulted in a sense of inferiority. Countries therefore opt for economic mobilization not only out of a desire for wealth or a longing finally to draw level with the industrial countries, but also out of fear of being exposed to the dictates of the more powerful. An obsession with growth is not infrequently a form of self-defence. Furthermore, growth is still considered a trump card in the struggle against poverty within nations. This assumption has acquired proverbial status in the metaphor of 'a rising tide' that will 'lift all boats' (not only luxury liners but also little sloops), which presides over so many development efforts: the forces of growth will raise the income of rich and poor alike; and, if the income of the poor is raised by more than the average, growth even has the potential to bring the hoped-for equality. In the long term everyone stands to gain, no one is expected to lose out. Those who manage to link justice with growth in this way can even delegate the hard issues of justice to the future.

This approach quite often stretches across political camps, uniting countries in both South and North, neoliberals and Keynesians, globalizers and critics of globalization. Most of them were and are caught up in a tradition of thinking that goes back to the early nineteenth century. This assumes that growth is a positive sum game which can go on adding new and useful things to the world, in far greater measure than it brings damage and loss. Economic theorists of different shades signed up to this rosy vision of the future, and the optimism of progress became to economics what faith was to theology. Although it was often disputed whether profit-oriented growth would automatically trickle down to those in real need, or whether some social steering would also be necessary to achieve this, the idea of growth itself was never really called into question. Justice did not have to be an issue, since no natural limits were foreseen for the expansion of wealth. Indeed, redistribution or self-limitation – the classical demands of the theory of justice – could only hold up the progress of growth and delay the coming of prosperity among the poor.

This conception of growth has lost its innocence, at least since the bio-physical limits became apparent. It can no longer be ruled out that growth is more like a zero sum game. It is beginning to look as if the creation of ecological 'disvalue' goes hand in hand with the creation of economic value. To a significant extent, the creation of value is fed by the free use of nature; therefore, beyond a certain threshold that is close or has already been reached, natural capital begins to shrink as a result of the growth of technological and financial capital. Of course, monetary growth is not tied to material growth in an unalterable relationship; the same gross national product may cause various degrees of environmental stress. But there can be no doubt that the overall tendency is for the material size of the economy to grow along with its monetary size, at least until the transition to a post-industrial phase occurs. Nothing changes in this respect as a result of the changed form of environmental stress often observable in the course of industrialization: whereas local air and water pollution is the rule at first, pressure on global energy and biological resources and on the global atmosphere later becomes increasingly important. The conclusion from these points may also be expressed the other way round: so long as the demand for justice remains coupled with conventional growth, it threatens to collide with the stability of the biosphere.

Here precisely is the dilemma of the drive to catch up, especially in the case of Asia. It may be debated whether the growth surges in China and India are bringing greater social equality internationally and less poverty nationally (see above), but it is certain that they are causing serious wear and tear to the biosphere. In absolute terms, China has become the world's second-largest emitter of carbon dioxide after the United States, as well as the second-largest importer of oil. Even more marked than the pressure on global resources has been the stress on local habitats: cities sick from polluted air, shrinking areas of cultivated land and dwindling water stocks are the emergency signs of a gathering crisis of nature.[55] The annual economic costs of environmental damage as a result of economic growth were estimated in the 1990s at 13 per cent of China's domestic product[56] – which would mean losses higher than the growth rate of the national economy! To be sure, China stands out because of the size of its population, but similar tendencies are at work in Brazil, India, Malaysia, Mexico, Indonesia and other 'take-off' countries. Given the composition and degree of effectiveness of traditional economic growth, the exit from poverty and powerlessness seems to lead straight into overuse and overexploitation. A higher income beckons, but in reality it means only a greater share in the pillage economy.

It is high time to place the affluent model of industrial modernity under the microscope. More justice in this world cannot be attained at the consumption levels of the industrial countries. It will not be ecologically possible to sustain a level of conventional economic development that might bring Western living standards to the whole of a growing world population; the resources needed for that are too great, too expensive and too destructive. The prospect, then, is that the kick start into industrial modernity will lead to further marginalization of the poor countries and regions and hence to global apartheid, and will even place them in danger. Already today the noose is tightening round the neck of dozens of peripheral countries, because China's colossal demand is driving up the world market prices for grain, oil and mineral ores. So, whoever wishes to keep the goal of a fairer and more just world should look very closely at the patterns of production and consumption with which the present hopes of prosperity are bound up (Chapter 5). To champion global justice within an ecological perspective therefore means nothing less than to reinvent the model of wealth in industrial modernity. A cosmopolitan society is conceivable only on the basis of resource-light kinds of prosperity. How else will it be possible around the year 2050 for the earth to offer hospitality to some nine billion people?

Notes

1 Scholz 2003: 56.
2 Barber 2003: 21.
3 Menzel 1998.
4 Beck 2000; Taylor 2003.
5 Sachs et al. 2002.
6 Arndt 1987: 35.
7 On the history and anatomy of the idea of development, see Sachs 1992 or Rist 1996.
8 CEPR 2001; Milanovic 2002: 14; Kozul-Wright/Rayment 2004: 26.
9 Milanovic 2003: 675.
10 World Bank 2002a: 64ff.
11 Ravallion and Chen 2004: 13.
12 Birdsall 1998: 80.
13 UNDP/TCDC 2001: 16.
14 Menzel 1998; Scholz 2002.
15 Milanovic 2002.
16 UNCTAD 1997: 106–8.
17 Cornia and Court 2001: 8, which also lists the countries in question.
18 Bourguignon et al. 2002: 65.
19 IFG 2001.
20 *Economist*, especially its issue of 27 May 2000, p. 94.
21 For the diverse methodological and conceptual problems in the measurement of poverty, see Ravaillon 2003 and (from a more sceptical position) Wade 2003.
22 World Bank 2000a: 51 reported an additional 200 million, contrary to Ravallion 2003: 22, here presented according to the recalculations in Ravallion and Chen 2004. Sala-I-Martin 2002 and Bhalla 2002 speak of a still greater fall in poverty, although their methodology is in dispute.
23 Ravallion and Chen 2004: 28.

24 Ibid.: 16.
25 Pogge 2003.
26 Ravaillon and Chen 2004: 32.
27 Deaton and Drèze 2002.
28 Meadows et al. 1972.
29 Georgescu-Roegen 1971.
30 Bevilacqua 2000.
31 Neumayer 1999: 112.
32 Davidson 2000.
33 Folke et al. 2002.
34 Arrow et al. 1995: 93.
35 IPCC 2001a.
36 Moser et al. 1996.
37 Steffen et al. 2004: 259.
38 Ibid.: 258.
39 UNEP 2002: 64.
40 Postel et al. 1996.
41 FAO 2001c.
42 UNECE 2003.
43 FAO 2000.
44 For a survey from the point of view of earth system sciences, see Steffen et al. 2004: 4ff. and 257ff.
45 Wackernagel and Rees 1997; Wackernagel et al. 2002.
46 WWF 2006.
47 Meyer-Abich 1991.
48 Berry 1999.
49 Earth Charter Initiative.
50 WCED 1987.
51 Brown Weiss 1992.
52 The American Movement for Environmental Justice and writers such as Juan Martinez Alier (2003) have repeatedly drawn attention to this.
53 Kapstein 1999.
54 Sachs 1998.
55 World Bank 2001.
56 Smil and Mao 1998.

2
Inequality in the Environment

It remains true, however, that the greatest inequalities stem from those who pursue excess, not from those who are driven by necessity. One does not become a tyrant to stop feeling cold.

Aristotle, 329 BC

In general, the environmentalists' picture of the world is marked by polarity. They divide the world into two spheres: humans over here, nature over there; anthroposphere against biosphere. They also perceive humans as a predatory species, which has blown up its ecological niche and is increasingly burdening all other creatures and ecosystems with its activities – thereby exposing itself to danger as well. Indeed, many an ecological theorist points to a looming disaster if man and his economic system continue to overload the carrying capacity of the system of nature.

Mankind, however, exists only as an abstraction. To be sure, each man and woman requires a minimum of nature to satisfy his or her existential needs. In bio-physical terms, this interchange with nature takes place first of all through the skin, the surface of the body, and is closely bound up with the human metabolism: breathing and perspiration, nourishment and the giving off of heat. At this elementary level, the annual material turnover comes to approximately 800 kg per person.[1] But, very early in history, hunter-gatherers acquired a kind of second skin in the form of clothing, huts and weapons, a way of life still present among some ethnic groups in remote parts of the world. Soon there came yet another cover, the one that surrounds peasant cultures. Here the economic system includes soil for cultivation, domesticated plants and animals, which produce food and raw materials. Tools and houses are formed out of stone, ores and other materials. Perhaps a good half of humanity presently makes this use of nature, which in the case of an Indian village accounts for 2 to 5 tonnes of materials per person per year.[2] A fourth cover, the one associated with industrial civilization, embraces far more than the local level and mainly consists of installations run by organizations at various levels of the system: high-rise buildings, steel plants, supermarkets, swimming baths, airports, armoured vehicles and so on. In industrial societies, the metabolism (without air and water) stands at roughly 40 to 70 tonnes per person per year,[3] which represents ten times the biologically indispensable level.

The broad categories 'mankind' and 'economic system' therefore conceal various realities. Different cultures, classes and modes of production make quite unequal demands on the biosphere for their survival and their large-scale operations. The global environment, with its natural goods that the life-serving action of the biosphere makes available for the needs of human existence, is very unevenly divided among the world's societies. Although this biosphere belongs to everyone and to no one in particular, it is used asymmetrically by different regions, classes and nations. So, world society is a long way from providing all earth-dwellers with equal access to the goods of nature.

In this chapter, we shall try to form a picture of how natural resources are distributed across the globe and appropriated by human beings. Who commandeers how much of the global environment? First we shall present the uneven distribution of resources among the nations of the world, then look in detail at asymmetrical trade relations, especially between Europe and the rest of the world. Next we shift our focus to the inequalities between social layers within the same society, and show that the resource-consuming classes of all countries have so much in common with one another that they may be regarded as a transnational middle or upper class.

The triad of omnivores

A total of 191 countries belong to the United Nations (UN), while the Triad of which we shall speak comprises only North America, the European Union and Japan. All states have a seat and voice in the United Nations, and under international law they count as units of equal value. In size, population and economic strength, however, they are extremely different from one another. To make meaningful statements about them – for example, about the distribution of natural resources – we must place them in groups correlated for the purpose in mind. The first great division – into a first, a second and a third world – was customary during the years of the Cold War but has long ceased to apply. The traditional division into industrial and developing countries is also too wide-meshed, as it obscures the huge differences that have developed over the past twenty years between developing countries, differences that are growing continually deeper. It is true that a country's income, usually calculated on a *per capita* basis, is still the most accurate indicator of its level of economic development, but precisely for the developing countries it exhibits distinct gradations. Since agencies such as the World Bank, the Food and Agriculture Organization (FAO) and the World Trade Organization (WTO) use different systems of classification, we have assembled the relevant data by special country groups. At a first level industrial countries are distinguished from developing countries, while at a second level the developing countries are broken down into five subgroups.

Groupings of countries used in this chapter

Industrial countries
Andorra, Australia, Austria, Belgium, Canada, Denmark, Faroe Islands, Finland, France, Germany, Gibraltar, Greece, Greenland, Iceland, Ireland, Israel, Italy, Japan, Liechtenstein, Luxemburg, Malta, Monaco, Netherlands, New Zealand, Norway, Portugal, San Marino, St Pierre and Miquelon, Spain, Sweden, Switzerland, United Kingdom, United States of America.

High-income developing countries
Aruba, Bahamas, Barbados, Bermuda, Brunei, Cayman Islands, Cyprus, French Polynesia, Guam, Hong Kong, Kuwait, Macau, Netherlands Antilles, New Caledonia, Northern Mariana Islands, Qatar, Singapore, Slovenia, United Arab Emirates, US Virgin Islands.

Upper-middle-income developing countries
Antigua and Barbuda, Argentina,★ Bahrain, Botswana, Brazil,★ Chile, Costa Rica, Croatia, Czech Republic, Dominican Republic, Estonia, Gabon, Grenada, Hungary, Republic of Korea,★ Lebanon, Libya, Malaysia,★ Mauritius, Mexico,★ Oman, Palau, Panama, Poland,★ Puerto Rico, St Kitts and Nevis, St Lucia, Samoa, Saudi Arabia,★ Seychelles, Slovakia, South Africa,★ Trinidad and Tobago, Turkey,★ Uruguay, Venezuela.★

★ 20 so-called new consumer countries, according to Meyers and Kent 2004. See page 68ff.

Lower-middle-income developing countries	Albania, Algeria, Belarus, Belize, Bolivia, Bosnia Herzegovina, Bulgaria, Cape Verde, China (People's Republic).* Colombia, Cuba, Djibouti, Dominican Republic, Ecuador, Egypt, El Salvador, Equatorial Guinea, Fiji, Guatemala, Guyana, Honduras, Iran,* Iraq, Jamaica, Jordan, Kazakhstan, Kiribati, Latvia, Lithuania, Macedonia, Maldives, Marshall Islands, Micronesia, Morocco, Namibia, Papua New Guinea, Paraguay, Peru, Philippines,* Romania, Russia,* St Vincent and the Grenadines, Samoa, Sri Lanka, Surinam, Swaziland, Syria, Thailand,* Tongo, Tunisia, Turkmenistan, Vanuatu, West Bank, Yugoslavia.
Low-income developing countries	Afghanistan, Angola, Armenia, Azerbaijan, Bangladesh, Benin, Bhutan, Burkina Faso, Burundi, Cameroon, Central African Republic, Chad, Comoros, Congo (Democratic Republic), Congo (Republic of), East Timor, Eritrea, Ethiopia, Gambia, Georgia, Ghana, Guinea, Guinea-Bissau, Haiti, India,* Indonesia,* Ivory Coast, Kampuchea, Kenya, Korea (Democratic People's Republic), Kyrghistan, Laos, Lesotho, Liberia, Madagascar, Malawi, Mali, Mauritania, Moldavia, Mongolia, Mozambique, Myanmar, Nepal, Nicaragua, Niger, Nigeria, Pakistan,* Rwanda, Sao Tome and Principe, Senegal, Sierra Leone, Solomon Islands, Somalia, Sudan, Tajikistan, Tanzania, Togo, Uganda, Ukraine,* Uzbekistan, Vietnam, Zambia, Zimbabwe.
Others	Anguilla, British Virgin Islands, Cocos Islands, Cook Islands, Falklands, Gaza Strip, Guadeloupe, Guyana, Martinique, Montserrat, Nauru, Niue, Norfolk Islands, Reunion, St Helena, Taiwan, Tokelau, Turks and Caicos Islands, Tuvalu, Wallis and Futuna.

Geographical distribution of resources

Geographical and climatic conditions ensure that nature already distributes resources unevenly around the globe. They are also subject to different rates of change over time. They depend on the frequency of bio-geo-chemical cycles, and thus on the time that it takes for a material to pass through the stages from initial formation to final disappearance.[4] The distinction between 'renewable' and 'non-renewable' resources rests upon the length of these cycles. Non-renewable raw materials present in the earth's crust – such as minerals, oil and metals – have cycles of millions of years and often appear only for a short time in a concentrated form. The material cycles of the biosphere, on the other hand, last in the region of ten years, involving substances that are incorporated into living creatures. Out of the biosphere cycles, raw materials such as forest then grow again over longer periods of time. The shortest material cycles, lasting ± 1 year, take place through the atmosphere: elemental acids and nitrogen, water and carbon dioxide. By means of photosynthesis and respiration they are metabolized by organisms in the biosphere.

Definition of natural resources[5]

Non-renewable raw materials	Fossil fuels, metal ores and other minerals, such as gypsum or kaolin, are non-renewable in the sense that they cannot be regenerated within a human time scale. Deposits are limited and dwindle as a result of human activities.
Renewable raw materials	Biomass is essentially renewed within a human time scale. It includes quickly renewable resources such as agriculturally useful plants and slowly renewable resources such as wood. However, when used as raw materials, these biological resources can run out.
Species diversity	Species diversity, also known as biodiversity, embraces the diversity of life itself: it denotes both the variety of species in a particular ecosystem and the genetic variety within a population. Species diversity is one of the basic preconditions for

stability of the global ecosystem, which is endangered by the extinction of species throughout the world.

Environmental media such as air, water and soil

These resources serve to sustain life and to produce biological resources. Their deterioration is a cause for concern. The total quantity of air and water on the planet does not change within a human time scale, but they are often in a poor condition as a result of contamination.

Flowing resources such as geothermic or solar energy

These resources cannot run out, but other resources are necessary to make use of them. For example, energy, materials and space are required to build wind turbines or solar cells.

Surface area

Evidently, physical space is needed for the production or maintenance of all the above resources. Examples are the use of land for human settlement, infrastructure, industry, mining, agriculture and forestry.

Renewable resources have comparatively short cycles; their distribution is more dynamic and can change appreciably within a human time scale.

Table 2.1 Global availability and use of land surface (1999)

	Land surface			Arable & permanent crops		
	mn ha	%	ha/head	mn ha	%	ha/head
Industrial countries	3,064	23.5	3.6	368	24.6	0.43
Developing countries	9,945	76.4	1.9	1,132	75.4	0.22
High-income	18	0.1	1.4	1	0.04	0.05
Upper-middle-income	2,305	17.7	3.9	214	14.3	0.37
Lower-middle-income	4,370	33.6	2.1	442	29.5	0.21
Low-income	3,252	25.0	1.3	475	31.6	0.19
Other	11	0.08	7.2	0	0.01	0.02
Whole world	13,020	100	2.2	1,501	100	0.25

Source: FAO 2001a. Data on forest availability from 1994, not 1999.

Their distribution and availability are bound up with the size and quality of the land areas – at least in the case of most of the humanly used biomass in agriculture and forestry.

The earth has a total land surface of approximately 13 billion hectares. The industrial countries, as listed above, occupy roughly one quarter of this area (Table 2.1), which is a lot in comparison with their 15 per cent share of the world population. For they include large countries with a low population density (USA, Canada, Australia), as well as others with a very high population density (Western Europe, Japan). Nevertheless, the distribution of land area is out of all proportion with the possibility of acquiring raw materials. Deserts and steppes cannot be used so easily, if at all. Roughly 30 per cent (approx. 4 billion hectares) of the land surface is covered by forest and should therefore be regarded as a potential source of renewable raw materials. Above-average levels of forest are to be found in the temperate regions of Northeast Europe and North America and the equatorial zone of South America. Altogether, then, barely two-fifths (5 billion hectares) of the land area available in the world can be used for farming. The great majority of this is pasture – 3.5 billion hectares. Only 1.5 billion hectares is actually used for agriculture. In the densely populated industrial countries of Japan and Europe, on the other hand, the great majority of farmland is used for agriculture and only a small part as pasture.

The area used for agriculture cannot be increased at will. In the last forty years it has risen by some ten per cent around the world. During

Permanent grassland			Forest			Population	Total area
mn ha	%	ha/head	mn ha	%	ha/head	mn	mn ha
749	21.7	0.88	1,050	25.2	1.23	850	3,207
2,704	78.3	0.53	3,114	74.6	0.61	5,125	10,178
1	0.03	0.08	3	0.07	0.21	13	19
776	22.5	1.33	847	20.3	1.45	584	2,333
1,017	29.5	0.49	1,326	31.8	0.64	2,057	4,442
910	26.3	0.37	938	22.5	0.38	2,462	3,373
1	0.03	0.13	8	0.19	0.90	9	11
3,454	100	0.58	4,172	100	0.70	5,975	13,384

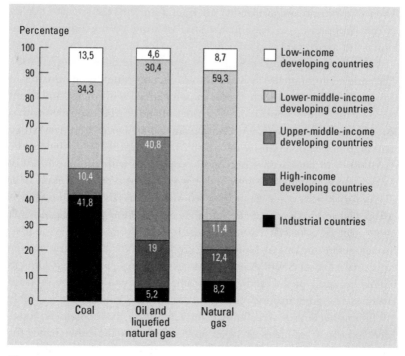

Figure 2.1 Proven reserves of fossil fuels (1998). The industrial countries dispose of more than 40 per cent of global reserves of coal, but only 5 per cent of oil and 8 per cent of gas reserves. A good part of the oil reserves is in developing countries with upper-middle incomes, and the overwhelming proportion of gas reserves is in developing countries with lower-middle incomes.

Source: World Energy Council 2001. The 'Others' category is not shown because the values are too low.

the same period, the world population has doubled, so that the amount available *per capita* has actually fallen from 1.46 to 0.8 hectares;[6] but agricultural productivity – that is, crop yield per hectare – has also doubled. Nevertheless, there are marked regional differences. South Asia, for example, because of its high demographic growth and limited natural spaces, has available only 0.17 hectares *per capita*. Crop yield per hectare in the industrial countries is nearly 30 per cent higher than in the developing countries. And in the European Union it is even twice as high, which is obviously connected with the greater outlay on energy and machinery as well as with the environmentally stressful overuse of fertilizers and pesticide. In fact, without the increased yields due to artificial fertilizer, the world's population would need roughly 30 per cent more high-quality arable land to satisfy the same level of demand.[7]

The industrial countries as a whole, but especially Canada and the US, are far better endowed than developing countries with agricultural land and forest. The potential of developing countries in biotic resources is considerably weaker, despite their higher population density. But the one exception is in respect of biodiversity. Of the 25 biodiversity 'hot spots', which have exceptional biological productivity and an abundance of plant and animal species, 21 are to be found in developing countries – such as Amazonia and the South African Cape. Since biodiversity is a resource for the genetic engineering industry, this uneven distribution may come to weigh politically and economically to the advantage of the South.

Mineral raw materials have long geological cycles. They are mainly distributed at discrete places on the earth's surface: coltan, for example, a tantalite ore used for the production of electronic devices such as mobile phones, digital cameras and computers, is found mainly in Central Africa. The reserves of platinum, another important raw material for the North's hi-tech industry, are confined to just a few areas, especially in South Africa and Siberia. The largest reserves of oil are concentrated in the Middle East and the Caspian Sea region.

Table 2.2 sets out current economic reserves for some important non-renewable resources. Economic reserves are that part of ascertained resources which, at the time of survey, it is economically rational to extract. Economic reserves may therefore change, because their quantity depends upon raw material prices and the state of extraction technology. The higher the raw material prices, the higher are the economic reserves, since fewer and fewer accessible deposits can be economically extracted.

The economic reserves in the industrial countries vary for each raw material. Chromium usually does not feature at all. For tin, phosphate and manganese, less than 10 per cent of economic reserves are to be found in the developed industrial countries. The North's economic reserves account for a fifth or less of the world's bauxite, copper and iron ore, but rather more of its nickel, lead, zinc and gold.

The picture is much the same for energy sources (Figure 2.1). Proven reserves of oil – today's most important fuel – are to be found overwhelmingly in developing countries; only 5 per cent of the world

Table 2.2 Economic reserves of selected raw materials (2004)

Material	Unit	Industrial countries	High-income developing countries
Bauxite	1,000 dry tonnes	4,420,000	700,000
	% of world total	19.0%	3.0%
Chromium	1,000 tonnes	–	0
	% of world total	–	0.0%
Copper	1,000 tonnes metal content	66,000	26,000
	% of world total	13.9%	5.5%
Gold	1,000 tonnes metal content	11,900	1,200
	% of world total	27.6%	2.8%
Iron ore	mn tonnes utilizable ore	30,100	21,000
	% of world total	20.5%	14.3%
Manganese	1,000 tonnes	32,000	40,000
	% of world total	10.5%	13.1%
Nickel	1,000 tonnes metal content	27,690,000	5,500,000
	% of world total	44.9%	8.9%
Phosphate (rock)	1,000 tonnes	1,282,000	6,600,000
	% of world total	7.2%	37.3%
Lead	1,000 tonnes metal content	25,600	–
	% of world total	38.5%	0.0%
Tin	1,000 tonnes metal content	200,000	1,700,000
	% of world total	3.3%	28.1%
Zinc	1,000 tonnes metal content	74,000	33,000
	% of world total	33.6%	15.0%

Source: US Department of the Interior/US Geological Survey 2004

total are in the industrial countries. A similar asymmetry applies in the case of natural gas, where the industrial countries have only 8 per cent of the global reserves. But the relationship is reversed in the case of coal, where they have a disproportionately high proportion of reserves.

All in all, then, the North disposes of relatively small reserves of non-renewable resources; the main share is to be found in the countries of the

Upper-middle-income developing countries	Lower-middle-income developing countries	Low-income developing countries	Non-attributable reserves	World total
2,220,000	3,480,000	8,170,000	4,300,000	23,290,000
9.5%	14.9%	35.1%	18.5%	
100,000	290,000	25,000	390,000	805,000
12.4%	36.0%	3.1%	48.4%	
207,000	64,000	51,000	60,000	474,000
43.7%	13.5%	10.8%	12.7%	
8,000	3,200	1,800	17,000	43,100
18.6%	7.4%	4.2%	39.4%	
12,600	35,100	37,300	11,000	147,100
8.6%	23.9%	25.4%	7.5%	
79,000	0	155,000	–	306,000
25.8%	0.0%	50.7%	–	
9,300,000	14,710,000	3,215,000	1,300,000	61,715,000
15.1%	23.8%	5.2%	2.1%	
1,760,000	7,100,000	170,000	800,000	17,712,000
9.9%	40.1%	1.0%	4.5%	
1,900	20,000		19,000	66,500
2.9%	30.1%	0.0%	28.6%	
1,540,000	1,630,000	800,000	180,000	6,050,000
25.5%	26.9%	13.2%	3.0%	
8,000	46,000	0	59,000	220,000
3.6%	20.9%	0.0%	26.8%	

South. Yet, since a whole series of these resources continue to provide important quantities of energy and raw materials for the industrial economy, the North consumes a disproportionately high share of them. This contradiction between possession and requirements is the basis for the geo-strategic conflicts that have repeatedly held the world in suspense for the past century or more (Chapter 3).

Table 2.3 Production and consumption of metallic raw materia

Material			World
Iron and steel	Iron ore production	mn tonnes	1051
		Share of world output	100%
	Domestic steel	mn tonnes	765
		Share of world consumption	100%
		kg per head	125
Bauxite and aluminium	Bauxite production	mn tonnes	146
		Share of world output	100%
	Primary aluminium consumption	mn tonnes	24
		Share of world consumption	100%
		kg per head	3.9
Lead	Mine production	mn tonnes	3
		Share of world output	100%
	Domestic consumption	mn tonnes	6.43
		Share of world consumption	100%
		kg per head	1.05
Copper	Mine production	mn tonnes	13.63
		Share of world output	100%
	Domestic consumption	mn tonnes	15.52
		Share of world consumption	100%
		kg per head	2.5
Nickel	Mine production	mn tonnes	1.23
		Share of world output	100%
	Domestic consumption	mn tonnes	1.11
		Share of world consumption	100%
		kg per head	0.18
Zinc	Mine production	mn tonnes	8.96
		Share of world output	100%
	Domestic consumption	mn tonnes	8.65
		Share of world consumption	100%
		kg per head	1.4

Source: Own calculations based on Natural Resources Canada 2002, International Iron and Steel Institute 2002 and World Bank 2003.

Appropriation between North and South

The type and quantity of resources that a country claims for itself only partly depend on its own natural endowment. Most countries (some more, some less) import additional nature from beyond their frontiers – for example, in the form of oil or food. For centuries the goods of nature

in selected countries (2001)

European Union (EU15)	USA	Japan	Africa	Latin America	China
22	63	0	46	249	224
2%	6%	0%	4%	24%	21%
142	103	73	15	40	170
19%	13%	10%	2%	5%	22%
376	362	576	19	77	134
0	0	0	18	36	8
0%	0%	0%	12%	25%	5%
5	5	2	0	1	3
20%	23%	8%	2%	4%	15%
12.6	19.1	15.8	0.5	1.6	2.7
0.19	0.47	0.01	0.15	0.47	0.6
6%	16%	0%	5%	16%	20%
1.74	1.69	0.28	0.13	0.41	0.65
27%	26%	4%	2%	6%	10%
4.62	5.94	2.23	0.16	0.78	0.51
0.18	1.34	0	0.52	6.05	0.56
1%	10%	0%	4%	44%	4%
1.84	1.8	1.43	0.41	4.03	1.43
12%	12%	9%	3%	26%	9%
4.9	6.3	11.2	0.5	7.7	1.1
0.02	0	0	0.07	0.22	0.05
2%	0%	0%	5%	17%	4%
0.41	0.13	0.16	0.03	0.02	0.09
37%	12%	15%	3%	2%	8%
1.1	0.46	1.27	0.04	0.05	0.07
0.67	0.84	0.04	0.23	1.85	1.57
7%	9%	0%	3%	21%	18%
2.16	1.11	0.63	0.16	0.58	1.46
25%	13%	7%	2%	7%	17%
5.7	3.9	5	0.2	1.1	1.1

have been distributed around the globe through international trade. These flows generally correspond to the lines of gravity of purchasing and political power; control over the movement of important and valuable materials has since time immemorial been a basic factor in economic superiority; trade thus becomes the driving force of uneven appropriation.

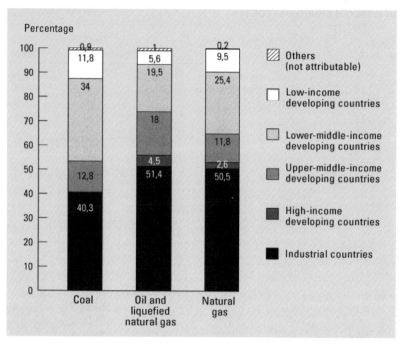

Figure 2.2 Consumption of fossil fuels (1999). The industrial countries account for approximately 50 per cent of global oil and gas and a good third of coal consumption. The group of lower-middle-income developing countries, registers the second-highest consumption of fossil fuels.
Source: World Energy Council 2001

The North–South gradient is immediately evident in a series of minerals. Bauxite, for example, which is used in the production of primary aluminium, is not extracted in any of the wealthy economies of the Triad. Most of the deposits of natural bauxite are in developing countries in the Americas (Jamaica, Brazil), which are significantly dependent on bauxite exports (to the tune of 55 per cent in the case of Jamaica). But more than a half of the world's primary aluminium is consumed in the Triad, especially for vehicle production, packing, machine–building and construction. The *per capita* consumption of the United States is some five times higher than the world average, and twenty times higher than the average for African countries.

The Triad also consumes more than it possesses of other metals (Table 2.3). For instance, only 8 per cent of the world's iron ore extraction is in

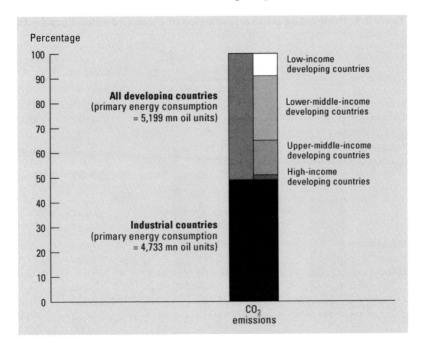

Figure 2.3 Energy consumption and CO$_2$ emissions (2000). All developing countries together already consume more primary energy and produce more CO$_2$ emissions than the group of industrial countries. The high-income developing countries emit as much *per capita* as the industrial countries; the *per capita* emissions of the other three groups of developing countries are significantly lower. Source: IEA 2004c

the United States and the European Union – roughly one billion tonnes a year, with Japan also having negligible deposits. Yet the Triad consumes 42 per cent of global steel production, and a Japanese citizen some thirty times more than the average African. Two-thirds of nickel, an important raw material for the refinement of steel, is consumed in the Triad, which has only 2 per cent of the world's reserves. As to lead, an important material for the automobile industry, this group of countries consumes well over half of global output, an American some twelve times more than a Chinese.

A similar picture emerges in relation to fossil fuels (Figure 2.2). The industrial countries consume a good half of oil and gas, although a somewhat smaller proportion of coal. Altogether they account for roughly 50

Table 2.4 Production and consumption of plant and animal products (1999

| | Root crops | | | |
| | Production | | Consumption | |
	mn tonnes	%	mn tonnes	%
World total	665,984	100	671,516	100
Industrial countries	83,442	12.5	96,445	14.4
Developing countries	582,129	87.4	574,657	85.6
High-income	432	0.1	723	0.1
Upper-middle-income	66,661	10.0	70,079	10.4
Lower-middle-income	283,694	42.6	273,429	40.7
Low-income	231,343	34.7	230,427	34.3

| | Fruit | | | |
| | Production | | Consumption | |
	mn tonnes	%	mn tonnes	%
World total	459,681	100	451,694	100
Industrial countries	98,820	21.5	122,506	27.1
Developing countries	360,658	78.5	328,974	72.8
High-income	926	0.2	2,346	0.5
Upper-middle-income	96,255	20.9	72,637	16.1
Lower-middle-income	143,712	31.3	134,922	29.9
Low-income	119,764	26.1	119,068	26.4

| | Oleaginous crops | | | |
| | Production | | Consumption | |
	mn tonnes	%	mn tonnes	%
World total	363,745	100	361,111	100
Industrial countries	126,567	34.8	124,281	34.4
Developing countries	237,178	65.2	236,827	65.6
High-income	110	0.0	259	0.1
Upper-middle-income	77,303	21.3	74,090	20.5
Lower-middle-income	77,062	21.2	80,650	22.3
Low-income	82,702	22.7	81,828	22.7

| | Cocoa beans | | | |
| | Production | | Consumption | |
	mn tonnes	%	mn tonnes	%
World total	2,943	100	3,277	100
Industrial countries	0	0.0	1,950	59.5
Developing countries	2,943	100	1,326	40.5
High-income	0	0.0	23	0.7
Upper-middle-income	349	11.9	571	17.4
Lower-middle-income	262	8.9	446	13.6
Low-income	2,332	79.2	287	8.7

Source: FAO 2001a. The difference between production and consumption is due to supply changes: that is, to additions and deductions.

Sugar plants

Production mn tonnes	%	Consumption mn tonnes	%
1,537,799	100	1,541,484	100
228,701	14.9	228,899	14.8
1,309,098	85.1	1,312,585	85.2
1,015	0.1	1,018	0.1
488,064	31.7	488,109	31.7
357,373	23.2	360,432	23.4
462,645	30.1	463,025	30.0

Vegetables

Production mn tonnes	%	Consumption mn tonnes	%
652,629	100	650,127	100
115,225	17.7	119,835	18.4
536,867	82.3	529,749	81.5
1,597	0.2	2,769	0.4
75,025	11.5	71,523	11.0
339,659	52.0	334,940	51.5
120,586	18.5	120,516	18.5

Cereals

Production mn tonnes	%	Consumption mn tonnes	%
1,872,129	100	1,865,742	100
635,902	34.0	518,358	27.8
1,235,930	66.0	1,346,652	72.2
604	0.0	4,784	0.3
208,516	11.1	251,370	13.5
588,142	31.4	638,536	34.2
438,668	23.4	451,962	24.2

Fish, seafood

Production mn tonnes	%	Consumption mn tonnes	%
120,601	100	115,758	100
27,317	22.7	34,851	30.1
93,281	77.3	80,907	69.9
359	0.3	661	0.6
16,131	13.4	11,262	9.7
58,064	48.1	54,045	46.7
18,727	15.5	14,939	12.9

Meat

Production mn tonnes	%	Consumption mn tonnes	%
228,591	100	227,392	100
86,525	37.9	81,594	35.9
142,016	62.1	145,712	64.1
756	0.3	1,817	0.8
36,749	16.1	36,496	16.0
82,878	36.3	85,619	37.7
21,632	9.5	21,779	9.6

Milk

Production mn tonnes	%	Consumption mn tonnes	%
570,796	100	568,404	100
245,894	43.1	224,865	39.6
324,436	56.8	343,060	60.4
944	0.2	2,171	0.4
83,233	14.6	87,380	15.4
93,041	16.3	102,121	18.0
147,217	25.8	151,388	26.6

Coffee

Production mn tonnes	%	Consumption mn tonnes	%
6,832	100	6,404	100
4	0.1	4,104	64.1
6,828	99.9	2,293	35.8
0	0.0	27	0.4
2,201	32.2	839	13.1
1,924	28.2	870	13.6
2,703	39.6	556	8.7

per cent of the world's total consumption of fossil fuels; the other half is spread among the developing countries. But since the population ratio between industrial and developing countries is 15:85, major disparities emerge in any *per capita* comparison. The industrial countries use an annual average of 4.5 tonnes of oil equivalent *per capita*, while the comparable figure in the developing countries is 0.8 tonnes. The appropriation of fossil fuels is thus five to six times higher in the industrial than in the developing countries, where, moreover, there is a wide variation in consumption levels. In a small group of countries with high income and a high level of development, including, for example, the United Arab Emirates, the annual consumption of 4.6 tonnes per head of the population is actually a little higher than in the industrial countries. But, at the other end of the spectrum, an impoverished group of populous developing countries, especially in Africa, consume a mere 0.3 tonnes of oil equivalent *per capita* – 14 times less than the industrial countries.

The burning of fossil fuels produces carbon dioxide. The CO_2 emissions produced by human activity came to a total of roughly 23.7 billion tonnes in the year 2001, or approximately 3.9 tonnes *per capita*. Climate scientists point to the necessity of halving this yearly rate by the middle of this century, if the climate change already under way is to be kept within tolerable bounds.[8] Nearly half (49 per cent) of worldwide CO_2 emissions can be laid at the door of the industrial countries (Figure 2.3). The inequalities here are similar to those in fuel consumption. At 12.6 tonnes *per capita*, CO_2 emissions in the industrial countries are 5 to 6 times higher than in the developing countries. There the average is 2.3 tonnes, but with a large range of variation: from 0.9 tonnes in the poorest countries to roughly 4.5 tonnes in those with an upper-middle income. The spectrum is also wide within the industrial countries: from 5.5 tonnes in Malta and Sweden to 20 tonnes in the United States. That is 200 times more than in some countries of central Africa.

In the last thirty years, it is true, the countries of the South have started to catch up in both energy consumption and CO_2 emissions. At the beginning of the 1970s the North's share was still around 60 per cent, but in recent years the South's CO_2 emissions have been increasing at the rate of 1.2 per cent per year, compared with 0.1 per cent in the industrial countries.

The food situation is on the whole more even. Table 2.4 compares national production and consumption of a series of major agricultural products. For root crops, sugar plants and vegetables, the industrial countries produce approximately as much as they consume, and their share of global consumption is more or less proportional to their population. For other product groups, their share of consumption is disproportionately higher, but they either cover the difference out of their own production (oil seeds, meat) or actually produce more than they consume (grain, milk). Fish and fruit, on the other hand, they import to a considerable extent from the developing countries. The disparities are even more marked in relation to tropical products such as coffee and cocoa beans, which are produced almost exclusively in the South but are consumed mainly (two-thirds) in the North. This explains why the North, despite its generally better endowment with agricultural land, appropriates additional land in the countries of the South.

Distribution of the damage

It is not only resources and emissions that are unevenly distributed between North and South, but also the resulting damage. In all probability, the bitter effects of climate change will hit first and most powerfully the countries and people who did least to cause it. For, contrary to what the film *The Day after Tomorrow* leads us to expect, the changes will most likely not appear as a sudden disaster but begin almost imperceptibly, and they will affect not so much North America and Europe as countries in the southern hemisphere. Great delta regions in China, Vietnam, Nigeria and especially Bangladesh, small island states in the South Seas, arid and semi–arid regions all around the world: these are all losers twice over, because they have fewer resources to convert into prosperity, and because it is mainly they which have to bear such consequences of climate change as drought, storms, water shortage, rising sea levels and reduced harvests. Far from being just a question of conservation, climate change will become the invisible hand behind agricultural decay, social erosion and forced emigration.

For, if the earth's atmosphere grows warmer, nature becomes unstable. Suddenly it is no longer possible to count on rain, groundwater, temperature, wind or seasons, all factors which, from time immemorial, have ensured the habitats of plants, animals and not least human beings. Changes in humidity and temperature will trigger changes in vegetation, species diversity, soil fertility and water levels. It is also to be expected that the environment will become unhealthier. Harvests will be plagued with vermin, people will fall ill with malaria and dengue fever or various other infections.[9] Research tells us that by the year 2050, with the rise of

2 degrees in global temperatures to be expected if emissions continue unchecked, 25 million people will be threatened with coastal flooding, 180 to 250 million with malaria, and 200 to 300 million with water shortage.[10]

Most scientists estimate that climate change will have a particular impact on food production in developing countries.[11] Along with gradual changes in temperature and humidity, it will be mainly extreme weather conditions that will directly affect food production. In the higher latitudes of industrial countries, however, agriculture may sometimes actually profit from global warming. Models suggest that, although a rise of 2 or even 3 degrees Celsius will not threaten global production, disparities will increase between climate zones and again industrial countries will be the winners, developing countries the losers. According to calculations of the Intergovernmental Panel on Climate Change (IPCC), developing countries will also suffer more severe economic damage as a result of rising sea levels.[12] The global water crisis due to climate change will aggravate the situation in already water-poor regions, where 1.1 billion people today lack sufficient access to safe drinking water. Above all else, then, it is the physical integrity of the poor that the affluent are undermining through their excessive burning of fossil fuels.

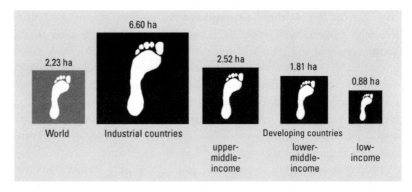

Figure 2.4 *Per capita* ecological footprint (2003). The average *per capita* footprint of the industrial countries is three times greater than the world average of 2.23 hectares per capita. Even upper-middle-income developing countries leave behind a larger footprint per head than the world average, whereas the largest group, the low-income developing countries, display less than half the world average.

Source: Our own calculations on the basis of data from WWF 2006. A lack of data accounts for the absence of upper-income developing countries from the diagram.

The above points may be graphically summarized in a set of *ecological footprints* (see Chapter 1).[13] In 2003 the ecological footprint of humanity came to approximately 14.1 billion hectares, while the globally available biocapacity stood at only 11.4 billion hectares: which means that the earth is already being overused in the order of 25 per cent. As far as the North–South comparison is concerned, the following relationships obtain. Of the 14.1 billion hectares that make up the global ecological footprint of humanity, the industrial countries remain responsible for 42 per cent or roughly 6.6 hectares *per capita* (Figure 2.4). The developing countries avail themselves of roughly 58 per cent of the global environment – but that amounts to no more than 1.5 hectares *per capita*. In proportion to their population, the industrial countries should take only 30 per cent or so of the available biocapacity, but in reality they avail themselves of an extra 2.5 billion hectares. Since all the developing countries together take roughly their proportionate share, the overuse is to be blamed entirely on the industrial countries.[14]

Although the inequalities between North and South have decreased only a little in the last few decades, the trend is set to change in the coming period. The hunger for raw materials of fast-developing countries like China, India or Brazil will ensure that *per capita* consumption in the South draws closer to the levels of the North. This 'catching up' will, however, have far-reaching consequences for the environment. It is realistically estimated that by the year 2050 approximately nine billion people will be living on the planet.[15] If they all require the same amount of raw materials as today's average citizen of the EU, humanity will be consuming somewhere in the region of 450 billion tonnes per annum:[16] that is, four times the current level.[17] And, if that happens, the chances are that environmental problems will increase in roughly the same degree. The conclusion is clearly that neither the industrial nor the developing countries can simply enlarge their footprint at will. If today's under-privileged are to have an opportunity for ecologically sustainable development, those who have hitherto imposed their demand for resources will have to limit themselves to the share to which they are entitled. Of this more will be said in Chapter 5.

Unequal ecological exchange

The epochal shift that goes by the name of 'globalization' has more than one aspect. It includes the rise of international television stations such as

CNN, as well as the rapid spread of epidemics such as SARS and AIDS, the growth of global air travel, and the ascendancy of the English language. But its best-known aspect is the omnipresence of the world market. The growing interconnection of the economy finds its statistical expression in the fact that global exports have been increasing faster than the global product. An ever greater share of raw materials, goods and services move across national borders. To be sure, world trade has less and less to do with the classical exchange of goods between nations; more and more it is a matter of transporting products between different sites of a cross-border production network, often within the same corporation. The increasing volume of trade reflects the economic denationalization of production, marketing and finance.[18]

Worldwide economic links have indeed soared since the middle of the twentieth century (Figure 2.5). Whereas the total global product has risen

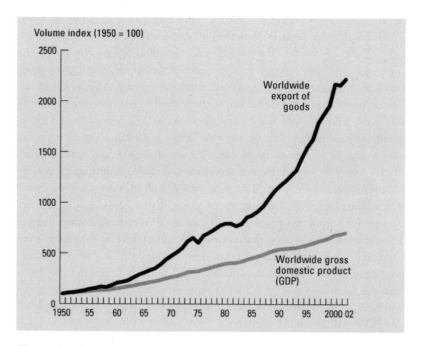

Figure 2.5 Growth of world trade and gross domestic product (1950– 2002). The volume of world trade has been growing faster than the world economy. Over the past fifty years global GDP has increased by a factor of 7, whereas world trade has expanded by a factor of 22.

Source: WTO 2003

approximately sevenfold since 1950, the global volume of goods exports (without services) has expanded by a factor of 22! Especially sharp was the increase in the 1990s. In fact, since 1990 the volume of world trade has doubled once more, while the world economy has grown by only 30 per cent. This unambiguously identifies the decade as the age of accelerated globalization.[19]

A large part of world trade involves material flows across frontiers, for the goods in question consist of various materials, whether tonnes of crude oil, finely modelled plastic casing or highly perishable flowers. Apart from the elements of information, communication and finance, all economic exchange is also a physical exchange. In what follows, we shall turn to the physical flows associated with international trade, looking at their composition and volume as well as their geographical direction. Do increased levels of trade reduce inequality between nations in the use of resources, or do they actually sharpen it? We will address this question mainly from a European perspective and, in doing so, refer to more detailed work previously conducted by the Wuppertal Institute.[20]

The Triad and its 'colonies'

Roughly one half of world trade takes place within the triad of the EU, North America and Japan. There can thus be no talk of trade globalization in the full sense of the word: the main share of world trade, measured in monetary terms, involves links among these three economic regions. But, if we distinguish between processed goods and raw materials, then significant differences emerge in the patterns of interconnection.

Table 2.5 shows world trade in processed goods by continental-geographical regions. Roughly half of the processed exports are exchanged between continents. The other half are traded within one of the regions. In Western Europe, for example, two-thirds of exports go to another country in the region. It is also apparent that the regions of the Triad mostly trade with one another. The largest intercontinental trade flows are between Asia and North America, Asia and Western Europe, and Western Europe and North America. Asia – especially Japan, China and the other Asian emerging countries (Hong Kong, Singapore, South Korea, Taiwan, Vietnam, Malaysia, Thailand and Indonesia) – plays an increasingly important role in the world trade in processed goods, whereas Africa scarcely participates in it at all.

Table 2.6 shows the world trade in raw materials or, to be more precise, in the products of agriculture and mining. The money value of

Table 2.5 World trade in processed goods by region (2002)

Trade in billions of US dollars	to North America	to Latin America	to West Europe	to East-Central Europe, Balkans & CIS	to Africa	to Middle East	to Asia & Australasia
North America	279.96	122.75	140.06	5.48	7.54	15.94	156.00
Latin America	158.81	29.09	12.45	0.21	1.29	0.58	5.91
West Europe	233.89	49.13	1,397.88	148.81	54.67	60.41	183.36
East-Central Europe, Balkans & CIS	7.48	1.92	110.43	38.91	2.50	4.32	13.51
Africa	3.92	0.54	19.41	0.15	5.45	1.33	4.06
Middle East	14.82	1.41	13.13	1.35	2.42	8.98	11.51
Asia & Australasia	367.98	35.05	231.47	18.18	20.26	40.36	614.90

Source: WTO 2003

the traded goods – again in US dollars – is here considerably lower than in the case of processed goods. But, measured in tonnes, raw materials count for more. Within Western Europe, the trade in raw materials mostly concerns energy (oil from Norway and the United Kingdom) and farming produce. Within Asia, Australia plays a prominent role as a supplier of raw materials to Japan and China. But between the two regions another configuration is apparent. There is very little trade in raw materials within the Triad; the largest material flows are from the Middle East to Asia, from Latin America to North America, from Africa to Western Europe, and from East-Central Europe to Western Europe. The Triad regions, then, draw raw materials from their respective hinterlands – one might almost say from their 'colonies', since the suppliers are mostly developing countries and, in the case of Western Europe, even former colonies.

Japan, a country poor in raw materials, obtains its energy supplies almost entirely from imports. North America also imports both energy sources and agricultural produce in large quantities, mostly from Latin America. And the European Union gets many of its agricultural raw materials from the developing countries in the South. In connection with

Table 2.6 World trade in agricultural and mining products by region (2002)

Trade in billions of US dollars	to North America	to Latin America	to West Europe	to East-Central Europe, Balkans & CIS	to Africa	to Middle East	to Asia & Austral-asia
North America	78.66	22.24	20.50	1.24	3.41	2.67	40.27
Latin America	55.89	24.92	29.71	3.17	3.05	3.94	17.47
West Europe	33.46	4.95	330.80	17.92	10.97	6.98	21.51
East-Central Europe, Balkans & CIS	6.50	4.00	60.16	40.56	1.21	3.00	10.45
Africa	19.75	4.09	47.60	0.77	5.90	1.83	18.54
Middle East	21.79	1.98	26.16	0.66	6.97	8.19	103.45
Asia & Australasia	19.19	2.87	20.98	2.65	3.93	6.10	155.84

Source: WTO 2003

these imports, the industrial countries occupy valuable tracts of farmland in the countries of the South, some 43 million hectares in the case of the European Union (the EU 15), which equals roughly a fifth of total EU territory.[21] By comparison, approximately 85 million hectares of agricultural land plus 56 million hectares of pasture are used within the EU itself. Roughly 80 per cent of foreign land used for EU agricultural imports (mostly soy beans and derivatives and coffee) lies in the developing countries, including 16 per cent (or 6 million hectares) in Africa, where cocoa is especially important. A lot of land is also used to produce animal feed (manioc), natural rubber and vegetable oils and fats – especially palm oil and coconut oil. The high share of feed in EU imports shows that European production (and consumption) of animal produce is a major reason for the occupation of land overseas.

Broadly speaking, then, world trade flows display the following pattern: exchange of high-value goods among the rich countries, exchange of goods with a lower monetary value between poor and rich countries, and very little exchange at all between the poor countries. The countries of the Triad mainly trade in processed goods in the upper value-creation brackets. In monetary terms, this trade in refined products accounts for roughly three-quarters of total world trade, with heavy industrial goods becoming established in the newly industrializing countries. But the initial materials for this refinement process largely originate in the developing countries. These may account for a small share of world trade, but not of its material volume.

The external trade of the European Union is a good illustration of the imbalance between flows of goods and flows of value. Raw materials make up three-quarters of total imports to the EU, measured in tonnes, and the largest part of this originates in the developing countries. In monetary terms, however, imports of raw materials make up only a fifth of the total. A typical example is the various levels of the metalworking industry. Only 2.5 per cent of the world's iron ore extraction takes place in Europe (EU 25 plus Norway, Switzerland, Bulgaria, Romania and Turkey),[22] yet it consumes between 25 and 30 per cent of the processed products: iron and steel. So, iron ore is imported at a favourable price, processed into steel, then worked into the high-value machinery or vehicles that are the export goods of the hi-tech economy. The outlets for these products are mostly in the industrial countries, even if the newly industrializing countries are also increasingly important buyers.

Much of the prosperity of the industrial countries is therefore based on finishing and polishing. The final stages of value creation, which rest on processing, innovation and symbolic production, are the preserve of the late-industrial economies and their highly skilled workers, engineers and managers. High-value processing brings with it certain linked effects, which in turn have a beneficial influence on the whole economic structure. The countries in the periphery lack all that. They supply the raw materials, but they endure the disadvantages of the trade, without any of its positive, strengthening effects. If such economies remain at the lower levels of processing, they require few skills and scarcely provide any stimulus for greater differentiation of the economic structure. They remain trapped in economic underdevelopment.

Ecological trade balance
Only rarely is it still smelly and noisy in the late-industrial economy, and winding towers and blast furnaces have all but disappeared from the landscape. But, even where the Internet and design have taken over, a national economy cannot get by without raw materials. The acquisition and processing of raw materials, including the environmental costs associated with them, have only dropped out of sight in Europe. The mobili-

zation of nature without which no data can flow has been moving steadily to far-flung parts.

The vivid indicator of the *ecological rucksack* can help to compensate for this failure of perception. It describes the total consumption of resources which, often unknown, has been used in the production of each product, and represents its comparative magnitude. Each raw material, each product and each service lugs around such an ecological rucksack. In fact, the greater part of the material flow never takes the form of a circulating object but remains somewhere along the product's life cycle as detritus or waste. To gain access to mineral raw materials, it is necessary to cut open mountains and divert watercourses, and in the same way the cultivation of crops or cotton involves considerable erosion of the soil. An ecological rucksack therefore contains all the resources needed to produce, use and dispose of one unit of a product or service – not counting the weight of the respective product itself. The rucksack is quantified in tonnes, and measured per tonne of the respective material or product.[23] The ecological rucksack of one tonne of primary aluminium, for example, weighs 7 to 8 tonnes, that of one tonne of copper approximately 500 tonnes, and that of one tonne of gold more than 500,000 tonnes.[24]

Material flow analysis provides a method with which to estimate the resource expenditure of economic areas, and thus of whole national economies. It also makes it possible to ascertain where the expenditure actually takes place.[25] For this the indicator 'Total Material Requirement' has been developed; it adds up all the primary materials (with the exception of air and water) that a national economy needs to extract from nature in the course of a year. This too is measured in tonnes or in tonnes *per capita*, and consists of materials extracted within the national economy as well as imported materials. In the latter case it also distinguishes between the weight of the imports themselves and their ecological rucksack. The following analysis will use this indicator to look at the external trade of the European Union.

In recent years, the EU's total material requirement has remained at a constantly high level – roughly 50 tonnes a year per head of the population since the middle of the 1980s. But in this the weight of imports and their ecological rucksack has increased from approximately 15 to 20 tonnes *per capita*.[26] The bulk of this increase is attributable to ores, mineral fuels, metalware and products such as glass, ceramics and precious stones. These four categories account for most of the ecological rucksacks of imports.[27] A good half of these originate in the developing countries, while fewer resources are extracted in Europe itself. Numerous mines have closed in Europe during the last few decades, either because of natural exhaustion or because they were uneconomic. In this way, environmental stresses have been reduced in Europe but have risen in other regions because of exports to Europe. The environmental costs have merely been displaced.

At the same time, the ecological rucksacks of imports into the EU have increased. The ratio between a product's own weight and its ecological rucksack has worsened, so that today the ecological rucksack averages five times the weight of an imported good.[28] In other words, one tonne of imports leaves behind an average of 5 tonnes in mining waste, emissions and erosion in the exporting country. This ratio has more than doubled over the past twenty-five years, and in the case of ores quadrupled from 1:4 to 1:16 tonnes. For imports from developing countries – which mainly consist of raw materials – the ecological rucksack has also increased appreciably, although the actual quantity of such imports has remained roughly the same (Figure 2.6). This suggests that the acquisition of raw materials is becoming more and more expensive, that more energy has to be used, and that more waste is left behind by mining operations. Analysis of the ecological rucksacks of imports to the EU makes it clear that increasingly environmental stresses connected to the acquisition of raw materials are relocated outside the EU.

On the whole, the turnover of materials and energy, and therefore the ecological burdens, are greater in the stages of simple industrial processing than in the final stages of the value creation chain. Mining involves large amounts of waste material and water, with a high level of energy input. Copper and gold are obtained with the help of large quantities of highly toxic substances. And, in conventional agriculture, even biotic raw materials are produced at a high environmental cost – for example, contamination of watercourses with fertilizer, climate damage due to methane emissions in animal farming, pollution of groundwater with pesticides, and so on. The processing of raw materials into basic inputs also makes intensive use of energy and environmental resources. Only the production process at the end of the value creation chain is relatively clean. German car factories, for example, are proverbially so spotless that one could eat off the floor.

With regard to toxic emissions (air, water, heavy metals), a study for the World Bank concluded that the following groups of products place

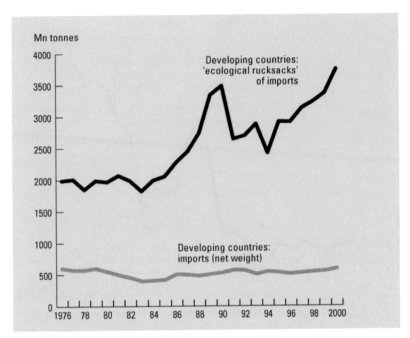

Figure 2.6 Ecological rucksacks of imports from developing countries to the EU (1976–2000). Imports from developing countries to the European Union (EU15) were for many years almost constant, at around 500 million tonnes per annum. The ecological rucksacks of the imports, however, have risen sharply since the mid-1980s and are by now six times higher than the imports themselves. Source: Schütz, Moll and Bringezu 2003

an especially heavy burden on the environment: iron and steel, non-ferrous metals, chemicals, mineral fuels, non-metallic mineral products, cellulose and paper, rubber goods, leather and metal.[29] The share of these goods in the EU import total has increased considerably in the last twenty-five years and currently stands at around 75 per cent. There has also been a marked shift towards the up-and-coming developing countries, whereas the more impoverished ones have become less significant. Production in the basic materials and textiles sectors, which create especially heavy burdens in terms of noise, waste, toxicity and landscape pollution, increasingly takes place in the up-and-coming developing countries, particularly in Eastern Europe, where it is partly a question of relocation outside the industrial heartlands.

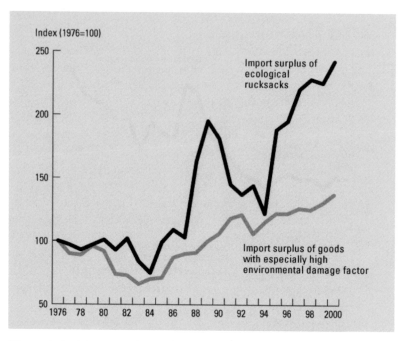

Figure 2.7 EU import surplus of goods with especially high environmental damage factor and ecological rucksacks of EU imports (1976–2000). In the foreign trade of the European Union (EU15), the import surplus of goods with an especially high environmental damage factor has increased since the mid-1990s. The import surplus of ecological rucksacks has also risen significantly in the EU's external trade.
Source: Our own calculations.

The European Union not only imports environmentally harmful raw materials and products; it also exports materials throughout the world, especially in the form of finished goods. It is possible to compare the imports and exports of materials: the ratio between them is known as the ecological trade balance, which, unlike the economic trade balance, is expressed in tonnes rather than monetary quantities. Unequal ecological exchange therefore takes place if Europe constantly imports a higher volume of energy, raw materials and (indirectly) land area than it exports.[30] To draw up an ecological balance sheet of the EU's external trade, one can base ecological rucksacks and especially damaging goods on the parameters introduced above.

In the last few decades, the EU's external trade balance has been more or less in monetary equilibrium. In physical terms, however, its external trade has been unbalanced, with imports standing at 1,400 million tonnes and exports at about 400 million tonnes. The discrepancy is to be explained by the difference between low-processed and high-processed goods. Europe mainly imports cheap goods requiring lower levels of processing, with an average value of 0.70 euros/ kg, but exports goods with a high average value of 2.20 euros/kg. For a long time, this inequality has meant that unfair exchange between North and South is a structural feature of world trade (see further Chapters 3, 4 and 6).

The ecological rucksacks of the EU's imports, hence the environmental stresses originating in the producer countries, also exceed the rucksacks of its exports. They came to 7.2 billion tonnes in the year 2000 total, against 2.3 billion tonnes for the EU's exports. That gives an import excess of nearly 5 billion tonnes, or approximately 14 tonnes per citizen of the EU. Europe thus places a considerably greater ecological burden on the countries of origin than it does on itself.

A similar picture emerges with regard to EU net imports of goods that place a special burden on the environment. In the year 2000 EU imports of these goods came to approximately 1,000 million tonnes, in comparison with exports of about 240 million tonnes. This also displays an ecologically unequal exchange. It increased especially fast in the 1990s, and this correlates with the timeframe for the general tendencies of globalization (Figure 2.7).

The post-industrial illusion

The geographical distribution of environmental burdens changes with the spread of transnational economic relations, as an increasingly high share falls to the industrializing countries in the South and in Eastern Europe. If power in the ecological sense is defined as the ability to internalize environmental advantages and to externalize environmental costs, then it may be thought of as a structural tendency in relations between the economies of the North and the South. In the wake of economic globalization, the rich countries managed to establish a greater geographical distance between places where the advantages of prosperity obtained and those where environmental burdens were incurred. Even if the main reasons for this may have been lower wages and taxes, the result is that environmentally stressful stages of an international production chain tend to be located in economically less developed regions, and that the cleaner stages are mainly in the industrial countries.

In basic industry, metalworking and chemicals, the share of the industrial countries is gradually declining, while that of the Southern countries is increasing.[31] In the aluminium industry, the extraction and bauxite conversion stages are to be found mainly (apart from Australia) in Guyana, Brazil, Jamaica and Guinea. At the processing stage, the smelting of aluminium moved in the 1980s more and more from the North to countries such as Brazil, Venezuela, Indonesia and Bahrain. And the low-pollution stage of material and application research continues to be located in the rich countries.[32] So, when industrial countries point with a superior air to their sometimes relatively favourable environmental data, they are displaying the 'rich country illusion effect'.[33] What allows people locally to breathe a sigh of relief turns out to be a fallacy globally.

We may speak schematically of a multilayered distribution of ecological burdens around the globe. At the top of the ladder stand the late-industrial economies, in which visible environmental pollution is on the decline, while imports, which pollute the countries of origin, are on the increase, bringing with them higher levels of carbon dioxide emissions into the global atmosphere. Cleanness is here largely achieved, but largely through relocation of the ecological burden. This group of countries also includes a number of oil producers, whose large-scale extraction of energy resources gives them the means to build up industrial economic structures of their own. Halfway up the ladder are the newly industrializing economies, which undertake heavy industrial production and therefore have to cope with classical forms of the pollution of water, air and soil – and people. Self-poisoning is the price they have to pay for a greater share of value creation, achieved in part by supplying the North with industrial goods. Right at the bottom stand the raw material economies of the poorest countries – or of poor regions within newly industrializing economies – which is where the great majority of people live. They supply raw metals and especially agricultural raw materials to the newly industrializing or affluent countries, and as a result they have to contend with waste, deforestation, soil erosion and water shortage. This especially affects peoples living close to nature and groups of small farmers who directly depend on it for their livelihood.

Resource claims of rising economies

The distinction between North and South – a rough classification that this book cannot dispense with either – proves misleading on closer examination. To be sure, until the 1980s it made sense to think of the world as bipolar, as structured into industrial and developing countries, rich and poor nations. But, at least since the collapse of the Communist bloc, there are two reasons why this distinction has lost much of its sharpness and actually blurs deeper lines of division.

First, it no longer grasps the reality of the world, since the newly dominant transnational economy has transformed the camp of the developing countries in particular. It has expanded since ex-Communist countries such as Kazakhstan or Georgia, but also Russia, Ukraine and China, have to be included, given their relatively modest economic performance *per capita*. But it has also shrunk, since in the last couple of decades 15 to 20 countries have notched up growth rates which soon distanced them from the majority of developing countries and enabled them to develop in more or less powerful leaps to the level of the industrial countries. So, beneath the category 'South' lie concealed the most diverse national interests and experiences. What exactly can Singapore and Mali be said to have in common?

Second, a comparison of country groups can only partly represent the crucial dividing line in today's world. Talk of North and South obscures the fact that the social cleavage within countries may be at least as dramatic as the gap between countries. There is much to suggest that only parts of a country are caught up in the world market, and that a dividing line runs between the globalized rich and the localized poor, even if the scale and proportions of the phenomenon vary from country to country.

What effect do these shifts within and between countries have on the appropriation of resources? Are the newly industrializing countries drawing level with the older industrial countries in terms of the consumption of resources? Or are we speaking not of countries that foist their expansive demands on the global environment, but above all of a transnational economic complex that is extending to all these countries? There can be no doubt that further countries and classes have been joining the long-established high consumers in a new alliance of 'omnivores'. In the conurbations of the South, there are several hundred million middle- and upper-class people whose purchasing power and consumer behaviour are already close to, if not level with, those of comparable layers in the North.

The new consumer countries

In a rapid, sometimes truly meteoric advance, all the newly industrializing countries have been acquiring a larger share of world economic activity. In the last ten to twenty years they have notched up growth rates far higher than those of the industrial countries, not to speak of the poorer developing countries. In various ways, they have thus come to occupy more favourable positions within the global division of labour: whether as energy suppliers (Saudi Arabia, Venezuela or Russia), as exporters of hardware and software (Thailand, China or India) or as sizeable markets (Brazil, China or Argentina). We shall therefore use the term 'new consumer countries' for emergent economies with a population above 20 million, since that is the size which makes the rise of their consumers globally significant.[34] According to Myers and Kent (2004), there are twenty of these new consumer countries: Argentina, Brazil, China, Colombia, India, Indonesia, Iran, Malaysia, Mexico, Pakistan, Philippines, Poland, Russia, Saudi Arabia, South Africa, South Korea, Thailand, Turkey, Ukraine and Venezuela. China has an especially prominent position among them, being home to a sixth of humanity and alone accounting for a big share of rising global consumption.

In these countries, to an admittedly varying extent, greater prosperity has brought with it a tendency for the consumption of energy, materials and land to increase. Economic success intensifies the claims on the natural environment. The demand for resources shoots up precisely because, under the prevailing economic model, income gains significantly increase the ability to convert natural values into lucrative commodity values. If we take primary energy use as the key indicator for environmentally intensive models of production and consumption, we gain a first impression of the growing resource hunger of the new consumer countries (Figure 2.8).

The industrial countries remain in the lead as far as absolute energy consumption is concerned, but their position is increasingly contested by the new consumer countries – although, of course, these have a larger number of inhabitants. Leaving aside the break in the statistical series due to the dissolution of the Soviet Union, it is clear that since the 1970s the new consumer countries have been catching up with the industrial

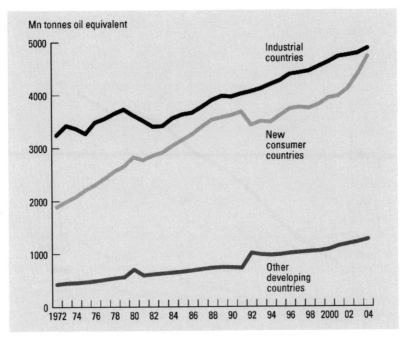

Figure 2.8 Absolute energy consumption in the new consumer countries (1972–2004). In the 1970s energy consumption in the new consumer countries was still midway between that of the industrial countries and other developing countries. Since then their absolute energy consumption has become similar to that of the industrial countries, although it should be remembered that they have a far larger combined population.

Source: World Bank 2003 and IEA 2006. On the basis of the available statistics, the whole USSR is counted among the new consumer countries until the year 1990.

countries in absolute energy consumption. At the same time, they have pulled away from the great majority of developing countries, whose energy use has been growing slowly but is still at a comparatively low level.

Major consumption of the environment is also associated with certain goods such as cars or televisions (Figures 2.9 and 2.10). If we compare their diffusion over the past few decades we get a similar picture, though with characteristic differences. Since the end of the 1980s, they spread in the new consumer countries at an initially slow but then much faster rate, especially in the case of televisions, which do not require such great

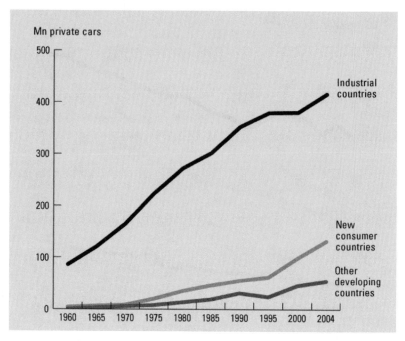

Mn private cars

Industrial countries

New consumer countries

Other developing countries

1960 1965 1970 1975 1980 1985 1990 1995 2000 2004

Figure 2.9 Number of registered private cars in the new consumer countries (1960–2004). The growth of car ownership has been slower than that of energy consumption and television ownership in the new consumer countries. Although the new consumer countries have far more inhabitants, the great majority of private cars are still in the industrial countries.

Source: VDA. On the basis of the available statistics, the whole USSR is counted among the new consumer countries until the year 1990.

purchasing power. This dynamic has led to a situation where the new consumer countries – with a larger population – have already overtaken the industrial countries in absolute ownership of TV sets. And there are quite a few predictions that the same will be true of cars within the next fifteen to twenty years.

Consumption habits are not determined only by income trends. Geographical, economic or cultural factors also exert an influence and may produce a varied range of consumer styles at similar income levels. Thus, although there is a strong correlation between rising income and car ownership,[35] cities with roughly the same *per capita* income display

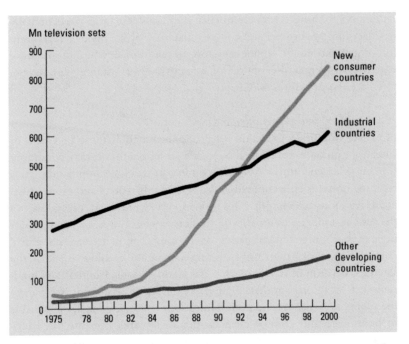

Figure 2.10 Number of television sets in the new consumer countries (1974–2000). Since the early 1990s the new consumer countries together have had more television sets than the developed industrial countries, whereas in the early 1980s they had scarcely any more than all the other developing countries.

Source: World Bank 2003; IEA 1997 and our own calculations. Figures not available for USSR before 1990.

clear differences in driving performance, depending upon how spatially dispersed and functionally divided they are.[36]

The new consumer countries must use such opportunities to shape their own future if they want to escape the dangers of a mere 'catching-up' development. It is sufficiently well known from the experience of the industrial countries how economic development leads to perceptions, habits and everyday routines that sink into the brain and make a change of direction considerably more difficult. The same is true of the major infrastructure underpinning consumption, without which neither TV sets nor cars could ever function. Televisions do not work without power stations, nor motor vehicles without road networks. But both of these represent very long-term investments: they condense, as it were, present-day decisions about steel and concrete that may prove disadvantageous to future generations. It would therefore be wise for newly industrializing countries to retain the option of a satisfying way of life without the intensive use of resources (Chapter 5).

'Global cities' and their hinterland

However important is the rise of economies such as those of China or India, it cannot have escaped anyone's attention that boom conditions scarcely ever encompass a whole country or a whole population. As a rule, the boom is concentrated in the central urban areas and more or less extensive industrial regions. This is not an accident but an integral part of the system. Under a transnational division of labour, it is not countries or peoples but only certain places or regions that participate in global competition – and then only so long as conditions allow it.[37] For the intended division of labour reaches out across national frontiers and binds remote areas to one another. Countless production chains cut right across the globe, as transport and communications technology make it possible to coordinate and control even far-flung networks. Against this back-ground, the success of the newly industrializing countries may be read as an upward surge not of nations but of regional or even local spaces that present one or more favourable characteristics for global investors. Growth regions should thus be regarded first and foremost as junctions of global production networks, not as trailblazers for a national economy. The fact that Shanghai and Shenzen are in China, or Mumbai and Bangalore in India, is of secondary importance: their booming districts are mainly locations for cross-border processes of capital formation.

So, the globalization of economic activities leads not to the same degree of growth around the world but to more intense inequality and differentiation.[38] Some regions are raised up, others fall behind; some locations boom, others face demolition. Regional and social conflicts grow deeper, because neighbouring areas may at the same time serve quite different functions for transnational production chains. We may distinguish three types of area with regard to such chains: global centres, their globalized hinterlands, and the excluded remainder of the world.[39]

In global cities such as Tokyo, Hong Kong, New York or London are to be found the commanding heights: the financial institutions, the corporate managements, the communications industries and the research centres. The globalized hinterland contains the networks producing

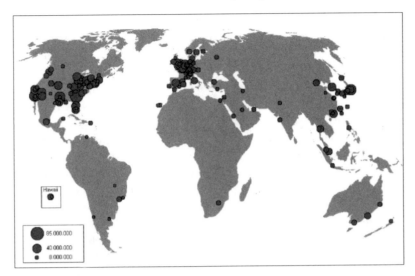

Figure 2.11 Size of 150 largest airports by passenger numbers (2000).
The most heavily used airports for passenger traffic are in North America and
Europe. Asia also has a significant share of the world's 150 largest airports,
while Africa has a mere two and Latin America six.
Source: Our own presentation, based on ACI 2002.

goods and services: software firms, factories for mass products, sources of
raw materials, and tourist areas. Examples of this kind are cities such as
Bangalore, Johannesburg and Naples, or regions such as southeast China
or Mauritius. Mention should also be made of the more than five
hundred special economic zones or tax-free enclaves, spread out over
seventy countries.[40] And the excluded remainder of the world is where
the majority of the population live, largely on the margins of the world
market or 'surplus to requirements'. These areas stretch from the
ghettoes of North America and the *favelas* of Brazil through the African
continent to the villages of India or Indonesia. Of course, locations and
regions may move into or out of a particular level, and in many places
there is lively competition over just this issue. But, from an economic
point of view, it remains the case that globalization brings not a levelling
but a hierarchical ordering of global space.

This hierarchy is mirrored in the flows of international transport. In
the end, despite the increasing importance of telecommunications for
processes of international exchange, the physical movement of persons

and goods continues to play a major role. Air transport serves as a transmission belt for an economy based on a global division of labour. The geographical distribution of personal air travel is plainly concentrated in the conurbations described above. As Figure 2.11 shows, the overwhelming majority of the 150 largest airports by passenger number are to be found in the northern hemisphere, with a mere six in South America, two in Africa and just one in the area of the former Soviet Union.

If we take into account that the data are distorted by people travelling from high-income to low-income countries, it is clear how the distribution of air transport reproduces the hierarchical order of global space. The first level, set apart from the rest, consists of the places and regions involved in globalization. The second contains a number of airports scattered around the globe, but with a much lower density and passenger totals. And at a third level, encompassing the largest land surfaces on the planet, there are no large airports at all. In keeping with this, it is variously estimated that only 1 per cent[41] to 5 per cent[42] of the world's population has experienced air travel. Greatly accelerated interaction is therefore a phenomenon that takes place overwhelmingly

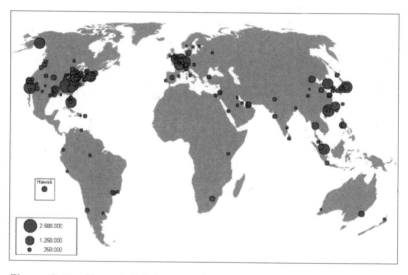

Figure 2.12 Size of 150 largest airports by freight tonnage (2000).
The most heavily used airports for freight traffic are in North America, Europe and Asia. East Asia and South America are more strongly represented than in the case of passenger traffic.

Source: Our own presentation, based on ACI statistics.

between a few parts of the world; the great metropolises, though scattered far and wide, keep in close contact with one another. The increase in passenger miles between 1975 and 1999 underlines the greater density that these contacts acquired precisely in the age of globalization.[43]

The geographical distribution of the largest freight airports makes still clearer the picture of a hierarchical order (Figure 2.12). The transport of goods by air, especially high-value goods such as machine or computer parts, is indispensable for global production networks, as otherwise the use of location advantages would be cancelled out by delays and the hazards of transport. This explains why civilian air freight, measured in tonne kilometres, grew by 449 per cent between 1975 and 1999.

To be sure, the geography of air freight has become more complex: Africa is still outside, but South America has already made an entrance and East Asia is much more strongly integrated than in the past. So, a larger number of regions are now involved in transnational production link-ups. The distribution of airports demonstrates the spread of international production networks, whose separate locations are often at a considerable distance from one another.

The infrastructure of the global production networks costs resources and puts additional pressure on the environment. If the demand for transport continues to grow by an average of 2.1 per cent per year, as the International Energy Agency predicts, it will mean an increase larger than in any other sector of consumption. In fact, over the next two decades transport will overtake industry as the largest final energy user.[44] Total air passenger transport is growing at a rate of approximately 6 per cent a year, after a temporary slowing in the wake of 9/11. Already in 1992 air traffic was estimated to be responsible for 3.5 per cent of all climate change due to human activity, and other components of exhaust fumes make a considerably larger contribution to this than does carbon dioxide. The effects of nitrogen oxides, vapour trails or cirrus clouds, and of atmospheric processes at an altitude of ten kilometres, have been only partly investigated. In respect of fuel consumption and carbon dioxide emissions, it is estimated that the climatic effects of air travel are two to four times greater than those of surface transport.[45] And, given the huge growth potential, the impact of air travel may be even greater in future and offset the efforts of other sectors to limit the damage to the world's climate.

Furthermore, aircraft consume various metals, while airports eat up land and terminal installations require steel and cement. The expansion of international air transport is achieved at the price of massive overuse of natural resources. The economic profit for certain parts of the world thus depends on the fact that the transport system can appropriate for itself a disproportionate share of global resources.

The transnational consumer class

Statistics sometimes distort the truth – not because they lie, but because they suggest categories that grasp reality only from a particular point of view. This is true of a good many statistics gathered by the United Nations. The World Bank tables, for instance, reconstruct the world in general through sets of data relating to countries, regardless of whether the information in question concerns national income or energy consumption. This is not surprising, since the United Nations has to rely heavily upon the statistical bureaux of its member states. However, this methodological nationalism is an obstacle to our understanding of globalization: that is, the emergence of transnational social spaces such as cross-frontier corporations, academic networks or consumption cultures. Thus, talk of the new consumer countries also tends to restrict our vision; statements about resource consumption by particular countries obscure the fact that this consumption is not shared equally by the whole population but is often limited to a relatively small minority.

The correlation between household income and energy use has been well substantiated in the case of industrial countries. Similarly, in the developing and newly industrializing countries, what separates the better-off from the have-nots is often the mode of energy consumption: the rich use quite different fuels from the poor, who frequently collect brushwood, tree branches or dried dung and only occasionally, in the big cities, have access to oil or electricity. The different fuels therefore constitute a kind of energy hierarchy, in accordance with household income levels.[46] Thus, for cooking purposes the bottom rungs of the ladder feature wood, dung and other biomass; the middle rungs, charcoal, coal and kerosene; and the top rungs, electricity, mains gas and petrol. The energy hierarchy corresponds to social stratification in many countries of the South.

In the main, however, class stratification takes shape in the *quantity* of energy consumption. Data from India and Pakistan show that the middle classes use roughly three to four times more electricity, and the upper classes four to five times more, than those among the lower classes who have any access to it.[47] The differences appear even more sharply in relation to transport. As people in the lower classes move around on foot or by bus, those who use their own car consume more than ten times as much energy. An Indian comparison of spending on private consumption gives similar results: the top 10 per cent of the population, living in the cities, spend almost ten times more *per capita* than the bottom 50 per cent in the countryside. Urban dwellers across the social spectrum spend three times more on energy than rural dwellers, three times more on transport services, more than twice as much on clothing and non-food consumption goods, but less than twice as much on food.[48] In many countries of Africa and South America, which have steeper social hierarchies than South Asia, the internal differentiation by class and region is even more conspicuous.

To sum up: the upper middle classes in South Asia use as much energy as their counterparts in many industrial countries. The uneven distribution of energy consumption between industrial and developing countries is repeated within the developing countries themselves, between the consumer class and the majority of the population. But the average consumption of the upper middle classes in developing countries is generally lower than in the industrial countries. In the North account must be taken not only of private consumption but of public services and social systems, while in the South the rich have to share with the rest of the population a rather scant infrastructure.[49] In any event, in the newly industrializing countries a consumer class of varying size is able to secure for itself a much larger share of natural resources than the majority of the population.

Finally, a passing observer in the big cities of the South cannot fail to be struck by their pockets of affluence: the glittering office towers, the shopping malls with their luxury shops, the screened-off districts with their villas and manicured gardens, not to speak of the stream of Mitsubishis and Mercedes alongside the battered trams and street traders. Sandton in Johannesburg, Alphaville in São Paulo, Ksour in Marrakesh or Sukhumvit in Bangkok are islands of wealth in a sea of simple houses and paupers' huts. The spatial fragmentation of the cities makes the social polarization visible; it demonstrates how remote the trend-setting classes are in their lifestyle from the ordinary citizens.

How large is the consumer class in various countries? It depends on the boundaries of the group in question. If the threshold is low, the consumer class becomes statistically sizeable, because it then encompasses the lower middle classes who have taken the first, relatively modest steps towards resource-intensive consumption. If the threshold is set higher, the consumer class shrinks in size and takes in only layers with some real purchasing power, whose style of consumption is comparable to that of the lower middle classes in industrial countries.

Norman Myers and Jennifer Kent take the first of these approaches.[50] They set a *per capita* income of US$2,500 a year, with the purchasing power this has in the respective country. Above this level people can gradually move beyond the satisfaction of basic needs and approach the kind of lifestyle they have learned from their models in the North. According to Myers and Kent, there are 1,059 million new consumers around the world. But the picture changes if the consumer class is more narrowly defined to include only those with an annual income above $7,000 (at purchasing power parity); this sum corresponds to the roughly measured poverty threshold in Western Europe, so that the transnational consumer class may be defined as a group possessing at least the income of the lower middle classes in Western Europe. On this basis Matthew Bentley calculates the number of new consumers to be 816 million.[51] These join the 912 million established consumers in the industrial countries, who, of course, dispose of an average income several times higher. If the net is drawn to include the whole consumer class at this level of purchasing power, then we are talking of a good 1.7 billion people already in the year 2000 – more than a quarter of the world's population.[52]

Figure 2.13 represents the countries with the largest number of (new) consumers, with the income threshold at US$7,000.[53] China and India alone account for more than 20 per cent of the global consumer class, a combined total of 362 million people (greater than in the whole of Western Europe, though with a considerably lower average income). The consumer class represents, for example, 19 per cent of the population in China, 33 per cent in Brazil and 43 per cent in Russia.[54] If we bear in mind that the equivalent figure for Western Europe is 89 per cent, it is not hard to picture the growth potential in these countries. At the same time, the figures show that in the North, too, in the age of globalization, more than one in ten are excluded from the prosperity of the transnational consumer class.

Roughly speaking, the transnational consumer class resides half in the South and half in the North. It comprises social groups which, despite their different skin colour, are less and less country-specific and tend to resemble one another more and more in their behaviour and lifestyle

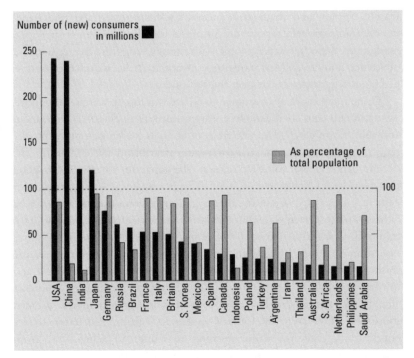

Figure 2.13 Consumers/new consumers in total figures and as share of population in 25 countries (2000). Of all global consumers, 53 per cent live in industrial countries and 47 per cent are 'new consumers' in developing and newly industrializing countries. Approximately one-third of the global consumer class live in three countries: USA, China and India.
Source: Bentley 2003: 153ff.

models. In many respects, a lawyer's family in Caracas has more in common with a businessman's family in Beijing than either has with fellow-countrymen in the respective hinterlands. In other words, they are not 'Venezuelan' or 'Chinese' so much as local representatives of a transnational consumer class. They shop in similar malls, buy the same hi-tech equipment, see the same films and TV series, roam around as tourists and dispose of the key instrument of assimilation: money. They are part of a transnational economic complex, which is now developing its markets on a global scale. Nokia supplies it everywhere with mobile telephones, Toyota with cars, Sony with televisions, Siemens with refrigerators, Burger King with fast-food joints, and Time-Warner with

DVDs. Supply and demand reinforce each other: on the one hand, mainly transnational corporations promote intensive consumerism in the market; on the other hand, people with money long for a higher standard of living. This two-sided expansion means that the world economy is placing a huge extra burden on the biosphere.

Three main types of consumer good are driving up the use of energy, materials and land area: namely, meat consumption, electrical equipment and motor vehicles.[55] The fattening of animals for consumption usually requires grain, and grain in turn requires farmland and water. In the decade from 1990 to 2000 alone, the quantity of livestock grain increased by 31 per cent in China, 52 per cent in Malaysia and 63 per cent in Indonesia.[56] Water for the irrigation of grain used as animal feed exhausts both surface water and groundwater: as much as 1,000 tonnes is required to produce one tonne of grain, and 16,000 tonnes to produce one tonne of beef.[57] Often enough, if farmland and water are running short, recourse to the world grain market drives up food prices and impacts negatively on the poorer countries; the new consumer countries already account for nearly 40 per cent of world grain imports. What is more, the whole range of electrical appliances – from refrigerators to air-conditioning systems, from washing machines to televisions, from microwaves to computers – increase the consumption of electricity, which is normally produced with fossil fuels. In 2002 as many as 1.2 billion households, comprising three-quarters of the world's population, owned at least one television set,[58] and through cable services 31 per cent can plug into the global circuit of fabricated images and get to know the goods they aspire to have. Finally there is the motor car. Whereas in 1990 the number of passenger cars in the new consumer countries stood at 62 million, by the year 2000 the figure had soared to 117 million, or 21 per cent of the world total. If these growth rates continue, the number of cars in the world will again almost double by the year 2010. It is hardly surprising that nearly all cities with the world's highest levels of pollution are to be found in the new consumer countries. As we see, the consumption of resources is spreading around the globe through the lifestyles of the North, whose offshoots in the South now compete with them for environmental space.

Notes

1　Baccini and Brunner 1991; Moll 1996.
2　Mehta and Winiwarter 1996.
3　Adriaanse et al. 1998; Bringezu 2004.
4　SRU 1994.
5　Source: our own presentation, borrowing from European Commission 2003.
6　Steger 2005.
7　McNeill 2003: 39.
8　IPCC 2001a; WBGU 2003a.
9　IPCC 2001b.
10　Parry et al. 2001.
11　IPCC 2001b; WBGU 2003a.
12　IPCC 2001b.
13　Wackernagel and Rees 1997.
14　WWF 2006.
15　United Nations Population Division 2002.
16　Bringezu 2004.
17　Bringezu, Schütz and Moll 2003.
18　Altvater and Mahnkopf 1996.
19　Enquete-Kommission 2002; *Le Monde Diplomatique* 2003.
20　Schütz, Moll and Bringezu 2003; Schütz, Moll and Steger 2003; Steger 2005.
21　Steger 2005.
22　British Geological Survey 2003.
23　Schmidt-Bleek 1998: 82.
24　Schmidt-Bleek 1998: 297.
25　Bringezu and Schütz 1995.
26　EEA 2003.
27　Schütz, Moll and Bringezu 2003.
28　Ibid. 2003.
29　Mani and Wheeler 1997.
30　Andersson and Lindroth 2001.
31　Sprenger 1997; Mason 1997.
32　Heerings and Zeldenrust 1995.
33　Andersson and Lindroth 2001; Muradian et al. 2002.
34　The definition and membership of the group have been taken from Myers and Kent 2004.
35　Ingram and Liu 1997: 32.
36　Kenworthy 2003: 3.
37　Scholz 2003: 12.
38　Knox et al. 2003: 113.
39　Scholz 2003.

40   Knox et al. 2003: 325.
41   Humphreys 2003: 20.
42   Whitelegg 2003: 235.
43   ICAO 1975–2001.
44   IEA 2002: 28.
45   IPCC 1999.
46   Goldemberg 2000.
47   Siddiqi 1995.
48   Ibid.
49   Parikh 2003.
50   Myers and Kent 2004.
51   Bentley 2003.
52   Ibid.
53   Ibid.
54   Ibid.; Gardner et al. 2004: 44.
55   Myers and Kent 2003: 4964ff.
56   Myers and Kent 2003.
57   Hoekstra 2003.
58   Gardner et al. 2004: 47.

3
Arenas of Appropriation

Man's power over nature turns out to be power exercised by some men over other men, with nature as its instrument.

C. S. Lewis, 1947

The earth's resources do not simply fall into the arms of the transnational consumer class. Usually the provision sites are a long way from the consumption sites, with provinces or even continents in between. How does it happen that transnational consumers are able to garner the lion's share of resources? Everyone knows the name of the gravitational force which ensures that resources move from near and far to the big consumers: it is called power. Yet power has not one but many faces; it does not spring from an arbitrary act but is part of the normal course of things. By virtue of its effects fleets of oil tankers set a safe course for the industrial countries, while tea, rice, soya and coffee find their way from poor areas of the world to supermarkets in the rich countries, and the swimming pools of the well-to-do remain supplied with water even in times of drought. So, the power of the transnational economic complex operates through force fields involving innumerable decisions, in such a way that in the end a quarter of the world's population can make disproportionate use of many valuable natural resources.

Power works through highly varied means. Most of these are familiar from history: for example, the use of military force, the quiet workings of world trade or the channelling effect of infrastructures. As we shall see in this chapter, power may also enlist the help of new instruments such as international agreements. It is difficult to extract resources without deploying overt or covert instruments of power, since resources are often neither freely accessible nor available in unlimited supply. There are several reasons for this. *First*, the great majority of resources exist not in a kind of no-man's-land but in the lived space of people who have often made a prior claim to them. Whether it is a question of natural gas, water, farmland or genetic material, many resources must first be transferred from the ownership of local inhabitants to that of the resource industries. *Second*, those who wish to gain control of certain resources usually have to compete with others who have the same end in view. States position themselves against other states, cities against rural areas, corporations against corporations, American consumers against European consumers – and meanwhile the number of people on earth keeps growing in comparison with the available natural resources. *Third*, there is no longer a plentiful supply of resources: most of the gifts of nature are now running short, and the competition becomes intense where, for example, oil reserves run low or the soil loses its fertility. Thus, the future limits of resources cast their shadows well into the present, and social conflicts often arise long before a resource is ecologically used up.

Far from being just a bio-physical fact, ecological limits are often the cause of a social explosion. In the various arenas of appropriation – geopolitics, trade, investment, international law – conflict is therefore quietly or noisily on the agenda. Through the force fields of power, transnational consumers and corporations try to gain the upper hand. But counterforces are also developing: the victory of the strongest is by no means assured, and the outcome is seldom clear-cut. Resource appropriation is therefore a conflictual process that constantly radiates out into the surrounding society. The struggle for resources is regularly associated with conflicts of a political or ethnic nature, as injustice on this issue is often what lies behind what may be called religious or tribal feuding. Neither the crisis in the Middle East nor the civil war in Sudan can be understood without reference to the role of oil, nor the plight of refugees in Pakistan or the genocide in Rwanda without reference to soil loss and degradation. Whether at international or subnational level, disputes over resources contribute to social destabilization whenever legitimate forms of conflict regulation are absent. It is therefore likely that, if the resource situation continues to grow tenser, conflicts will flare up in many places and make the world as a whole more inflammable.

In this chapter we shall look more closely at four arenas for resource conflict, taking four patterns of appropriation for illustrative purposes. (1) The demand for oil, in a situation of limited supply, gives rise to geopolitical strategies to ensure a constant flow from source to final consumer. (2) Agricultural imports into the transnational centres are underpinned by the force field of the global market, which spurs the countries of the South to gear their farm output to exports. (3) The flow of water is directed mainly by investment in dams, canals and mains systems, which take a common good and ultimately employ it for one-sided industrial or consumption-related purposes. (4) The patenting of plants, with the protection of international law, allows corporations to make lucrative use of genetic material, while depriving the poor of the free use of plant resources.

Geopolitics: the hands on the oil

Nowadays, if one talks of resource appropriation, one thinks first of oil. It is certainly more important than gold ever was. All structures significant for human civilization are geared to the 'black gold', and without it the industrial economy would collapse. Large parts of industry and many jobs are based on the use or processing of crude oil; transport and mobility – by water, land and air – mainly rely upon refined oil products,[1] as do plastics, pharmaceuticals, fertilizers, construction materials, paints and dyes, textiles and much else besides. This dependence on oil has continually increased since the middle of the last century, making it a politically, economically and even culturally irreplaceable resource. Oil leaves its mark as no other substance on global lifestyles. And this means that its strategic value multiplies its economic value.

Secure access to oil has long been a central factor in geopolitical strategies. Governments gear their economic, military and other foreign policies to the gaining of political influence over major resources in other countries and continents. The recent armed interventions of the United States and its allies, for instance, have not only aimed to free Kuwait, to overthrow the Iraqi dictatorship or to break up the Al Qaida terror network, but also concerned themselves with the Middle Eastern oil reserves. Although oil has kept growing in importance to the industrial countries, they mostly have little or none of it on their own territory (see Chapter 2). Access to oil in other regions is therefore such a high priority that their efforts in the last few decades to control oil reserves have more than once led to large-scale conflicts and wars.

In the main, the countries that have moved to gain secure access to oil have been those with an already strong position in the international arena: the countries of North America and Europe, Japan and Australasia – that is, today's industrial heartlands. And countries from the developing world that seem to be winning the catching-up race, such as China, closely follow suit. Inequality in relation to oil has been extended and cemented with the aid of geopolitical strategies.

Spheres of influence

In the Middle East, the most important oil region, the United States has long been present through its Saudi Arabian ally. Close relations between the two countries date back to 1945, when President Roosevelt signed an accord with the Saudi king of the time, Abd al-Aziz ibn Saud, offering military protection in return for access rights to oil reserves. Since then the United States has been the largest Saudi trading partner. The state oil corporation, ARAMCO, was originally a Saudi-American joint enterprise. In the race to establish commercial relations, Washington proved faster than all others and managed to secure its supply of oil and its long-term influence over the world oil market. In 1991, during the Gulf war following Iraq's annexation of Kuwait, Riyadh even permitted US troops to be stationed on its territory for the first time. In exchange, operation 'Desert Storm' was launched to 'liberate' the Kuwaiti oilfields.

From the American viewpoint, there are important reasons for their presence in Saudi Arabia: the country extracts nine million barrels of oil a day, which makes it the world's largest producer, followed by Russia and the USA.[2] If a power hostile to the United States were to gain influence over the Saudi reserves, it would put major pressure on the USA and the rest of the oil-dependent world. Besides, for many years Saudi Arabia had free production capacity that could be used for a time to replace other producers and thereby guarantee the total oil requirement.[3] In this way Riyadh – and indirectly also Washington – had in its hands the most important instrument for stabilizing the world supply and price of oil. The attacks of 11 September 2001, involving contacts and money from Saudi Arabia, dramatically altered the situation; Saudi Arabia now counts as an unreliable partner for the United States. This throws light on the most recent Iraq war, since now the key issue for Washington's oil geopolitics is how to assert American influence in the region while freeing itself from dependence on Riyadh.

Whereas the spheres of activity are marked out in the Middle East, the struggle for oil in the Caspian Sea region is currently in full swing. In the first few years after the break-up of the Soviet Union, Moscow showed little interest in Central Asia, as internal problems and financial shortages restricted its ability to exert political and economic influence there. The United States, however, already in the early 1990s supported the striving of the Central Asian states for independence and invested in their oil industries.[4] The politically insecure position of the Caspian region harbours a major potential for crisis. The US responds to this by strengthening its political and military involvement: a thousand troops have been stationed in Uzbekistan for humanitarian purposes in recent years; a massive international deployment has taken place in Afghanistan, as part of the 'war on terror'; American soldiers are also on duty in Kyrgzstan; and in 1997 US special forces engaged in joint manoeuvres with Kazakh soldiers.[5]

Washington has not been alone in linking the military and economic aspects of energy supplies; NATO's current strategic conception states that 'Alliance security interests can be affected by other risks of a wider nature, including ... disruption of the flow of vital resources.'[6] Already in November 1990, before the beginning of the Gulf War, NATO's general secretary of the time, Manfred Wörner, maintained that its intervention in the area was justified not only to liberate Kuwait but to safeguard the supply of oil.[7] Such threatening gestures should be understood as part of a general attempt to intimidate anyone toying with the idea of withholding key energy resources from NATO or one of its members. Meanwhile no secret is made of the fact that democratic countries will also resort to military means to ensure their energy supplies – and to defend a system that has led to such dependence.

War or military threats are not the only means of gaining more favourable access to oil. The world oil market is by no means a free one where price and quantity develop in accordance with supply and demand. Major producers, such as those in the cartelized Organization of Petroleum Exporting Countries (OPEC), attempt to direct the market. And the ability of their customers to seek out the most advantageous suppliers is limited by production capacities and political influence, as well as by the very indispensability of oil. Current needs must be covered at almost any price, as there is no alternative on offer. What this means in practice was demonstrated during the first oil crisis in 1973, when an Arab sales boycott following the Yom Kippur War suddenly quadrupled the price of oil. Output and export levels were cut by 5 per cent, leading to worldwide economic stagnation (zero growth in Germany in 1974, for example, and a 1 per cent fall in GDP the following year).[8]

Oil-importing countries therefore have a special interest in influencing market trends, rather than allowing the supply and price of oil to be governed by market forces. Two objectives underlie the geopolitical strategies: to guarantee supplies, and to keep prices low. The poorest countries in the South, or industrial countries such as Japan that have no oil on their territory, are especially concerned to pay the lowest possible price. The configuration of interests is more complex in the case of the United States. As the world's largest consumer, it too has an interest in low prices, but on the other hand it has an extensive oil industry of its own. This leads to a constant conflict. For, whereas low oil prices are advantageous from the point of view of the US economy as a whole, they must not be so low as to ruin the domestic oil industry – given that North American oil is more expensive to produce than Middle Eastern.

Countries such as Saudi Arabia whose main exports are oil and natural gas have an interest in low-to-medium oil prices. The reason for this is that many of the oil-exporting countries invest so much money abroad in the form of joint enterprises and financial operations that a global economic recession due to high oil prices would cause them considerable losses. So, cheap oil is not only in the interests of import-dependent countries; oil producers would also like to avoid turbulence in the world economy.

Besides, a higher oil price makes alternative energy financially attract-ive, with the result that the demand for oil might permanently fall. Forward-looking investment in renewable energy sources would be a more viable option in the long run than the imperialist strategy of ensuring access to oil by military means. But, in the short-term view of those who have an interest in maintaining the structures of the last half-century, such an alternative is not available. They would themselves have to help replace the structures in which they have invested and from which up to now they have derived a profit.

Peak oil

Oil has such geopolitical importance not only because it is still the basic energy source for the world economy, but also – indeed especially – because it will soon be in short supply. Until a few decades ago, the oil developers could be happy that reserves were still sharply increasing, and announced that newly discovered fields held more oil than the amount produced annually from existing ones. Since the early 1980s, however, things have turned around. Annual output has significantly outstripped the quantity available from new discoveries. Roughly four barrels of crude are now being extracted for every one newly discovered barrel.[9]

When it is a question of the oil available, the discussion has for a long time centred on absolute reserves. But what do such figures tell us? Very little about the availability of oil. The only figures of predictive value are those which compare present and future productive capacity. This is what gives the measure of how much oil can be produced for a given unit of time. The exploitation of an oil field follows a bell-shaped curve: output rises very sharply at first, peaks at roughly half of the maximum production capacity, and is then followed by a period of decline in which output continually decreases because of falling pressure. Supportive measures can delay things slightly but by no means reverse the tendency. At some point the quantity of oil from the field becomes so small that further production is no longer worthwhile. A halt to production therefore occurs before the field is totally exhausted. For all the oil fields in the world, there is a point of maximum output – the so-called 'depletion midpoint' – after which production levels go into irreversible decline.

There is heated debate about precisely when output will peak at this global maximum. The problem is that analysis and evaluation of the available statistics are usually interest-driven: representatives of the oil corporations quoted on the stock exchange claim that such a level will never be reached,[10] while optimists at America's official Energy Information Authority or the Paris-based International Energy Agency place it in a very wide time corridor that allows of very few predictions.[11] But, although it seems scarcely tenable to name a precise year, it is not impossible to set clearer temporal parameters. If we weigh up the various factors, we may conclude that the level of maximum oil output will be reached sometime between the years 2008 and 2015.[12]

Against this background, geopolitical strategies to guarantee oil supplies at stable prices acquire even greater significance. For those in charge of the war in Iraq, the aim is not only to ensure oil reserves in the medium term but to ward off an impending crisis of the world economy. For, once depletion midpoint is reached, oil prices will increase rapidly and a vicious circle similar to that of the 1970s may well appear – except that this time there will be no end in sight to the supply shortages. If output is no longer able to keep pace with demand, all countries, and especially those dependent on oil, will be heading for an economic crisis.

Discussion on the basis of absolute reserves is therefore misconceived. But it is also deliberate: it serves to produce a clear psychological effect. If there is enough oil for the next forty years or more, then we are talking about a problem that lies in the future, and meanwhile new production technologies will emerge, as they did in the past, to give another breathing space. In this way, discussion is deflected from the ever more acute question of availability and the risk of skyrocketing prices.

More demand, fewer suppliers

The crisis is looming at a time when the world's thirst for oil is constantly increasing; all prognoses speak of a dramatic rise in oil consumption.[13] In fact, nearly every country on earth is banking on economic growth that can be attained only through increased use of fossil fuels. Apart from the old industrial heartlands, the demand for oil has for some time also been growing in the new consumer countries (see Chapter 2), especially China, India and Brazil. Their soaring need for oil – still irreplaceable as a raw material and means of propulsion – has given them a new prominence on the world market. The newly industrializing countries of Asia, in particular, where there are relatively few reserves of oil and gas, are becoming increasingly involved in the competition for resources. China is already the world's second-largest importer of oil, and even a country like Malaysia, which is today still a net exporter, will turn into a net importer over the coming decade. Since the industrial countries are far from reining in their own consumption of oil, and in many cases are still even expanding it, the situation is becoming truly tight. The emerging economies insist on their claims, the old users will not give ground, and the deposits are beginning to run short. This is a perfect scenario for explosive rivalries over the next few decades.

What is more, oil production is set to become concentrated in the hands of fewer and fewer suppliers. At present a fairly large number of producers still operate on the international oil market, making up quite a motley bunch of states and corporations. Approximately 30 per cent of the world's supplies come from OPEC countries; North America accounts for just under 20 per cent; and Africa, South America, Asia, the former Soviet Union and Europe for roughly 10 per cent each.[14] Over the past thirty years, however, the relative shares have shifted quite considerably. Under the impact of the oil crises of the 1970s, the Western industrial countries made huge efforts to reduce their dependence on OPEC, but this expansion of their own production exacted a heavy toll. Some of the countries in question already passed their depletion midpoint a number of years ago: the United States reached it in 1970 and is today pumping out only 60 per cent of what it produced then; Russia in 2003 was extracting no more than 70 per cent of its 1988 peak. Norway, Mexico and Venezuela reached their depletion midpoint in the last five years.[15] In future more and more producers will reach their maximum output level, and then oil production will start falling. The field of oil producers is growing smaller, and only a few giants will survive. If they come to an agreement among themselves, there will be even less of a free choice of suppliers or a free play of market forces than there is today.

Exit from oil as security policy

A short-term view might lead to the conclusion that the cheap-oil policy described above served the industrial countries as well as the oil producers, and that the poor countries of the South, which had no other alternative, benefited from it as much as anyone else. What this overlooks, of course, is the fact that the low price for oil and the assurance of a constant supply everywhere built up an infrastructure dependent on that single resource. This was all right so long as there was enough cheap oil to go round. But now, when the cake is getting smaller but the hunger is growing and the number of guests is increasing, a permanent field of conflict is opening up. In the wars in the Gulf and Afghanistan, but also the tensions in the Caspian, the war in Chechnya or the fighting in Sudan, the great contest of the future is already casting its shadows. The powerful states are seeking to guarantee their oil supplies by military means, and for the less powerful this can only mean that they too will have to employ violent action if they are not to fall into greater dependence.

The greatest costs will be borne by the poor countries. As analysts at the International Energy Agency have shown, an oil price rise from 15 to 25 dollars has an immediate effect in the industrial countries of reducing economic growth by 0.4 per cent, but the oil-importing developing countries are hit even harder: the Asian developing countries lose 0.8 per cent, and African countries south of the Sahara as much as 3.0 per cent.[16] The national debt will grow there, as it did during the oil crisis of 1973, and fossil fuels will move out of reach for large sections of the population. Economic growth will also be blocked – indeed, petrol shortages are already immobilizing commercial vehicles in many African countries. If we are to believe the forecasts of long-term oil prices above $50 a barrel, with temporary peaks well in excess of that, it is clear that such problems are only a taste of things to come.[17] The prospects for the poor look truly grim. It is likely that countries with little purchasing power will be driven into economic apartheid by the evolution of oil prices. Inequality in the world will increase instead of diminishing. And it cannot be excluded that, in the resource wars that may develop, the rich countries will be pitted not only against the poor but also against one another.

So, the social limits of fossil fuel use are discernible far in advance of the ecological limits. The finite reserves of oil are becoming a destabilizing factor, long before the last barrel has been pumped out of the earth. The 'limits to growth' are returning in the shape of geopolitical conflicts. Against this background, it is scarcely an exaggeration to say that conventional economic development based on fossil fuels has become a major risk for the security of the world. This has turned around an assumption that was taken for granted during the second half of the twentieth century. For now development does not promote peace but – so long as it is based on oil, gas or coal – leads to a situation where peace can never to be found. Consequently, strategies for a more efficient use of fossil fuels and a changeover to regenerative forms of energy (Chapter 5) serve not only to protect the biosphere but also to prevent poverty, conflict and wars. Resource productivity strategies have become an indispensable part of a policy for world peace.

Foreign trade: the appropriation of land

Meanwhile agricultural land has also become a coveted global resource. It is not exported, of course, but often cultivated for export crops. For, above all else, globalization means gearing production no longer to the local or national market but to the world market. Through long-distance trade, agricultural land that is inevitably tied to a particular place effectively becomes a contested, limited resource; vast and sparsely populated areas become available for the needs of densely populated regions, and consumers everywhere with money in their pockets gain access to farmland on the other side of the globe. The European Union (EU 15) alone, by importing agricultural raw materials and produce from their lands of origin, stakes a claim to an area of some 43 million hectares – equivalent to more than a fifth of its own territory (see Chapter 2).

Where rice or maize used to be grown for the producers' own consumption or for local markets, exotic fruits have now often stepped in to supply distant consumers. As much as 50 per cent of farmland on the Philippines island of Mindanao, for example, is today controlled by foreign corporations: from Del Monte's or Dole's pineapple or banana monoculture through Nestlé's coffee plantations, Japanese timber concessions and Guthrie's British–Malaysian palm oil plantations to the lands producing cocoa for Henkel and Mars. Over the years small farmers have been squeezed out, often by far from courteous methods. And those who have leased their little plot to the corporations soon realize that the rent plus any wages they might earn at the canning plants are not enough to provide a living. Usually they did not take into account the elements of a livelihood that they signed away with the lease: the provision of food for their own needs, or the possibility of raising animals and hunting or fishing on their own land. Moreover, bananas wear out the soil, making it difficult to contemplate a return to rice or maize.[18]

Especially in the South, the production of agricultural goods for export competes with production for people's local needs. This has led to a highly contradictory form of development. Although large parts of the local population suffer from undernourishment, many countries in the South extensively pursue an export agriculture that involves concentration on a single product and a heavy use of resources.[19] Often the country is no longer in a position to cover internal demand for food (especially the cereals that are by far the most important food world-wide) with its own national output. In the mid-1970s all developing countries together were producing 4 per cent less cereals than they needed; by the end of the 1990s the figure had climbed to 9 per cent, and by 2030 the shortfall is expected to be as high as 14 per cent.[20] The countries of the South are thus increasingly dependent on food imports. At the same time large parts of their population are sinking into poverty and migrating from the land to the overcrowded cities – which brings about a dangerous polarization between rich and poor, town and country.

But why do so many countries specialize in export produce? What makes it so difficult for them to provide for themselves? Why do the countries of the South, where population growth is the highest, push ahead with an economic structure that again and again results in repression and impoverishment? Usually they are forced to earn foreign currency to pay off their external debt. So long as they have to export relatively cheap raw materials and to import relatively expensive industrial goods, it is only with great difficulty, if at all, that they can earn enough income to pay more than the interest on their loans. Once they have fallen into the debt trap, they have scarcely any other choice than to deprive their own population for the benefit of consumers in distant, financially strong parts of the world. And, even without excessive levels of debt, many countries in the South are forced to develop their export sector because they have to offset the continual loss of value of their goods in the world market. Through protection of their markets for higher-value goods, the industrial countries make it difficult for them to improve their exchange relations, and so they often have no other option than to increase their agricultural (and mineral) exports.

Food first or exports first?

Already in colonial times the states of the North pursued a policy that tied the countries of the South to agricultural production and the extraction of raw materials, preventing them from building up processed or finished product sectors. Bengal, for instance, before the colonization of India, had been an economically self-sufficient country with agricultural surpluses and extensive production of high-quality cotton, silk and muslin. But the British colonizers trimmed the economically autarkic country back to the role of a supplier for colonial needs. They set up large numbers of jute or paper factories and cotton-spinning mills, and prohibited any industry that did not fit in with their conception, such as iron and steel, not to speak of machine building.[21]

This interest in protecting their own economies from the competition of industry in the South has its contemporary sequel in the trade policies of the countries of the North. Their aim is still to ensure that their own lead in many sectors is not challenged, and that the countries of the South remain available as producers of cheap agricultural goods and raw materials. On the one hand, they hinder the import of industrial goods so as to protect national firms from competitors producing more cheaply in the South (see Chapter 6); this forces the South to supply unfinished goods at a low price and to buy processed industrial goods at a high price from the North. On the other hand, the rich countries promote their own agricultural sector with subsidies and export its surplus at such reduced prices that the countries of the South, often characterized by traditional and labour-intensive small farming systems, are forced to introduce capital-intensive methods of industrial agriculture.

The combination of these two strategies is especially unfavourable to the poorest countries. For the scissors between their income from low-priced raw materials and their expenditure on high-priced finished goods from the industrial countries opens ever wider as technological advances increase the value of finished products. Furthermore, government subsidies in industrial exporting countries expose the poorest countries to unfair competition from cheaper products. Whereas one kilo of cotton cost $2.50 in August 1995, it fetched a mere $0.84 in January 2002 – a record low for some thirty years. The income of many cotton producers, who received no subsidies, was thus cut to one-third of its previous level, and the export revenue of producer countries in the South was seriously reduced.[22] The countries of the South were therefore compelled to export ever-larger quantities of agricultural produce in order to import the same quantity of industrial goods. But the fact that everyone was producing more meant that agricultural prices tended to fall, since there was hardly any change in demand. Between 1980 and 2000, the world market prices of eighteen important agricultural goods fell by an average of 25 per cent – and by as much as 47 per cent for cotton, 64 per cent for coffee, 60.8 per cent for rice, 71.1 per cent for cocoa and 76.6 per cent for sugar.[23] As a result, the trade balance deteriorated in many parts of the South: 64 countries now have to contend with a negative balance and a chronic shortage of foreign currency.[24] In turn, the high level of debt in the poorer countries is causing a severe export dependence.

Since the countries of the South must export ever-larger quantities of agricultural produce, they shift on an ever-larger scale to industrial methods of capital-intensive and chemical-intensive farming. The production of agricultural goods, however, uses more land than the production of finished goods. The industrial countries therefore require more land in Southern countries for their own imports than they make available to the latter through their production of export goods (see Chapter 2). Evidently the land they require is no longer available for the provision of the local population. Tanzania, for example, mainly exports coffee, cotton and cashew nuts, and is one of the world's largest producers of cloves. But, in bad years, its production of maize, millet, rice and pulses is no longer sufficient to cover its people's needs, and these staples then have to be imported. In 2004, despite debt forgiveness of $3 billion three years earlier, Tanzania was still in debt to the tune of $6.6 billion.[25]

It seems justifiable to conclude that the industrial countries have shaped their trade policy into a powerful instrument for extracting more from the South than they give back to it. In the countries of the North, the appropriation of cheap raw materials increases productive capacity, while cheap imports of food and clothing directly raise purchasing power. Both boost the possession of goods and money beyond the level that would otherwise be attained. Consumers and producers alike profit from the enrichment, but, as we shall see, it is of special benefit to mobile capital. The corresponding impoverishment in the countries of the South has the opposite effect on their economies; it does not hit all social groups there equally, but it hits some hard and many very hard indeed. Their productive location and living conditions deteriorate so much that they become marginalized and have scarcely any share in the opportunities for economic activity and social integration.

Marginalization of farmers and land

The concept of marginalization refers primarily to workers who have been driven to the margins of society and are permanently excluded from prosperity and social respect.[26] In the countries of the South, income and lifestyle often depend upon access to natural resources, and so the marginalization of nature not uncommonly entails the marginalization of people living on it. Where nature is regarded purely as a factor of production, it is neglected as soon as its profitability becomes too narrow. In the case of export-oriented agriculture this occurs when it conforms to the industrial principle: that is, when it uses few workers and only the most fertile soil, dispensing with less productive land that used to be worked but is now regarded as marginal (at or outside the limits of profitability).

In many cotton-producing areas, for instance, the soil is damaged through pollution and salinization; indeed, a large proportion of the world's pesticides, defoliants and growth regulators are sprayed on cotton fields. Cotton thrives on artificially irrigated dry soil, and so every year 200 to 1,500 litres of water are employed per square metre and 3,600 to 26,900 cubic metres of water per tonne of cotton. As much as 20,000 litres of water may thus be used to produce a single T-shirt. Regular doses of water gradually add salt to the upper soil, so that in the Russian Federation, for instance, but also in countries of the South, salinization and pollution have already rendered large areas of land useless for agriculture and in many cases resulted in outright desertification. Fields, pasture, forest and lakes are going to ruin because people have lost a sense of how to cultivate nature in a way that serves both the production of goods and the needs of conservation.

Often, the marginalization of nature is a result of an export orientation that gears agriculture to the industrial production and markets of the North, instead of producing with methods suited to the local soil and climate and exporting only the surpluses left over after domestic needs have been met. As Ivan Illich noted some years ago: 'Paradoxically, the attempt to counter famine by further increases in industrially efficient agriculture only widens the scope of the catastrophe by depressing the use of marginal lands. Famines will increase until the trend towards capital-intensive food production by the poor for the rich has been replaced by a new kind of labor-intensive, regional, rural autonomy.'[27]

So, export orientation, neglect of nature and displacement of labour are internally related to one another. When corporations in the North invest in the industrial agriculture of the South, they save on conservation costs because lower standards are the general rule there, but they also save because of the lower wages and social spending in the South. The export orientation imposed there causes poverty and environmental strains which are no longer considered justifiable in the North.

The export economy can absorb only small numbers of those who used to be engaged in subsistence economy. Things are different if a national economy remains largely closed, exchanging goods but keeping labour and capital inside the country. Then there may well be temporary unemployment, but labour-saving technological progress will bring down the price of the old products and provide a stimulus for the production of new ones. These new goods will be made with the released manpower, and demand will come from the greater internal purchasing power. The industrial countries practised such an orientation to the internal market for much of the twentieth century, but there too it is in danger of dissolution in the wake of globalization. For globalization means that technological progress releases labour without making goods cheaper at home. If goods do become cheaper this does not boost internal purchasing power, since they are actually sold abroad. Nor are export profits ploughed back into the production of new goods for the internal market, since demand is lacking there and other countries protect themselves against industrial imports.[28]

In Europe, where the development of industry began centuries ago, small or medium-sized agricultural and craft enterprises gradually appeared alongside, and partly in the place of, an economy geared to self-provision. It was mainly they which absorbed the labour shaken out of the subsistence economy. In the countries of the South, however, the danger today is that small and medium-sized enterprises will not get past the starting-post. The development process advances so rapidly that forms of large landownership often eliminate self-provision without adequately replacing it; they are not a substitute for it but its opposite, just as export-oriented agriculture is the opposite of farming adapted to the local region and does not perform the same tasks. For the large corporations pursue export-oriented strategies that simply push traditional self-provision out of the picture. People lose their work and livelihood and crowd into the cities.

Who gains from rural exodus?

The displacement of self-provision and the dominance of industrial production are ubiquitous phenomena, but in the countries of the South they have led to a self-destructive polarization. To a large extent, they are also responsible for the migration to the cities. Of course, it is not poverty as such or the prospect of a better income elsewhere which induces people to migrate, but also the dissolution of the social fabric that has held their lives together. When a country becomes a centre of migration, it has already been reduced to a hinterland.[29] Only the sub-ordination of a territory to outside forces creates the disequilibrium which leads to deracination and migration.

Rural areas are drained of more and more of their population, while the cities burst at the seams and become ungovernable time bombs. 'By the year 2020 nine of the ten most populous cities in the world will probably be in the South, with three of them in India alone.... It is expected that by 2020 Mumbai will have pushed into first place, with 28.5 million instead of today's 18 million, and that Lagos will have taken third place.'[30] A majority of people in these megacities will live in slums – as a billion already do around the world.

It is true that migration may be seen as not only a consequence but also an instrument of the expansion of big capital. This position has been clearly formulated by Saskia Sassen,[31] in three related points. First, migration from the countryside to the cities increases the pressure on the urban labour force, setting up competition for the jobs left in the wake of the digitalization of labour processes. Second, low-paid work is the base on which the activity of global corporations rests. Even in virtual space, corporate players have to rely upon points of spatial support, and the information industries also need a physical-technological infrastructure to be present at certain strategic nodes. Third, 'global cities' are therefore increasingly important as nodal points. This is often overlooked as attention is focused on the mobility of finance capital, highly skilled labour, knowledge and production; the significance of locally attached capital and labour remains unnoticed. Yet the profitability of the global corporations largely rests on low-paid labour, which is made possible especially through the invisible, unpaid subsistence labour of women.

So, even the informal economy makes its contribution to polarization, as those with high incomes profit from the fact that they can command cheap goods and services in the orbit of the global corporations. The growing presence of immigrants in the big cities or 'special economic zones' of the South, together with the formation of a new, largely female proletariat, has created the basis for the low-paid labour on which the corporate operations depend. This would not be possible if migration had not created and maintained a huge pool of people prepared to take on undervalued labour. But the cause of migration is not so much the attractiveness of cities as the degradation of life in the regions from which the migrants originate. And this is closely bound up with the export orientation.

A caricature of free trade

In fact, the affluent countries to which the agricultural exports are sent may also suffer from the export orientation. For the import of goods of identical quality that have been produced in another region at lower cost often brings with it huge social costs.[32] It may trigger 'displacement trade',[33] which drives out domestic goods and jobs by introducing more cheaply produced products of the same kind. Some decades ago, for example, Japan replaced the American production of video recorders and cameras, television sets and stereo systems, by imitating these products and producing them more cheaply. This shift meant that by 1980 the US imported from Japan goods to the value of $33 billion, while it sold to Japan goods to the value of only $21 billion. The resulting demise of whole branches cost several hundred thousand jobs.[34]

We therefore need to consider who stands to gain from the export orientation. There can be no doubt that it is in the interests of the politically and economically most powerful layer: finance capital. The internal market is largely saturated and high profits are not expected there. But the expansion of exports opens up new markets and promises higher sales and profits that cannot be achieved in an overcapacity economy. So, an export orientation may well serve the transnational corporations and global finance capital, even if it pushes out small and medium-sized enterprises geared to the internal market.

The supremacy of finance capital rests today on bringing together the mobile factors of production – footloose capital, knowledge-based and highly specialized labour, mobile and standardized transformation of nature – in ways that take advantage of the absolutely lowest costs. This pushes out capital that is tied to a particular place. In former times, such capital increased the prosperity of nations by using the comparative advantages of its own particular location, in accordance with Ricardo's theory that all countries stand to gain by producing goods in which they have a comparative advantage and purchasing other goods from abroad. Their combined social product is then greater than it would be if each country were itself to produce all the goods it needs. According to Herman Daly, however,[35] this works only if labour, capital and nature remain inside the country, so that only goods are traded internationally, and if the countries engaged in trade are at roughly the same level of development. It does not work if capital and labour can be relocated at random and if nature can be transferred in the shape of externalized environmental costs, since in that case all cost advantages can be assembled in a single location. The places where this happens today are the global cities, where the differences of interest between transnational corporations and self-providing regional economies are mostly resolved at the expense of the latter.

A possible solution to this problem may have been suggested long ago by Aristotle.[36] In Polanyi's view, his distinction between production for one's own needs ('economics') and production for trade and profit ('chresmatics') contains the most prophetic advice ever given in the realm of the social sciences: namely, that regional self-provision should not be subordinated to export production.

> Aristotle insists on production for use as against production for gain as the essence of householding proper; yet accessory production for the market need not, he argues, destroy the self-sufficiency of the household as long as the cash crop would also otherwise be raised on the farm for sustenance, as cattle or grain; the sale of the surpluses need not destroy the basis of householding.[37]

To conclude: export-oriented production that endangers self-provision will undermine the foundations of regional or national economy. And that is precisely what happens through the industrial and agrarian strategies with which the industrial countries make a caricature of free trade.

Investment: the monopolization of water

Nowhere are resource conflicts more aptly described than in the case of water. For the word 'resource' is derived from the Latin *surgere* (pour forth); it should be understood as a metaphor for life itself.[38] And, in conflicts over water, what is directly at stake is life – and survival. Approximately 20 per cent of people on earth have no access to safe drinking water, and 40 per cent suffer from an inadequate supply of water. It is estimated that by the year 2050 a total of 2 billion people (in the best case) or 7 billion (in the worst case) will face a water shortage.[39]

At first sight, fresh water may still not be a global resource. Certainly water-poor areas of the world are making increasingly vocal demands on water-rich regions, and already water is traded internationally by means of tankers, pipelines and bottles. But direct water transfers of this kind have until now played a subordinate role. On the other hand, there is considerable indirect access to other countries' water resources: for example, through the export of goods that require water for their production, or through the pollution of water in industrial production. Here, too, corporations and consumers from distant lands dispute a scarce resource that they need on a day-to-day basis.

Regional disputes usually lie behind today's open conflicts over drinking water. These reflect the contest between regional elites and the local population. A role is always played here by investment in specific projects, which first create the structures to move water from one location to another. Infrastructural investment in dams, canals or pipelines diverts water from rural areas to the moneyed centres; investment in thirsty processing industries takes water from the local population or makes it dirty and undrinkable; and investment in export-oriented agriculture means that water is transported in the form of arable crops to distant consumers. The corporations that engage in such projects are mainly interested in their own profits. The governments that promote them are interested in the associated prestige, in the support of urban middle and upper layers, and in the growth of the economy. Although such investments are usually trumpeted as development projects useful to the poor, they often result in a degradation of living conditions for the local population.

Water conflicts share certain common features. In all cases it is a question of defending an existential resource and the ecosystems dependent on it against the demands of non-resident players: not so much for the sake of natural conservation as because the natural areas in question – wetlands, rivers, valleys and deltas – provide living space for a human community. Springs, lakes and rivers are an integral part of the cultural spaces that link people to their ancestors and to the world of their gods. Major incursions into these spaces therefore always have a social as well as an ecological significance. The threat to the community gives rise to ecological resistance, 'the environmentalism of the poor',[40] which defends the right to life of local people against faraway claimants of the transnational consumer class. Two questions are always at the heart of the dispute. To whom does the water belong? And do we have a right to existence in the places where we belong?

Trapped water

Conflicts and protests over access to water are most visible in relation to dam construction, where the reshaping of nature takes especially dramatic forms. Huge dam projects completely trap water, change the flow of rivers, inundate valleys and destroy ecosystems. By 1949 some 5,000 large dams had been built in the world, three-quarters of them in the industrial countries; by the end of the century there were already 45,000, two-thirds of them in the countries of the South.[41] They were intended mostly for the irrigation of industrial agriculture, but also for electricity generation and the collection of drinking water for the cities.

The displacement of families and village communities has been at the heart of the resulting conflicts. It is estimated that, between 1986 and 1993 alone, four million people had to retreat before the dams. Case studies put together by the World Commission on Dams (WCD) show that the negative effects mainly concerned subsistence farmers, indigenous groups, ethnic minorities and especially women, whereas the positive effects were mainly enjoyed by towndwellers, large landowners and industrial enterprises.[42] The water resource certainly has its winners and losers.

Conflicts over dam projects in China have aroused especially lively discussion. In China water is a scarce good: the country has only 6 per cent of the world's supply of drinking water, but more than one-sixth of the world's population. Moreover, in China itself the greatest problem is the distribution of water and population. More than one-third of its water resources are in or south of the Yangtse, while some 400 of the 600 large cities in the North suffer from a shortage of water. The government has therefore planned a series of giant projects to divert water through canals and pipelines from the rural areas in the South to the population centres of the North.[43]

In addition to their incalculable ecological consequences, these projects call for massive resettlement – as we have seen in the case of the Three Gorges dam. According to official reports, 1.13 million people have had to move for it to be built, while critical voices speak of as many as 1.9 million. The land and jobs promised in other areas often fail to materialize, and where new land is made available it is often of worse quality than before. Compensation has not been paid in full, and before resettlement those affected have had to buy new housing at a much higher price than the compensation award. Because of major soil erosion, it has not been possible for local people to move elsewhere in the Three Gorges region, and the government has forced some 125,000 of them to move to faraway areas. On top of all their other problems, such people have thus had to cope with living in a new and unfamiliar physical-social environment, where the loss of social networks has often irreversibly deprived them of informal sources of employment.[44]

Virtual water

Use conflicts also arise when water is required for the mass production of goods. 'Virtual water' is the category that tells us how much water is embedded in a product or used in its production. By analogy with the ecological rucksack (see Chapter 2) containing the total material outlay, the concept of virtual water expresses what we might call the 'aquatic rucksack' of goods and services.

Nearly every product contains virtual water. For example, the production of a 32-megabyte computer chip weighing two grams requires the consumption of 32 litres of water; the manufacture of a motor car soaks up as much as 400,000 litres. The heaviest user of all is agriculture, which accounts for 65 to 70 per cent of the global consumption of fresh water. Depending on the region of origin, one kilo of grain conceals 1,000 to 2,000 litres of virtual water, depending on the local climate; 5,000 to 5,500 litres go into the production of one kilo of cheese, and as much as 16,000 litres into a kilo of beef. Water consumption figures for various nations must therefore include virtual water in the reckoning; they cannot limit themselves to the direct consumption of water for drinks, showers or car washing. An average citizen of the United States, for example, uses about 2,000 litres of water a day just for his or her consumption of beef.[45]

The export of goods with a high component of virtual water is especially conducive to conflict in regions where water is already scarce – for example, in the case of Kenyan flowers. In 2001 Kenya produced 52 million tonnes of flowers for the European, Japanese and North American markets, at a time when 3 million Kenyans were suffering from water shortages. In 2000 the European Union alone imported flowers from Kenya with a total value of 153 million euros. The flowers are watered mainly from the economically and ecologically important Lake Naivasha, in and around which live 350 species of birds, as well as hippopotami, buffaloes, apes and other rare animals; the Masai nomads also use it to water their herds. Both the shortage of water and its contamination with fertilizer and pesticide represent a threat to the lake's future. Without realizing it, flower lovers in distant lands are thus eating away at the existence of that part of the local population which does not share in the proceeds of flower production.[46]

It is not only on the fringes of the world market and in the South that the extraction of water as virtual water poses existential problems for the local population. It can also threaten people in the North, in the back-yards of the global consumer class. One striking illustration of this is the Black Mesa/Kayenta coal mine in the American Southwest. Here the Peabody Western Coal Company, the world's largest private producer, breaks up the coal after extraction, mixes it with (drinking) water and pumps it along huge pipelines to Nevada, where it is then processed and shipped. Peabody pipes away some 43,000 tonnes of coal sludge every day, using approximately 480,000 tonnes of water an hour for the purpose; the annual consumption of water comes to a total of approximately 5 billion tonnes. This water is taken from the Navajo aquifer, which is the only one in the area with water suitable for drinking, and which also supplies most of the headstreams in the Black Mesa. In this arid region, the social, spiritual and cultural life of the local Hopi people revolves around the spring water; they use the biodiversity of the wet-lands for their ceremonies and revere a kind of water snake that lives in the springs. They work some fields around the larger springs and draw their drinking water from them. But the springs are visibly drying up – and this is endangering the social existence and agriculture of the Hopi. Already in 1995 studies convincingly showed that two-thirds of the fall in the groundwater table was due to Peabody and its coal production. It is thought that by the year 2011 a large number of the Hopi springs will have completely dried up.[47]

Contaminated water

Many governments of Southern countries still argue at international conferences that environmental pollution is mainly a problem of the industrial countries, and that protection is a luxury which becomes attainable only with a certain degree of prosperity. In reality, however, it is everywhere the poor who suffer from environmental pollution. For them, living as they often do directly from nature, the quality of their natural surroundings is synonymous with access to clean drinking water.

Water pollution is today a threat to 1.2 billion people around the world and each year leads to the deaths of some 15 million children.[48] It may have local causes, such as untreated sewage or toxic residue from nearby farms. But the sewage and residue may also originate much further away, and the contamination may also come from cities and industries on the headwaters. The further the pollution is from one's own area and the more distant the beneficiaries are from the consequences of their action, the less interest there usually is in the sustainable use of water.

Extreme cases of water pollution are caused by industries that extract and process raw materials for export. One example is near the village of Kinari, in the Indian state of Orissa, where the Indian firm Sterlite Industries India Limited (SIIL) digs for bauxite and processes it into aluminium. The mineral is extracted in opencast mines in the Nyamgiri hills, after they have been cleared of trees. The deforestation impairs the ability of the soil to absorb precipitation and therefore causes a lowering of the groundwater table, and this in turn leads to the drying up of two nearby rivers and other smaller watercourses. During the aluminium production toxic substances develop in an insoluble red sludge, which contaminates the water and makes the soil infertile. However, the groundwater, rivers and estates provide the only means of subsistence for the local population.[49]

Another example concerns the extraction of oil in Ecuador's rainforest. Some three hundred sources here yield just under 20 million tonnes of oil a year, or 0.4 per cent of world output. The concessions granted to multinational corporations, affecting a total area of some 1.2 billion hectares of rainforest, often lie in the territories of indigenous peoples. Theirs are mainly subsistence societies, dependent on the natural forest spaces, flooded areas and river banks, where agriculture is combined with hunting, gathering and fishing. The interplay of forest and water makes it one of the regions in the world with the richest variety of species. So, the consequences of water pollution by the oil industry are here especially grave. Oil seeps into the soil and water through numerous leaks in the pipeline system, and over the last twenty years more than half a million barrels have flowed by this route into watercourses that provide Ecuador's inhabitants with drinking water. Disease and malnutrition are on the rise, and the other consequences include social disintegration and the driving of people from their native lands.[50]

Lucrative water

Poorer sections of the population, especially in the urban areas, are the hardest hit by water price rises, as they usually have no way of responding with a different structure of demand. Higher water prices therefore directly threaten their life chances. In recent years there have been a number of disputes over privatization of the water supply in the cities of the South. Corporations have been buying up water rights, and if customers are unable to pay they risk being cut off. The protests have been quite major in places as far apart as Cochabamba, Soweto, Jakarta and Manila. Until the 1990s some 30 per cent of people in Manila had no connection to the water supply, and the capital had no sewage system worth speaking of. Manila's public corporation in charge of the service had been rendered virtually inoperative as a result of falling revenue and a high burden of debt. The city government therefore expected a lot from the privatization, which handed over to Mayniland Water Services International and Manila Water Company Inc. the right to supply water. The two companies promised to reduce old debts and to make new investments, to lower charges and to ensure that the whole area was covered within a maximum of ten years. By the end of 2002, it is true, they could claim some success with their Water for the Community programme, as more people than before had a mains connection. But anyone who cannot afford the price of a connection is now worse off: the public water distribution points have been closed down, and users of illegal connections are consistently reported for theft by the water companies. So, the poorest layers of the population, especially women, are forced to make hour-long journeys to obtain water, while the water companies have not kept their promise to invest in infrastructure but have tried to offset the losses from pipes by raising their charges. Consumers now have to face the expense of connecting to the mains as well as higher prices. By 2002 they were already paying three times more than in 1997, and this was expected to rise even further in the future.

Along with privatization of the water supply, the market for bottled water has offered other ways of squeezing money from this scarce resource. That the worldwide boom in bottled water may be to the disadvantage of whole sections of the population is illustrated by the example of Plachimada, in the southern Indian state of Kerala, where Coca-Cola, together with Hindustan Coca-Cola Beverages Private Ltd, has built a plant and is pumping out 600,000 litres a day from the earth through specially installed pipes. This has led to a rapid drop in the groundwater table and caused a number of insoluble problems. One is that over-exploitation is constantly increasing the hardness of the water, so that it is more and more difficult to drink and becomes unsuitable for either human consumption or agricultural purposes. Furthermore, Coca-Cola has long been advising residents to use the plant's sludge-like residue as fertilizer. This has led to failed harvests, and the consumption of bitter water and contaminated rice has increased the incidence of gastro-intestinal disorders, sight defects, skin irritations and other illnesses. Anyone who wants clean water must travel three kilometres or so to the nearest source. The failed harvests mean that farmers lose income and can no longer afford to employ labourers. Many are therefore forced into seasonal migrant labour; it is a disaster for the local area, where most people are dependent on wage labour. In December 2003 Kerala's Court of Justice compelled Coca-Cola to look for alternative supplies of water and to use only as much as a landowner with a similar surface area would be allowed. In March 2004 Coca-Cola ceased production, as its permit was not renewed.[51]

The conflicts that result from water pollution, excessively high prices and the real or virtual diversion of water erode the basis of life mainly for the poor and those living in the self-provision economy. The right to life includes what people need to satisfy their basic human rights: drinkable water, fertile land, adequate food, a roof over their heads, and so on.[52] In the conflict over natural resources such as water, it is therefore especially important to guarantee the ecological living space of such populations. Respect for the right to life means recognizing and strengthening the rights of communities to their local resources. Lakes, rivers and ground-water are in the end the indispensable sources for food, health and hygiene – and hence also for freedom and a dignified life. To strengthen the right to life is therefore a central part of a strategy to achieve global justice with limited resources (see Chapter 4).

International law: patents on plants

When it is a question of oil, water or soil, resources appear as materials of nature that enter into the economic process of production. But, in the transition from an industrial to a service economy, knowledge of how to use natural goods becomes a central resource alongside those goods themselves. Competition for oil reserves or productive farmland has for long been supplemented by the struggle to take the lead in inventions and technology. For, especially through exclusive know-how and the allocation of intellectual property rights, knowledge may become a resource that places one competitor in a special position *vis-à-vis* all others.

Intellectual property rights are formally certified rights: for example, patents on inventions, new technologies, designs or discoveries such as genetic codes. They give protection for a limited period (usually twenty years) to inventors and developers of ideas or products, and exclusive control over commercial use of their ideas. The fees charged for such use are supposed to fund further work on the technologies and to encourage new research and product development.

With regard to natural resource conflicts, the object of greatest dispute is provided by the genetic codes of living organisms such as plants, animals and micro-organisms. For, in the case of bio-patents, the globalization era has been leading not to deregulation but to the first-ever cases of regulation. The aim is to use international patent agreements, such as the Agreement on Trade-Related Intellectual Property Rights (TRIPS), to impose a uniform international system of laws governing intellectual property rights. And, since patents come into being only through national and international legislation, the conflicts apply less to the plants in question than to the rules under which patents are issued. The patent controversy surrounding plant genes has been raging for a good decade at intergovernmental summits, international conferences and diplomatic levels, especially with regard to what are to be considered fair rules. The parties to the dispute have unequal weapons. Poor and small countries usually have fewer funds, personnel and political influence to negotiate on an equal footing with the rich countries over rules that will satisfy everyone. Thus, in the jungle of diplomacy, one can see how the interests of powerful states are endowed with the force of international law; how corporations are granted rights that are withheld from local communities; how governments in the South are skilfully played off against one another; and how the North step by step establishes its competitive lead in knowledge.

The rise of biopiracy

Most people around the world see species diversity as a common legacy from which no one should be shut out. Claims to dispose of plant genes as an exclusive resource, through the assigning of patents to particular individuals or corporations, are alien to the public spirit. Indeed in 1983, in one of the first international legal agreements on plant genes, the UN Food and Agriculture Organization enshrined the conception of species diversity as a common legacy of humanity.

However, this agreement immediately came under fire from various sides. Corporations that 'bred' plants commercially saw it as a threat to plant variety protection under civil law and feared that their profits would be eroded if they did not have some exclusive rights to market the new strains they developed. Local communities from areas with high species diversity, supported by various civil society groups, objected that their traditional stocks of knowledge would not be recognized. Certain governments resisted what they saw as an attack on their territorial sovereignty. And many countries of the South (which is home to by far the greatest number of species) regarded their rich diversity and their store of traditional knowledge as a national resource; free access would place the financially and technologically more endowed countries of the North in a position to derive unilateral advantage from the 'green gold'. These governments of the South were not opposed to patents in principle, however, so long as they were given a share in the revenue from them and from the sales of patented products.

For some time now, biotech corporations from the North have been on the look-out for genetic material to optimize their products. With the help of modern biotechnologies as well as the traditional knowledge of local peoples, they have been seeking to identify active plant agents whose properties might assist product development in the pharmaceuticals, cosmetics and pesticides industries. The genes responsible for certain properties are isolated and redirected to the breeding of new economically useful plants or the development of drugs and cosmetics. If the corporations in question manage to patent the properties of the agents or products, they are able to determine the market price and to chalk up higher profits.[53]

Since the discovery of plant properties and the development of new plant genes are patented by corporations, people living in areas where the corporations have helped themselves to local knowledge feel passed over − or threatened in their very existence. This gives rise to the accusation of biopiracy, a term used in different ways by various interest groups.[54] Thus, it is called biopiracy when corporations appropriate biogenetic resources without the consent of the local community or country and without giving them a share of the profits. The Pfizer company, for example, tried to use South Africa's hoodia plant, whose hunger-quelling properties have been known to the San bushmen for generations, without informing the San or allowing them a share of the profits. It is true that, after the San subsequently protested, a profit-sharing agreement was worked out, but this assigns them less than 0.003 per cent of the expected income from marketing of the hoodia plant and denies them any right to use their knowledge commercially in other ways.[55]

Transnational corporations, for their part, consider it biopiracy when their products are used without authorization and the payment of patent fees. In 2001 Monsanto sued for damages the Canadian farmer Percy Schmeiser, on the grounds that its patented seeds had been found in his fields, while he claimed to know nothing about them and maintained that they had spread in pollen from a neighbouring farm. In May 2004 Canada's supreme court found Schmeiser guilty but excused him from having to pay damages or court costs.[56]

Civil society groups and local community representatives from around the world have taken the idea of biopiracy much further. Since the use of biodiversity often goes together with cultural practices, they consider that its privatization by law is altogether illegitimate and plays into the hands of transnational corporations. Even if companies agree to share the profits with local communities, this conflicts with the public and collective use of resources that are regarded as a common legacy of humanity and should be protected as such.[57]

Intellectual property rights over plant genes may actually contribute to the decline of global biodiversity, as patenting requires that the development of plant varieties is genetically uniform around the world. The cultivation of single varieties may entail a loss of biodiversity and speed up genetic erosion, as a result of which plants become more susceptible to pests and pathogens. During the 'Green Revolution' in the second half of the twentieth century, for instance, this led in a few decades to the reduction of Indian rice varieties from 50,000 to no more than 30 to 50 survivors,[58] and sometimes to dramatic losses for farmers who had previously used better-adapted and more resistant seeds.

Whose knowledge?

The long-lasting effects of patents on species diversity have meanwhile become associated directly with social conflicts. Indigenous communities are tied in manifold ways to the plant genetic resources in their surroundings, which provide them with food and medicine, clothing and housing materials, and are also closely bound up with the spiritual life of the community. Since patents restrict access to parts of the biosphere, they endanger traditional ways of life – and result in a loss of biodiversity. For traditional lifestyles have adapted over many centuries to the conditions of the natural environment, and by ensuring their own survival they make a significant contribution to the maintenance and further development of biodiversity.[59]

Often women play a special role in preserving knowledge about the production and conservation of medicines or seeds. This role commonly lies outside the market economy – for example, in care for the well-being of their family and community.[60] Patents that commercialize their store of knowledge may change traditional gender relations, frequently leading to a deterioration in women's social status and sphere of influence, while patents as an object of economics and politics belong to a social sphere in which women are usually underrepresented.[61]

The 'global players' control this sphere. A mere six transnational corporations (Aventis, Dow, DuPont, Mitsui, Monsanto and Syngenta) together hold 98 per cent of the world market in genetically modified organisms in agriculture. It is above all they who have an interest in patenting and high patent fees. They assert that genetically improved seeds can produce a larger harvest over a smaller area of land – and that this can help to reduce world poverty. But this scarcely applies to the products patented until now. Monsanto, for instance, has been advertising its genetically modified bt cotton with the promise that it will lead to higher yields and lower production costs.[62] Yet studies in India suggest that harvests have been lower than with traditional cotton seeds, and that this has contributed to the farmers' indebtedness.[63] Since the aim of patents is ostensibly to refinance product development, the priority focus for research is commercially lucrative procedures, not the needs of individuals or communities living in poverty and hunger. Up to now there has been hardly any serious investment in the five crops (sorghum, millet, chick peas, pigeon peas, groundnuts) that are of major importance to people in poor and arid countries. And only 1 per cent or so of the research and development budget of transnational corporations is invested in crops that might be useful to the population in the South.[64] The great majority of patented seeds have been intended to raise the pesticide tolerance of plants – not surprisingly, as the above six corporations hold 70 per cent of the market share in pesticides.[65]

For 1.4 billion people around the world, the free exchange of seeds is an indispensable basis for next year's crop and the guaranteeing of agricultural yields; a high diversity of plants and plant varieties, adapted to local conditions and the changing seasons, is their only way of ensuring adequate nourishment. Ruchi Tripathi reports that, out of 918 patents on rice, maize, wheat, soya and sorghum, 633 have had directly negative effects on small farmers.[66] Not only do the poor face worse conditions of production as a result of seed patents; they also have to find the patent fees to pay to the corporations.

Forum shifting

Access to seeds and natural resources in areas of great species diversity, the uses made of traditional knowledge, and the distribution of profits resulting from such knowledge: these are the key issues in the political conflict over patents on plant genetic resources. How did the international regulations come about which favour corporate interests and work to the disadvantage of local communities and poor sections of the population?

At the heart of the conflict is the rivalry between the UN Convention on Biological Diversity (CBD) and the Agreement on Trade-Related Aspects of Intellectual Property Rights (TRIPS) of the World Trade Organization. The former came into force in 1993 and has been signed by 188 states; it defines genetic resources as 'genetic material of actual or potential value' derived from plants, animals or micro-organisms, and recognizes the sovereignty of national governments over their use. The Convention on Biological Diversity not only seeks to preserve species diversity and its sustainable use, but also demands, as the first international agreement, that access to resources should always rest on the consent of those affected and involve fair and equitable distribution of the resulting benefits. This may take various forms, ranging from monetary compensation through the transfer of biotechnologies to the involvement of authorized parties in research activity. Since no binding international agreement yet exists on this issue of 'access and benefit sharing', the actual formulation of the principle remains at the discretion of individual states.

In parallel to the negotiations on the biodiversity convention, the international community acting within the framework of the World Trade Organization (WTO) reached the TRIPS agreement on the legal protection of intellectual property, which came into force in 1995. This binds the 149 member states of the WTO to make national legislation on patents conform to certain minimum standards, the aim being to establish a single global regime for intellectual property rights. Since many countries in the South do not yet have a regime governing patents, they must first introduce the concept of private intellectual property rights. The TRIPS agreement prescribes patents for any invention in any field of technology, whether it is a question of products or processes. It does allow for the patenting of plants and animals to be excluded, but demands patent protection in the case of micro-organisms. As to plant varieties modified in the laboratory or through special cultivation, the TRIPS agreement concedes a degree of flexibility and allows for other national forms of protection apart from patents.

Although most of the countries and governments were on the same wavelength in the negotiations, the bestowal of exclusive patent rights through TRIPS conflicts with some central provisions of the Convention on Biological Diversity. For the TRIPS agreement recognizes neither the principle of national sovereignty nor the protection of the traditional knowledge of indigenous communities. It therefore calls into question the principle of access and benefit sharing.[67] This contradiction did not arise by chance. In the WTO, governments work mainly with trade experts, economists and business leaders to design the future architecture of the world trade system. Those active in relation to the biodiversity convention, on the other hand, wish to protect species diversity and the environment, traditional knowledge and the concerns of indigenous communities. Since the biodiversity convention is an agreement under international law without any sanction mechanisms, and since it therefore has scarcely any means to force the implementation of its political goals, the representatives of economic interests and the lobbyists for transnational corporations have opted for the WTO and its disputes mechanism, backed up by powerful sanctions. Violations of the TRIPS agreement can be punished by tariffs on any goods or services that have a considerable impact on the respective national economy.[68] So, the attempt to balance the competing interests of North and South, corporations and local communities, within the Convention on Biological Diversity is petering out in a series of inconsequential appeals.

Another strategy of denying protection to the store of knowledge held by local groups is to shift the responsibilities from one court of international law to another. The group of African states has long refused in principle to negotiate over traditional collective knowledge within the framework of the TRIPS agreement, on the grounds that it is an agreement for the protection of private intellectual property. But, fearing that the biodiversity convention will be ineffectual and succumb to TRIPS, they now demand a new WTO accord to protect traditional knowledge and genetic resources. The EU, USA and some other industrial countries reject this proposal, arguing that the WTO is not the proper place and that such matters should be discussed within an ongoing forum of the World Intellectual Property Organization (WIPO).[69] In fact, however, the protection of private intellectual property was already discusssed in WIPO before the TRIPS agreement and was placed on the WTO agenda only in response to massive pressure from the industrial countries.[70] Earlier they had refused to allow negotiations there on the protection of traditional knowledge.

It is true that WIPO has a committee of its own on the issues of 'intellectual property and genetic resources, traditional knowledge and folklore'. But, even after three years of discussing an international legal regime for the protection of traditional knowledge, it was impossible to reach agreement. The United States, in particular, feared that such protection would conflict with existing patent law and might lead to claims on patent holders; it also refuses to accept that patenting should not be available for a large part of plant genetic resources.[71]

In the Convention on Biological Diversity, too, further progress has up to now been successfully held up. The member states of the convention, to which the United States is one of the few major countries not to belong, have still not clarified what role intellectual property rights are supposed to play in protecting traditional knowledge. The non-binding Bonn Guidelines define them as only one possible source for the fair sharing of benefits from biogenetic resources, and propose joint patent holding by local communities and marketing corporations. There is not even agreement about whether the consent of communities in which the traditional knowledge originates must be obtained before the allocation of intellectual property rights. And, although the international community agreed in 2002 at the World Summit on Sustainable Development in Johannesburg that a benefit-sharing regime should be developed, negotiations have been dragging on because it is a matter of dispute whether such a regime should be binding under international law or should merely have the force of an appeal.[72]

Bilaterals as a gateway

The countries of the North do not always act as a brake on inter-governmental negotiations. If the accelerator offers greater success, they are happy to engage in bilateral talks at which the countries of the South cannot group together to defend a common position. In well over a hundred bilateral trade agreements, the USA, EU and other industrial countries have got governments of the South to allow stronger protection of private intellectual property rights, in return for improved market access for selected products.[73] As the clauses contained in such agreements usually go far beyond the minimum TRIPS standards, they are also referred to as TRIPS-plus. But then the high protection of private rights by no means applies only to the two signatories, as it is written into the TRIPS agreement that all member states of the WTO must enjoy the same privileges; the country in question must therefore extend the standards of the bilateral agreement to all other members of the WTO. Bilateral agreements thus become an effective way of getting round multilaterally negotiated WTO agreements, or of adjusting them by the back door to the interests of the powerful industrial states.

This strategy proved its worth especially in the protection of plant breeding. Since 1961 the industrial countries, acting through the International Union for the Protection of New Varieties of Plants (UPOV), have protected the intellectual property rights of their plant breeders. Up to now few countries of the South have had an interest in signing up to the UPOV Agreement, since the Union represents the interests of large agro-industrial breeders far better than it does those of smaller ones. For example, the costs of UPOV certification are well in excess of what small farmers can afford, and UPOV's assignment of exclusive monopoly rights to newly bred varieties cuts across the widespread practice in the South of exchanging seeds. Furthermore, one of UPOV's criteria in assigning rights is that the breeding should produce largely uniform plants – and this, as we have seen, may contribute to the erosion of species diversity. With the help of bilateral agreements, governments can now be forced to introduce UPOV-like standards or even to accede to the latest and strictest UPOV agreement. This agreement also makes it possible to compel governments to accept patents on animals and micro-organisms. The slight flexibility in the protection of intellectual property that the countries of the South managed to impose in the TRIPS agreement has thus been cancelled out in the aftermath.

Again, the interests of local peoples and small farmers are being deflected to international legal forums that have far less potential for enforcement than bilateral agreements. In 1994, after 25 years of negotiations in the UN Food and Agriculture Organization, the International Treaty on Plant Genetic Resources for Food and Agriculture came into force. Yet the agreement guarantees no rights for farmers and small breeders over their existing varieties; it merely postulates the protection of traditional knowledge and calls for a fair sharing of the benefits from agricultural plant breeding. At least, in a relic of the original conception of a common legacy of humanity, the agreement demands a ban on patents for 64 of the most important food and fodder plants and calls for easier access to them.[74] But the ban covers only native varieties and ceases to apply as soon as they are genetically modified. As in the case of the biodiversity convention, it is left open how far and with what means governments will enforce these requirements; there is a lack not only of sanction mechanisms but even of guidelines or good examples. Nor does the treaty clarify the relationship in which it stands to the TRIPS agreement. The wording may turn out to be farcical when it states that farmers are free to exchange seeds that they themselves have multiplied, so long as this is in accordance with national legislation; the problem is that the TRIPS and TRIPS-plus agreements specify that national laws must be introduced to protect intellectual property rights over plant breeding.[75]

So, the tussle over patents on plant genetic resources makes one suspect that, instead of establishing justice, the force of the law often helps the powerful to gain new rights. Yet only the law can give the countries of the South and local communities a greater scope for action in relation to their resources, or ensure that they have a fair share of the benefits of enterprise. Partial successes may be scored in the heat of battle at summit conferences. But, in order to establish justice, the law must be used not as a tool to advance certain powerful interests but as a means to balance differences of power, as we shall see in Chapter 4.

Notes

1   BWA 2003; MWV 2004.
2   IEA 2003.

3   Salameh 2004.
4   EIA 2004a.
5   Klare 2000.
6   NATO 1999.
7   Wörner 1990.
8   In 1995 prices. Personal communication from the Federal Statistical Office, August 2004.
9   Salameh 2004.
10 See, for example, Exxon/Mobil 2004.
11 IEA 2004a; USGS 2000; EIA 2000.
12 Hennicke and Müller 2005, and for a similar view Duncan and Youngquist 1998; ASPO 2004.
13 EIA 2004b; IEA 2002.
14 BMWi 2002.
15 Schindler and Zittel 2000a; 2000b; the authors' own calculations.
16 IEA 2004a; IEA 2004b.
17 EIA 2004b; al-Husseini 2004.
18 Brassel and Windfuhr 1995; Raina et al. 1999.
19 Steger 2005; Thrupp 1995.
20 FAO 2002: 33.
21 Schweizer 2004: 110.
22 Paulitsch et al. 2004.
23 WCSDG 2004: 83.
24 World Bank 2003.
25 Paulitsch et al. 2004: 48.
26 Nun et al. 1968; Nickel 1973.
27 Illich 1976: 264.
28 Jenner 2004.
29 Parnreiter 1999: 130ff.
30 Stiftung Entwicklung und Frieden 2001: 102ff.
31 Sassen 1998.
32 Daly 1993: 41; Stiglitz 2002.
33 Jenner 1997: 83ff.
34 Ibid.
35 Daly 1993; Daly 1996.
36 The discussion here is based on the free interpretation in Polanyi 1968.
37 Polanyi 1968: 17.
38 Shiva 1992.
39 UNESCO 2003.
40 Martinez-Alier et al. 2003.
41 WCD 2000.
42 Ibid.
43 Barlow and Clarke 2003; China Ministry of Water Resources 2004; *Economist* 2003.
44 International Rivers Network 2003; Haggart and Chongqing 2003.

45 The authors' own calculations, based on MHR 2003; Hoekstra 2003.
46 Fachverband Deutscher Floristen 2004; Alfarra 2004; Hargreaves-Allen 2003.
47 USGS 1995; Whiteley and Masayesva 1998; Beckman et al. 2000.
48 UNEP 2000.
49 FIAN 2004; Hindu Business Line 2003.
50 Haller 2000; Sachs 2003.
51 Kürschner-Pelkmann 2003; Llorente and Zerah 2003; Pabst et al. 2004.
52 Shue 1980: 23.
53 WRI 2000.
54 Ribeiro 2002.
55 Wynberg 2002.
56 Öko-Institut 2002; 2004.
57 Ribeiro 2002; Brouns 2004.
58 Görg 1998.
59 UNEP 1999; Posey 1999; Enquete-Kommission 2002; Kuppe 2002.
60 Aguilar and Blanco 2004.
61 Quiroz 1994; UNDP/TCDC 2001; Barwa and Rai 2002; Howard 2003.
62 James 2002.
63 Sahai and Rahman 2003; Chandrasekar and Gujar 2004.
64 Pingali and Traxler 2002.
65 Madeley 2001.
66 Tripathi 2001.
67 CEAS 2000; WTO 2002b; Brouns 2004.
68 Santarius et al. 2003.
69 Lasén Díaz 2005.
70 Steinberg 2002.
71 Lasén Díaz 2005.
72 Ibid.
73 GRAIN 2003 and 2004.
74 Brouns 2004.
75 Lasén Díaz 2005.

4
Models of Resource Justice

When someone asked him where he came from, he gave the answer: 'I am a citizen of the world.'

Diogenes Laertius, fourth century AD

Justice, like love and freedom, has an elusive utopian content. Beyond all definition, it acquires its features more from concrete histories of bitterness and suffering, resistance and counterforce. Indeed, no one knows what justice means, although what constitutes injustice is known to all. The cotton growers in Mali whose harvest brings in less money every year, the farmers in Nigeria who are driven from their land because an oil field lies beneath it, the rice farmers in Bangladesh who are forced to buy their seeds instead of exchanging them: they can all tell you of the justice they are denied through violence and intimidation, poverty and repression. At the same time, their protest and rebellion indicate what greater justice might mean: more independence and security, more freedom and influence would loosen the grip of injustice over them. Justice is the understanding that develops out of continual efforts to overcome injustice.

Models of justice therefore offer no blueprint, no instructions for a better world, but articulate the hidden ideals that drive the resistance to injustice. Which principles come into play, consciously or unconsciously, in the struggles for greater justice? The present chapter first tries to explain the special challenge posed by a transnational ethics. In a number of broad strokes, it sketches two basic dimensions of our understanding of justice: recognition and distribution. Against this background, an attempt is then made to outline four models of resource justice that might inform a commitment to fairness in international relations: securing livelihood rights; cutting back resource claims; shaping fair exchange; and compensating for disadvantages.

Ethics and distance

Most theories of justice present a handicap: they are designed for nationally constituted societies. Their thinking has as its basis a territorially demarcated society, whose architecture is guaranteed by the state and whose members are held together by social cooperation and shared basic values. In short, principles of justice often depend on a 'container' theory of society.[1] When such theories are applied to the international level, they lay emphasis – in accordance with the tradition of international law – upon the state realm and discuss relations among nations. This gives them only limited usefulness for any consideration of the globalized world.

For the point of globalization, however understood, is that people live less and less in closed societies (see Chapter 1). This trend has taken the ground from under traditional thinking about justice. More and more cross-frontier social relations are developing with distant countries and people, but in a space from which justice is largely absent. Whereas the nation established itself long ago as a community of justice, this is not at all true for global society. A law-based community encompassing all inhabitants of our planet has hardly taken shape as yet. Why should the concern for justice go beyond the borders of one's own society? What motives impel people to include foreign societies in this 'community of justice'? Three reasons may be identified: a desire for security, for self-respect and for world citizenship.

Interest in security

An opened door sets up a draught, a demolished frontier wall releases streams of traffic. In so far as national containers break up, interactions become a habit that sometimes stretches over large distances: Turks in Germany suffer because of events in Turkey that seem part of their lives; computer programmers in Atlanta and Bangalore work day and night shifts on the same software project; a textile factory closes in Denmark and moves to Romania because of the lower wage costs there. The same happens with economic, cultural and ecological interaction: oil managers in Saudi Arabia influence the price at petrol pumps in Japan; the path of the monsoon in South Asia is linked to carbon dioxide emissions in the United States; and the collapse of the currency in Mauretania sends refugees fleeing to Europe. It is ever more difficult to draw a clear distinction between internal and external, as transnational social corridors and patterns of interaction bind proximity indistinguishably to distance. The result is the 'overlapping communities of fate' that David Held sees as the distinguishing feature of a globalized world.[2]

But open borders make people vulnerable. If the territorial state offered a degree of protection from challenges and acts of aggression, the sites and organizations of today's society are exposed to the influences of distant actors and forces. An undefined sense of insecurity therefore permeates many areas of society, and experiences of dependence and loss of control keep being repeated. Factory closures or financial crises, for example, often obey an external logic; they are symptoms of a complexity whose pace-makers elude domestic influence, even if its effects unfailingly make themselves felt. For countries on the periphery this experience of vulnerability is certainly not new, but in the age of globalization powerful countries also have to cope for the first time with an insecurity imported from outside. In general, the darker aspects of reciprocal transnational relations form an important layer of the globalization experience. 'The everyday experiential space of cosmopolitan interdependence does not come into being as a love relationship of all with all. It arises and persists in the perceived emergency of global threats.'[3]

Forms of warfare have also been overtaken by denationalization processes. No longer is it only states that line up against one another; armed subnational or supranational formations also take the field. No longer are armies the only forces that do battle; warlords and assassins also operate from the underground. And zones where the state has collapsed and law and order have gone by the board develop into breeding grounds for transnational illegality. One form of this illegality, cross-border terrorism, has brought about an especially acute and menacing transnational threat, but in geographical structure it has a lot in common with other dangers such as financial movements, arms deals or cut-throat economic competition. It is a question of threats that force every society to wrestle with processes outside its frontiers for the sake of its own security.

There are three competing answers to the problem: enclosure, supremacy and cooperation. The first of these wagers on renationalization and exclusion; the EU's policy towards asylum seekers and refugees speaks volumes. The supremacy option is available only to relatively powerful nations, which can seek to extend their powers of control beyond their borders – in the American case, to the whole planet. That leaves cooperation, which also also counts on prevention abroad, albeit with different means. For common, multilateral action is expected to remove, or at least to dampen down, the causes of threats. This is probably the most promising of the three options. Transnational threats demand a cooperative security policy, though less in the military sense than in relation to police matters and the economy – a policy that seeks to influence situations and players by reconciling interests and promoting joint action. Whether the aim is to produce collective results or to ward off collective threats, such systems of cooperation can obviously tolerate asymmetrical relations to only a limited extent. They are geared to joint work and can function only when they are governed by fairness and mutual consideration. Gross injustices in international relations undermine the willingness to cooperate, as we can see from the operations against terrorism or in respect of climate change. This way, the darker consequences of globalization create a demand for a multilateral architecture of cooperation. The structural insecurity of a globalized world might actually give rise to a transnational community of law (see Chapter 6).

Interest in self-respect

Porous frontiers allow influences not only to enter from outside but also to be carried from inside a country into the wider world. Globalization is not a one-way street: it increases both vulnerability and mutual influence. Powerful countries in particular – or rather, powerful metropolises that keep the flow of trade, finance and images in movement – have acquired enormous influence beyond their frontiers in today's transnational world. Even the British Empire, on which the sun supposedly never set, pales before the sphere of influence of the World Bank or, in another context, the global reach of Hollywood.

The greater the distance from the field of action, the less is it possible to sustain the ethical priority of proximity.[4] In the end, the prime loyalty to family and fellow-citizens developed at a time when the effects of people's actions were by and large restricted to their own territory. Traditional ethics was therefore largely a national ethics; moral duties had validity when it was a question of dependants, friends or other members of one's own society. Foreigners generally had no claim to moral consideration, unless they were guests, travellers or people in need of help. To be sure, the frontier between inner and outer was repeatedly crossed, but only one's own community came into account as the terrain of justice: for example, it was members of the same nation-state who were entitled to expect moves towards social equality, a guarantee of civil rights or welfare support. In international relations it was the law of the jungle that prevailed.

Even if this conception is still prevalent today, it has been severely dented by the denationalization of social relations. When money, people and goods ceaselessly cross frontiers, should not morality too become a cross-border phenomenon? To ask the question is already to answer it. In so far as the sphere of activity of social players becomes transnational, their sphere of responsibility cannot remain national. When production chains span entire continents and trade is regulated at a global level, the newly emerging social spaces cannot remain an ethical no man's land; they too require debates and agreements about the proper way to live together. This is already happening in parliaments and conferences, on demonstrations and in planning exercises. After all, what underlies the controversies over world trade or the demands for corporate codes of behaviour is ultimately a search for adequate forms of transnational justice. In future, a transnational politics worthy of the name will regard not only national but also denationalized social spaces as contexts for justice.

Of course, this extension of the space of responsibility does not mean that the powerful should be responsible for everything; many an ideology of domination has been grounded on the idea of responsibility for the well-being of distant peoples. The concept of justice is bound up with an idea of the common good, which, however, comes in diverse shapes and forms. Among contemporary theorists of justice, it is the 'communitarians' who have emphasized this point.[5] What justice should be, grows out of the understanding that a society has of itself, out of its specific memories and its special ideals. For this reason, no society is responsible for greater justice in another society – except in the case of major violations of human rights. But a society certainly does have a responsibility not to inflict injustices on others. To help cause and perpetuate unjust conditions in another country through one's own policies is not a morally trivial matter – on the contrary, it is just as blameworthy in a transnational framework as in a national one. The core of transnational responsibility is the avoidance of harm, not primarily the increase of prosperity.

This is true also for reasons of self-respect. It conflicts with an elementary sense of fairness to deny others what we claim for ourselves. The prosperous one-fifth of worldwide society therefore has few grounds to consider itself the culmination of human history.[6] In so far as it lives on the overexploitation of nature and the wealth of others, it remains – as Klaus Töpfer once said – trapped in the lie of prosperity. Transnational responsibility moved by self-respect does not imply total responsibility for the happiness of the world; it requires self-inspection so as not to bring unhappiness on others. It may be possible for a morality to develop that seeks to defuse global conditions, though without tending towards interventionism. In other words, it is advisable to understand transnational responsibility not as transitive but first and foremost as intransitive; not as action on others but as action on ourselves.

Interest in world citizenship

The development path of children – psychologists such as Jean Piaget teach – reveals how, in their perception of others, they move from a phase of egocentrism in which the other person is disregarded or instrumentalized to a phase of decentring in which they learn to see themselves through the eyes of others and to incorporate this insight into the way they behave.[7] Empathy and a certain distance from oneself are thus basic faculties of moral behaviour. A comparable path of development may also be observed for human societies. The space of loyalty gradually extended from the family through the community and local principalities to the central state, and is now slowly coming to embrace global society. On the cultural learning curve of nations, a leap ahead in decentring is on the cards for the coming years; a broadening of vision will mean that one's own point is view is arranged within a transnational reference system, so that it includes the ways of seeing of distant others.

Of course, the expansion of moral sensibility has little to do with an advance of altruism; it represents a cognitive and emotional adjustment to the worldwide networking of social relations. People as *citoyens* – in contrast to *bourgeois* – know that their own selves are woven by countless threads into society, and so concern for society is a part of our concern for ourselves. Anyone who wishes to be a citizen of the world is aware that his or her self is transnationally bound up with distant events and persons; concern for the world cannot be separated from concern for oneself. It is not possible to insist on your own rights if you turn a cold shoulder to the basic interests of others. Sooner or later, injustice towards others rebounds in one way or another on yourself and your life plans.

Three convictions define the terrain of world citizenship. First, moral recognition is due mainly to individuals, not to clans or states. Second, this recognition should apply equally to all living people, not just to males, Christians or whatever. And third, every human being brings moral recognition to all other human beings. 'It is the central idea of moral cosmopolitanism that every person possesses moral stature as the ultimate bearer of moral significance.'[8] In a cosmopolitan perspective, the world is a community of people and not a set of countries or states: that is, it is a community in which all have a claim to justice, just as they themselves owe justice to others.

Strictly speaking, the cosmopolitan perspective is grounded upon a human nature common to all; it is not simply the result of transnational interdependency. Nevertheless, borderless intercourse between people creates a new sounding board for cosmopolitan thinking. Anyone who mixes with people of other cultures and races in a sporting competition or a team project finds it natural to see the other first of all as a human being, and only then as a Hindu or a coloured person. It is therefore right to emphasize the power of globalization to bind nations together. It is also true that moral respect is owed first of all to members of our own society – but that does not exclude moral regard for the extended community, in accordance with the model of concentric circles. Moral obligations can vary in strength: stronger in restricted communities, weaker in global society. An ethics of distance is compatible with an ethics of proximity.

Recognition and distribution

People who feel unjustly treated are convinced that they are being denied something to which they are entitled. This can be seen in archetypal situations of the human life story in which justice is demanded of others: children *vis-à-vis* parents, pupils *vis-à-vis* teachers, employees *vis-à-vis* the boss, defendants *vis-à-vis* the judge. In each case a person in authority is expected to assign advantages and disadvantages impartially. In the iconography of the West, the figure of *iustitia* is accordingly often represented as blindfold. The semantic core of justice may be understood as the claim that no one should be preferred if others are thereby put at a disadvantage, and that no one should be harmed for someone else's advantage. *Suum cuique*, to each his own, has been the rule of thumb for justice since antiquity, and it explains why the controversy over justice concerns who can demand what on the basis of which claim.

Pursuit of this claim involves argument over which rules should be considered binding. If it is handled fairly, certain recognized rules will apply, especially those tying down the action of the powerful. The aim of justice may be seen as protecting the weak, in particular, against arbitrariness and violence; it is a matter of social obligation, of rights that someone else has a duty to respect. This distinguishes justice from generosity or charity, which people can only hope for or request. 'We do not regard the recognition of justice as an act of mercy for which we ask our fellow-humans or "the authorities", and which they grant us out of sympathy or pity. It is demanded that justice be done. In the face of injustice one does not turn away in disappointment; one is indignant or incensed and makes a protest.'[9]

The indignation is by no means necessarily directed against individuals; it may also apply to social structures. Since Aristotle, thinking about justice has developed as a doctrine of virtue, and philosophers have concentrated on personal justice. Numerous treatises sought to draw up a model of the just paterfamilias or the just ruler, usually with personal qualities such as incorruptibility and consistency. But modern times brought political justice to the centre of attention, along with the procedures, laws and institutions that mark coexistence in society. It was thought, for example, that an institution or society was unjust if it was so constituted as to make it possible for some to gain advantages or superiority at the expense of, and against the will of, others.[10] Or, in John Rawls's positive formulation, justice is the primary virtue of social institutions.[11]

Justice as recognition

The last few decades have witnessed disputes over justice that mainly focus not on a different distribution of goods but on the recognition of others as members of society with full rights. One thinks of the women's movement or the anti-apartheid movement, of the struggles of indigenous peoples, or of various calls for national independence. In all these examples, the demand for recognition without discrimination is at the forefront. Indeed, the major conflicts through which the world is passing today, from that between North and South through the Arab–Israeli confrontation to the clash between Islam and the West, cannot be understood simply as distribution conflicts but must also be thought of as recognition disputes in which the demand for equality and respect plays a major role. The point, then, is to keep the full meaning of justice in view. This is true also of a current in contemporary philosophical debate which understands justice as a *blend* of recognition and distribution, without having yet reached agreement about the relationship between the two.[12]

Recognition conflicts, then, may be analytically distinguished from distribution conflicts: they generally revolve around questions of group identity rather than class interests, and they are directed more against cultural disparagement than against economic exploitation. Both personal and collective self-esteem are threatened when they are continually belittled by others. Few things are as wounding as behaviour that treats you 'as if you were not there'. 'Non-recognition or misrecognition shows not just a lack of due respect. It can inflict a grievous wound, saddling its victims with a crippling self-hatred. Due recognition is not just a courtesy we owe people. It is a vital human need.'[13] And, we might add, it is also a vital collective need for all who are treated condescendingly in the prevailing hierarchy – for blacks and women, for Muslims as well as Mayas.

It is therefore advisable not to equate resource justice too hurriedly with justice in the distribution of resources. For resource conflicts also arise out of resistance to disrespect, out of a desire for participation and recognition. Whether in conflicts over water or patents, over the natural habitat or even over oil, the demand for recognition is always one factor among others of varying strength. It is a question not of equal but of sufficient access to resources – sufficient for individual physical existence, for the culture of an ethnic group, for the development of a society. The quarrel over natural resources is thus associated with the striving for self-affirmation and participation. Thus, in all variants of human rights, national rights and development rights, the main issue is justice as recognition; in so far as the possession of natural resources plays a role, it is often seen as the material expression of recognition.

Furthermore, under conditions of globalization, the demand for recognition has become more pressing. The world is shrinking, and often the old structures no longer provide a home. People meet and mingle with one another more as a result of migration, travelling or even watching television. The foreigner, the person who thinks differently, the rival is coming ever closer and triggering the desire for demarcation. The great opposing camps of communism and the free West have dissolved; institutions such as churches and trade unions have faded in significance; and states are becoming porous or even collapsing altogether. Who can feel in good hands? In this context, identity-generating differences become more important, as do defensive affiliations, especially when protective powers such as the state can no longer be relied upon. A borderless world – this is one paradox of globalization – prompts a search for new borders, since the demand for belonging seems both indelible and open to constant exploitation. Serbs against Croats, Hindus against Muslims, Islamists against the West: the desire for recognition has turned out to be a highly inflammable substance.

Justice as distribution

Whoever fights against exclusion and for recognition will sooner or later require, as the pledge of recognition, a share in the material possessions of a society. It is true that recognition can run on ahead of distribution, but without consequences in terms of distribution it will remain empty and dishonest. In this sense distribution cannot be separated from recognition, nor recognition from distribution. Justice revolves now around the concept of equality, now around the concept of dignity.[14] A full understanding of justice will include both meanings. But distributive justice in the narrow sense focuses on the proper relationship among social groups.

Distributive justice was, above all, the battlefield of the bourgeois revolution and the workers' movement; both appeared on the scene with the demand that life prospects should be equal, the former in conflict with the aristocracy, the latter with the bourgeoisie. Two circumstances were mainly responsible for the fact that this concept of justice came to the fore: on the one hand, welfare took over from courage, piety or class honour as the most important good in society; on the other hand, it became generally accepted that no one may assert a position by birth in the distribution of welfare. A worker's daughter should not be denied in advance what is customary for a businessman's son. In industrial societies these have become self-evident truths, on the basis of which the tug-of-war in wage bargaining or even the struggle over unemployment benefit is fought out. At the international level, however, it is not so clear how far the principles of welfare and equality apply, nor how deeply they have penetrated the various cultures. When caste membership determines people's lives, welfare is a lower-ranking good. And when only male offspring can inherit legal title, distribution continues to be partly shaped by birth.

In the West, at any rate, the model of just distribution involves the equalization of life chances. Of course, since Aristotle it has not been possible to doubt that to treat unlike as like may signify the greatest injustice. A verdict of injustice cannot be delivered on each and every hierarchy; a differentiating justice is called for in normal cases. A philosophy of distributive justice must therefore establish to what extent and in what measure inequality may be justified. Who is entitled to how much of what is to be distributed? On the basis of which claim and with what justification? These are the issues in all kinds of dispute over distribution. Three principles are traditionally introduced to make unjust distribution seem just: everyone is to be taken into account in accordance with their rights, their needs or their performance. The conflict among these principles permeates many a quarrel: it is in large part the substance of struggles over justice.

Nevertheless, these tensions may to some extent be defused if we ask a more precise question: equality in what? According to John Rawls, it is advisable to distinguish among equality in relation to basic freedoms, equality in relation to economic goods and equality in relation to opportunities. Equal respect for all members of society requires that there should be equality for all in basic freedoms; it would be unjust to refuse them, since that would be to exclude certain people from the context of mutual recognition that underlies social cooperation. In other words, too little equality is here the enemy of liberty. Things are different with regard to the distribution of economic goods. To distribute equally salaries or profits, an art collection or a landholding may redound to everyone's disadvantage if it blocks the forces driving social differentiation and certain increased benefits for society that this process creates. A degree of inequality may thus be socially useful: the needs principle should not abolish the performance principle. Freedom may also go by the board if there is too much equality. Yet it is essential to reconnect distribution by performance to distribution by right and by need, and it is for this purpose that Rawls introduces his well-known 'difference principle': 'Social and economic inequalities are to satisfy two conditions: they must be (a) to the greatest benefit of the least advantaged members of society; and (b) attached to offices and positions open to all under conditions of fair equality of opportunity.'[15] This allows a provisional reckoning of social justice to be made: a society is sufficiently just if it affords equal basic rights to all its citizens and fair and equal opportunity of access to privileged positions, and if it is so organized that things are better for the most disadvantaged than they would be if society were otherwise organized.[16]

It should not be overlooked that the difference principle contains some really explosive material, precisely with regard to resource justice. It represents a condemnation of the existing distribution of resources, as it would be hard to claim that sharp environmental inequality improves the lot of the least advantaged people in the world. The same is true of the confrontations that have been occurring at international forums. Neither the world climate talks nor the agricultural negotiations in the WTO, to take just two examples, are conducted with an eye to the fate of the economically peripheral majority of the world. Systematic respect for the difference principle would considerably change their character, but fairness towards the poor is certainly not the first thing they have had in mind.

Securing livelihood rights

The idea of cosmopolitan law found expression in the Universal Declaration of Human Rights. It was in December 1948, three years after the world had re-emerged from the horrors of war and the Holocaust, that the United Nations adopted the principles whose explosive charge is today greater than ever: 'All human beings are born free and equal in dignity and rights' (Article 1); and 'Everyone has the right to life, liberty and security of person' (Article 3).

For the first time, the rights of the individual were thus solemnly rooted at an international level. Until the Second World War, international law had regarded the planet as nothing more than an arena for competing states; rights could therefore be claimed only by national states. Now, however, the human rights charter identified the people living on earth as a moral community, whose members possessed equal and inalienable rights that took precedence over the jurisdiction of national states. All six billion people on earth (or, at that time, three billion), whether rich or poor, male or female, white or black, were bearers of certain rights and duties; they were citizens of a transnational legal space. This may be regarded as the juridical revolution of human rights.[17]

Habitats and human rights

The Universal Declaration states that every inhabitant of the planet, by virtue of being human, has the right to lead a dignified life: that is, a life which is physically secure and permits the exercise of a free will. For, without bodily integrity, without the basis for a livelihood and the freedom of action and expression, no one is capable of leading an unmutilated life. Human rights are directed not against any particular viciousness but against attempts by governments and other powers to treat people as objects to be manipulated in their own interests. In fact, the idea of human rights reverses the traditional relationship: it affirms that, before society can assert a claim against individuals, those same individuals can make legitimate claims on society. This means that human rights can be used as a political weapon in the hands of the powerless.

By now it is widely accepted that human rights are indivisible and interdependent.[18] Indeed it would be hard to understand why malnutrition or disease should impair people's capacity for action less than press censorship or religious persecution does. If someone's economic-social rights are denied, their civil-political rights are usually not worth the paper on which they are written. And, conversely, civil-political rights are often suppressed in order to avoid making any economic-social concessions to the have-nots. Livelihood rights, understood as the most elementary part of human rights, therefore define what people need for their development as living beings: healthy air and drinkable water, basic health care, suitable nourishment, clothing and housing[19] – but also the right to social participation and freedom of action. Existential rights form the core of economic, social and cultural rights, as these were established in 1966 in the International Pact on Economic, Social and Cultural Rights.

Very often the humiliation of poverty goes back to a denial of livelihood rights, for widespread poverty stems less from lack of money than from lack of power. In terms of resource justice, the crucial point is that natural habitats have a great value for the security of existential rights. Since savannah, forest, water or fields may, along with fishes, birds and cattle, be valuable means of providing a livelihood, the interest in subsistence coincides with the interest in environmental protection. And no one is more dependent upon intact ecosystems than the third of the world's population who rely directly on access to natural resources for their food, clothing, housing and medicine. The destruction of natural spaces therefore undermines their existential rights.

These very groups, however, are in latent or sometimes open conflict with the resource hunger of local and global upper and middle classes.[20]

For dams are built to carry water to the cities; the best land is used to grow exotic fruit for the global consumer class; mountains are broken up and rivers poisoned so that metals can be delivered to industry; and biopiracy is conducted to produce genetically engineered pharmaceutical products. Thus, in October 2000 a murmur of outrage went through the world's press when the Indian writer Arundhati Roy spent a day in jail for contempt of court. A green light for the continuation of work on the massive Narmada dam! 'In India over the last ten years,' Roy wrote,

> the fight against the Sardar Sarovar Dam has come to represent far more than the fight for one river.... What is at issue now is the very nature of our democracy. Who owns this land? Who owns its rivers? Its forests? Its fish? These are huge questions. They are being taken hugely seriously by the State. They are being answered in one voice by every institution at its command – the army, the police, the bureaucracy, the courts. And not just answered, but answered unambiguously, in bitter, brutal ways.[21]

The natural habitat of the poor is again and again targeted by the international resource economy. The search for raw materials has been penetrating the remotest areas of continents and oceans, as more accessible sources have been tapped or exhausted. The age-old territories of indigenous peoples are also incorporated into the worldwide flow of resources, and their landscapes are degraded and desecrated. The history of colonization down to the global age is at the same time a history of land grabbing. From tea and sugar cane through cotton and eucalyptus trees to kiwi fruit and king prawns, farming systems are put in place to cover the tables of distant consumers. The resource conflict between subsistence and market economies is at the root of today's struggles over the conversion of nature for plantations, aquaculture and water reservoirs. Even seeds or certain plant and animal varieties may have a price tag attached to them, now that patents protect property rights over genetically modified forms of life. Farmers who have hitherto been able to exchange seeds, to gather cuttings or to reproduce animals must now pay licence fees for their use of nature (see Chapter 3).

As an economic space, such a natural habitat provides essential resources for both subsistence and market production. As a cultural space, it often provides the link between the local community and its ancestors and the transcendent world of its gods. Major incursions into the natural space are therefore not only of ecological and economic significance but also have social consequences; they threaten the foundations of life for local communities. Then stresses and strains turn into injustice, as the people in question are threatened in their fundamental rights. Resource injustice throws up human rights issues and the basic question of democracy: Do we have a right to stay and live in this land?

Human rights, human duties

The rights of some are the duties of others: the right to freedom requires that those in positions of power should not oppress others; livelihood rights require that society should make the means of life available to individuals. In the international debate, however, this complementarity of rights and duties has up to now remained a blind spot; there is often talk of human rights but more rarely of human duties. But how can the universality of human rights ever be made a reality if there is not also a universality of human duties? Can we postulate global civil rights without at the same time envisaging global civil duties?

Whereas Article 29 of the Human Rights Declaration only mentions in passing that 'everyone has duties to the community in which alone the free and full development of his personality is possible'; the declaration on human duties and responsibilities, issued in 1999 under UNESCO auspices, is much more abreast of the times in stating that 'members of the international community bear individual and collective responsibility for promoting respect for human rights and basic freedoms'.[22] The first point worth noting here is that the addressees are not only governments but also international institutions, transnational corporations, non-governmental organizations and communities in general. The sovereignty principle is growing dimmer today, while multilateral and private players are both in the ascendancy. They all have some influence over whether a political-economic order respects human existential rights. Human rights would be in a bad way if, in an age when power relations are becoming transnational, national states were to remain the only bearers of duties. In a globalized world, non-governmental players also have a responsibility for the realization of human rights.[23] Indeed, German law speaks of the 'third party effect' (*Drittwirkung*) of basic rights, applying them also to relations among private individuals. At world level, too, it is time to accept the third party effect of human rights – in their economic as well as political significance (see Chapter 6).

It is not only acts of violence that infringe livelihood rights. The smooth operation of institutions can also mean withholding them. To guarantee existential rights is therefore not only to refrain from actual curbs but also to take measures which ensure that they are respected; a human rights policy involves the deployment of power as well as the limitation of power. Furthermore, it implies three levels of responsibility: respect, protection and realization. Fundamental respect requires the shaping of social institutions in such a way that they do not structurally or permanently undermine basic rights.[24] Protection may require new legislation on trade, cartels or resources to provide a cushion against the pressures of power. And realization may require (through land reform, for example) putting people in a position to ensure their livelihoods.[25] Realization of these livelihood rights takes precedence. Survival comes before a better life.[26] This formula indicates that the recognition of livelihood rights is a basic duty for institutions, both nationally and, to an increasing extent, internationally (see Chapter 6).

A dual strategy is necessary to strengthen environmental human rights: it must give the powerless greater scope and limit the power of the well-to-do. Numerous conflicts, especially in rural areas of the South, centre on recognition and enforcement of the rights of local communities. Pastureland and forest, fields and seeds, fresh water and clean air are indispensable sources of food, health, materials and medicine. It is here that the right to a livelihood overlaps with the interest in environmental protection. Since intact ecosystems reduce the vulnerability of the poor, the protection of nature is a core component of a policy that takes seriously the ending of poverty. And conversely, since effective rights provide the best guarantee that the resources of the poor will no longer be so easily diverted to the rich, the right to a livelihood is a core component of the protection of nature and species diversity. Ecology and survival rights are most closely intertwined with each other.

For this reason, conflicts over the human right to an intact environment can only grow sharper if the global class of high consumers asserts its demand for natural resources. Only if the demand for oil decreases will it no longer be worth prospecting in virgin forest; only if agriculture and industry limit their thirst for water will enough groundwater remain for village wells; and only if the excessive burning of fossil fuels is ended will insidious climate changes no longer threaten the existential rights of the poor. This means that only resource-light patterns of production and consumption in the prosperous economies can create the basis for a world economy where human rights are guaranteed. Recognition of basic economic and social rights creates a duty to pursue a form of economy that does not undermine such rights (see Chapter 5).

Cutting back resource claims

The appropriation of natural wealth is highly uneven on our planet. Once again the rule of thumb applies: 25 per cent of the world's population appropriates roughly 75 per cent of the world's resources. Nor is it difficult to find concrete examples that bear out what the abstract figures tell us; we have only to think of the contrast between an average family in the United States and in Bangladesh. Some, with their cars, refrigerators, household appliances and air conditioning, dispose of more than 300 energy slaves, while others, with their single light-bulb, communal water pump, gas canister and the father's moped, dispose of no more than three energy slaves (that is, three times the labour power of one person for twenty-fours hours a day throughout the year).[27] The example points to gross inequality in the distribution of resources. But can inequality be described *a priori* as unjust? After all, a lot of things in the world are unfairly distributed. Under what conditions does inequality turn into injustice?

Egalitarianism as the exception

The first idea to suggest itself is that, for all human beings to be equal, Bangladeshis should have the same share of resource use as Americans. The natural goods of our planet are the common property of all human beings. Atmosphere and oceans, flora and fauna together constitute the tissue of life that sustains each one of us. It is given as an unearned legacy to each generation, which should use it and pass it on intact to the next generation. All are equal with regard to the biosphere, we might say, and this is why all have an equal right to the earth's resources. In as much as the biosphere is common property, it makes sense to speak of an ecologically equal right of all human beings to the resources of the earth.

Closer inspection raises some doubts, however. For, over and against the postulate of equality stands the wealth of ecological and cultural difference. From an ecological point of view, the majority of resources – one thinks of oil, forest, fishes, water, soil and ores – are not at all part of the global ecosystem; rather, they are components of regional or local ecosystems. They are global only in an indirect, systemic sense; directly and tangibly they are bound to a particular territory and are subject to the ownership claims of those who live there and use its resources. It would obviously be wrong to describe as global resources, on which everyone has a claim, the pastures of Alpine Europe or the mangrove forests along

Tanzania's coastal strip. Even if local users have an obligation as trustees to preserve their natural goods for the sake of the greater whole, those goods do not in any concrete sense belong to the global community. It is precisely the difference of natural spaces which gives the biosphere its multifarious character.

The earth's cultural spaces are as varied as its natural spaces. Whether money, honour or power is the most important good, whether they are achieved through family status, effort or favour: this arises first of all from the history and culture of a country. Ideas about distributive justice are as varied as the cultures with which they are bound up. Hence, on a global scale, distributive justice may not mean that people should be accorded equal positions or resources regardless of the political–cultural community in which they live.[28]

This rule does not apply, however, if it is a question of resources on which all (or very many) who are tied to no territory are dependent, or which are in demand by all societies and are in danger of exhaustion. The atmosphere, as a sink for carbon dioxide emissions from the burning of fossil fuels, is the most important resource of this kind: it is not inserted into a local ecosystem, but is a global system in great demand that is by now used beyond the limits of its absorption capacity. No country and no individual can therefore claim, to the detriment of others, permanent access rights to this global common good, unless a deviation from the principle of equality has been negotiated and accepted. The equal entitlement approach therefore holds especially in climate policy;[29] most other resources jib at a simple formula of equal distribution (see Chapter 6).

Survival before prosperity

Unequal resource appropriation may be entirely justified. By no means every country has to use as much wood as Finland, as much water as Germany, as much fish as Bangladesh, or as much oil as Qatar. Moreover, world society is a society still in the balance: it is certainly becoming more integrated, but it is hardly possible to speak of an ever more unified institutional structure or even a commonly shared world-view. This is why Rawls held back from extending his difference principle to global relations;[30] he indeed warned, with his methodological patriotism, of the dangers of a cosmopolitan illusion. Nevertheless, such caution can no longer be sustained; at least the beginnings of distributive justice must apply to the still weak global society. A continuation of

Rawls's argument would suggest that a principle of external damage avoidance should be set beside his internal difference principle. In other words, all national or international regulations should be so framed that they do not worsen the position of the least advantaged.[31] This may be regarded as the basic rule of distributive justice. What it aims at is not redistribution but fairness. And to elicit advantages by exploiting the position of the weak may be regarded as the main violation of fairness.

If this seemingly rather modest rule is made the criterion for decisions in international economics and politics, a considerable change in priorities becomes due. At present, both investment decisions and political negotiations seek to maximize each side's advantage in opposition to that of rivals – with no great regard for the costs to the least advantaged, who usually have no place at all at the boardroom table. There is no shortage of examples. In multilateral talks on agricultural issues, competitive advantages are a matter for dispute among exporter countries, but no account is taken of the position of small farmers. In the world climate talks, emission thresholds are fixed which keep to a minimum the losses to industrial countries but happily accept the loss of survival rights among fishing communities, farmers and delta inhabitants in the southern hemisphere. It is contrary to justice when some gain advantages for themselves at the cost of great disadvantages for others. Fairness demands shelving advantages to oneself if they would further harm those who are already weak. The minimal rule of distributive justice thus coincides with the respect for existential rights throughout the world. It is anyway unjust to sacrifice the survival needs of some to the prosperity needs of others.

Freedom before overconsumption

The point of justice is not to guarantee a good life to every citizen of the world, but rather to leave everyone free to follow their own project for a good life. A theory of justice should therefore take the form of a theory of freedom, not a theory of happiness.[32] A cosmopolitan theory of justice will start from the fact that people and societies differ fundamentally in their ways of life and their ambitions for the future. Equality does not mean sameness. Yet everyone does have a common interest in the freedom to live in their own way and by their own lights. A duty-centred theory of justice – whose most prominent representative was Immanuel Kant – will ground the injunction of responsible behaviour on the demand to respect the freedom of others.

Ways of handling natural resources in an interdependent world must also measure up to the criterion of freedom. They correspond to the spirit of global responsibility only if they do not seek to restrict the freedom of people and societies around the world. And the freedom of countries and societies is respected if they are not denied the natural resources necessary for their development. After the waves of industrialization that have washed over the world, every society is now dependent not only on food, plants and intact ecosystems but also on energy, fuel, metals and minerals. If, following Amaryta Sen,[33] we understand development as a process that enlarges the real freedoms of human beings, then the freedom of societies to enjoy equal but self-chosen development cannot be at hand without a sufficiently strong resource base. But, however 'development' is defined, it is a code word for the longing to draw level with the most powerful countries. In short, development stands for the overcoming of inequality among nations.

Now, the overcoming of inequality may mean many things – from poverty relief to the promotion of growth, from huge dam projects to Marshall plans. But, if the maxim of justice is seen as respect for the freedom of others, one will choose the core rather than the periphery as the field for the overcoming of injustice. But such an approach is by no means a matter of course, since most initiatives launched in the name of greater justice (for example, the war on poverty, the AIDS programme or the granting of microcredits) attempt to change people or structures in the weaker country. They are interventionist. They concentrate on feeding the poor, and seldom enough on setting limits on the rich. However, to stand up for the freedom of others means to focus not on the rights of the weak but on the duties of the strong.

The key move in Kant's ethics was to place universal duties rather than universal rights at the centre of attention. If all are to enjoy their space of freedom, then the freedom of some is the limit to the freedom of others. This sets a standard for every player: no one may base their conduct on principles which are not universalizable, that is, which cannot be basically adopted by everyone else. Or, to quote the first formulation of the categorical imperative in the *Groundwork of the Metaphysics of Morals*: 'I ought never to act except in such a way that I can also will that my maxim should become a universal law.' In a Kantian perspective, then, injustice may be defined in such a way that political or economic institutions are unjust if they are based upon principles which cannot be adopted by all nations. They are just if their principles could be adopted by all, because then they do not curtail anyone else's space of freedom.[34]

Kant's theory applies to scarcely any other field as well as it does to that of international resource distribution. Environmental space is largely monopolized by the strong nations, to such a degree that the weaker nations can no longer access the shares they need for autonomous and equal development. The external freedom of economically less strong societies is already severely restricted, and will be even more so in the future, in favour of opportunities made available to stronger societies. The present system of resource distribution is therefore unjust, and two additional factors will reinforce this injustice: the number of citizens and the finite nature of resources. Since the weaker countries face the challenge of providing a home for a fast-growing number of people, a curtailment of their rights and freedoms is doubly onerous. Yet, more than ever before, the increasing scarcity of major resources is intensifying the injustice of uneven distribution. It is becoming a zero sum game, in which the gains of some mean losses for others; excessive appropriation of the environment is turning into outright robbery. It is therefore the intertwining of inequality and limitation which gives global resource distribution its explosive potential.

Kant's theory also shows us in outline what a just distribution of global resources would mean: each society would organize its resource consumption in accordance with rules which, in principle, could be adopted by all other societies. Overappropriation of the environment by a few strong countries at the expense of many weaker ones contradicts such rules. The cutting back of resource consumption in the rich countries therefore becomes the categorical imperative for resource justice (see Chapter 5).

Shaping fair exchange

It is part of a cosmopolitan paradigm that trade safeguards the interests of all involved in it. People have been exchanging goods since time immemorial: it is one of the activities that make humans into social beings. Besides, the rules for trade justice are much less controversial than those for distributive justice; the distinguishing characteristic of fair trade is the equal value of what is given and what is taken. A successful relationship can develop through exchange only if neither of the parties to it is permanently worse off – otherwise it would no longer be possible to count on the loser's willingness to cooperate, and a means of communal bonding would turn into a mixture for blasting it apart.

The issue of just exchange has given rise to repeated conflict. To be sure, like must be exchanged for like – but what does that mean? How is one to measure the value of the goods or services in question? How can one tell when like is being exchanged for unlike? The answers more or less oscillate between two poles. Those who hold an objective theory of value – from Thomas Aquinas through Karl Marx to Nicholas Georgescu-Roegen – maintain that the quantum of labour or nature contained in a product is ultimately what determines its value. Those who hold a subjective theory of value – a small minority until the rise of neoclassical economics – insist that value depends on the scarcity of a product in the interplay of supply and demand.

As so often in the case of insoluble basic questions, both positions are right and wrong; they arise out of different perspectives. One springs from the interest in efficiency, the other from the interest in justice. Whoever chooses to focus on the injustice of exchange relations will start from the assumption that the losers are denied something to which they are entitled. In this context, what matters is often not an objectively measurable deficit but the nature of the relationship between the players. An exchange relation may be described as unjust if the transactions associated with it permanently worsen the relative position of the weaker party. If a relation is dramatically unbalanced, the effort that the weaker side invests in it finds too little recognition, and so any discussion of injustice cannot proceed without a judgement on the objective facts of the case. The inequality in exchange would then reflect a lack of equivalence in the relations between the two sides. An investigation of exchange justice at international level thus takes us back to the question of the kind of relations that the emerging global society wishes to generate. Serge Latouche sums this up as follows: 'We should look for the just relationship of exchange by keeping in mind that together with our partners we are shaping a society, and that their problems are ours and our problems are theirs.'[35]

Value created and creamed off
At present there can be little talk of exchange justice in trade relations between the northern and southern hemispheres. To those who have shall it be given – this motto governs proceedings on the global markets. However, fine manners have rarely been the norm, especially in long-

distance trade. Neither the city republic of Venice, whose merchants brought pepper, cinnamon and silk from the Orient to sell by auction on the Rialto bridge, nor England, whose trading ships carried back cotton, sugar and indigo from the Indies, refrained from ruse and violence to drive down costs on the supply markets, in order then to make a fortune on the sales markets. And, for several hundred years, there was no exchange relation through which the victims of the colonial powers could have retaliated for the humiliation they suffered. In today's shrinking, ever more integrated world, however, the context of injustice and exploitation has undergone dramatic changes. The losers are turning from distant strangers into networked citizens of the world. But what can they be expected to put up with?

Inequality still governs exchange relations between those who supply the resources and those who market the products created with them. In this, patterns of ecologically unequal exchange are mixed in with patterns of economically unequal exchange. From an ecological point of view, industrial countries and regions import more materials and energy than they export; their material trade balance with the countries of the South is anything other than balanced (see Chapter 2). But the sheer volume of oil barrels, timber and copper is only one side of the story; the other is their quality. In terms of thermodynamics, the transformation of raw materials generally involves a reorganization that reduces the content of useable energy. Just as the conversion of coal into electric current necessarily releases waste heat, so does the processing of bauxite into motor cars or of iron ore into steel girders involve a loss of useable energy; in other words, the amount of entropy increases. The exchange relations that develop in world trade lead to a net transfer of highly useable energy – so-called syntropy – from the periphery to the core. In thermodynamic terms this means that the South delivers syntropy, while the North produces entropy. The economic prosperity of the trans-national consumer class crucially depends on its ability to tap into the sources of materials with high internal energy – the earth's syntropy isles, as it were.[36]

The conversion of bauxite into cars also requires an enormous input of labour. The fairness of an exchange of 'high labour' products for 'high syntropy' raw materials – but also the exchange of many tonnes of raw materials for relatively few final products – depends to a large extent on the price relationship between imports and exports. The less a country must spend on imports and the more it can earn from exports, the easier

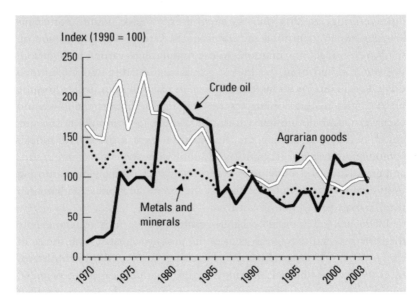

Figure 4.1 Declining commodity prices on the world market (1970–2003). Between 1980 and 2002 prices for agrarian goods fell by 47 per cent, and for minerals by 35 per cent. However, the falls were accompanied by sharp price fluctuations.   Source: World Bank 2004

it is for the exchange to take place. But good fortune on one side is bad fortune on the other. Falling prices for raw materials and rising prices for industrial goods or capital put the countries of the South in a tight corner (Figure 4.1): they are compelled, for better or worse, to export ever greater quantities of raw materials for the same counterpart (see Chapter 3). In economic terms, there is indeed a secular trend worsening the terms of trade between North and South. All through the twentieth century, the prices of raw materials (except oil) fell by an annual average of roughly 1 per cent relative to industrial products; real prices have fallen by two-thirds since the early 1970s.[37] Numerous countries in the South are therefore under chronic pressure to earn foreign currency by increasing their exports of raw materials. The terms of trade operate as a lubricant for the South–North syntropy transfer; economic asymmetry is the basis for the ecological asymmetry.

The structures of inequality that have taken shape in international trade are also reflected in the relations within transnational production chains. In the age of globalization, the cross-frontier mobility of capital has been eroding the usual pattern of trade; 'trade' no longer means that countries are able to acquire things they do not have themselves. Rather, the world is becoming a universal economic arena, in which the same kinds of products generally compete with one another. Value creation chains stretch far across the globe, positioning individual members at the most favourable locations so that the sum of rationalization gains can ensure a crucial market edge. Unequal exchange, both ecological and economic, now takes place in the relations among these links more than among nations. For one T-shirt – some 90 per cent of clothing items sold in Germany come from abroad[38] – the value creation chain stretches from cotton growing in Punjab and spinning in Lahore to dyeing in Vietnam and stitching in southern China, before it is delivered to a Swedish brand name which then, after inputs from a design office in Milan and a marketing firm in Switzerland, sells it through the retail trade in German cities. At each stage materials and wages are paid for, and at each stage the seller tries to gain an advantage by imposing a price as far as possible above his costs. This means that the producers are often the weakest link in the chain: they can be blackmailed because their 'capital' – whether land, crop rotation, climate or physical strength – cannot be easily invested elsewhere. Thus in global trade the payment to the producer is seen as the 'soft' element in the product price,[39] whereas the later stages of commerce, design and sales take the lion's share of the difference between the producer's and the consumer's price. In the textile chain, for example, only a few per cent of the final price goes to the raw materials producer and barely 20 per cent to the processer; the rest is eaten up by service workers, who mainly live in the country of consumption. In the end, it depends on the strength of the various players how gains and losses, both ecological and economic, are distributed along the chain. The question of fair trade in global production networks, which is coming back on to the agenda of debate, certainly has many different facets. But its relevance is plainly visible in the gulf between producer and consumer prices.

Learning from Fair Trade
In the debates of the 1970s on a new international economic order, there was also a tug-of-war over the price stabilization fund for raw materials. Since then, however, high-level politics has bidden farewell to the theme of exchange justice. The market and the TNCs that dominate the

production chains perform their deskilling work in silence, while governments seem powerless in the face of the systemic marginalization of
numerous countries and major population groups within global society.
In these cases, the market brings about segregation instead of integration
in the world community. But, although just pricing is no longer on the
agenda for summit diplomacy, it is becoming the lodestar of the
grassroots movement for fair trade. With the TransFair brand in
Germany, Max Havelaar in the Netherlands or FairTrade in Britain,
trading associations have been formed that aim to make the exchange
between producers and consumers the driving force for greater justice
and environmental protection.

   Their starting point is that trade is the alternative to charity. The
slogan 'Trade, Not Aid' crystallizes the idea that the claim to be paid for
goods produced through one's own effort and intelligence is the only
dignified path out of want and marginality.[40] Obviously not every kind of
trade builds this bridge. So, the Fair Trade organizations set about forging
trade chains that would give a fair price to producers in the South and
offer the possibility of ethically more responsible consumption to people
in the North. Whether the product is bananas, coffee or children's toys,
the principle is always the same: a higher final price ensures a better
income for the producer and – increasingly – a better ecological quality
for the consumer. This strategy aims at breaking the disastrous tendency
of profit-oriented markets to externalize as much as possible social and
ecological costs: that is, to pile them on the shoulders of the weak.
'Untrue' prices not only degrade labour and the environment but also
turn consumers into unwilling accomplices of disdain for other people
and destruction of the environment. Expressed in the language of
economics, a fair price is a price that reflects the full costs of production;
it is also meant to facilitate a decent living with a margin for investment
in the future, and to ensure that the capacity of nature to regenerate itself
is not diminished.

   It would not be surprising if future historians looked back to the Fair
Trade movement as a laboratory for the reshaping of the world
economy. It is a niche where principles have been tried out that may one
day become building blocks for a sustainable system of world trade. One
can imagine the principles of Fair Trade gaining influence at two levels:
in intergovernmental trade agreements and in cooperation among players
in a global production network. Instead of enforcing only deregulation,
trade agreements in the spirit of Fair Trade would aim at a balancing of

interests, so that the economic opportunities, social rights and natural resources of the weaker countries were not harmed as a result. An agreement may contain rules and standards that move away from the subsidies disguised as low producer prices that result in pauperization and environmental destruction (see Chapter 6). At the same time, purchasers may be able to assert their interest in dignified human relations or in goods produced in an environmentally sustainable manner.

Similar measures may come into operation among the players in a transnational value-creation chain: for example, special delivery clauses may ensure social and environmental sustainability in preliminary stages of production, and purchasers may be required to support such targets and to honour the agreement by paying higher prices. The Body Shop cosmetics chain has shown through its Community Trade Programme how fair trade principles can be incorporated into business relations with suppliers. In obtaining natural materials for body lotions and shampoos from plant-rich regions of the South, the company seeks to establish a fair relationship of cooperation with local communities: on the one side, purchasers guarantee market access, a reasonable price, long-term contracts and assistance for commercial or social investment; on the other side, producers make sure that their activity is worker-friendly, environmentally sustainable and supportive of community.[41] Such agreements fit in with the tendency to bind together the layers of global production chains through logistical requirements – who supplies what, where and when? – and through common quality and efficiency standards. If corporations seek to use 'supply chain management' to improve systemic integration, there is much to be said for making common social and environmental standards the distinguishing characteristic of a production network. For global corporate networks are more than just commercial alliances for a certain purpose; they are subsystems of world society which cannot be permitted to operate in ways that conflict with cosmopolitan values. Only if global production networks are in synergy with human rights and environmental protection will it be possible to hope for a world society capable of facing up to the future (see Chapter 6).

Compensating for disadvantages

In a rush of sarcasm, Anatole France once mocked 'the majestic egalitarianism of the law, which forbids rich and poor alike to sleep under bridges, to beg in the streets, and to steal bread'. This aphorism again pinpoints the injustice that can arise when everyone is treated equally, emphasizing that everything depends on the starting conditions. To recognize everyone as equal does not necessarily imply treating everyone in an equal fashion; on the contrary, it is just to treat equally only those of equal strength, and to treat unequally those of unequal strength. Hence the age-old art of *iustitia correctiva*, or counterbalancing justice, which means allowing initial compensatory advantages to the disadvantaged. If this function is disregarded, the equality imperative leads under unequal starting conditions to a perpetuation of inequality. In a world of gross inequalities, to treat all nations equally comes down to the stabilization of privileges; greater justice can be expected only if the weak are specially favoured and the strong are placed under a special handicap.

Common but differentiated responsibilities

The insight that there is no fairness when the strong are able to exploit the weak under the guise of equality is not even alien to the rules of the World Trade Organization; its formulation of 'special and differential treatment' introduces the principle that trade regulations should vary in accordance with the degree of economic development. Thus, once in a while, developing countries are entitled not to go as far in opening their markets as stronger countries, while the latter are expected to offer weaker countries preferential market access. According to Article XI, 2 of the Marrakesh Agreement establishing the WTO, the least-developed countries are only required to undertake obligations consistent with their individual capacities. This recognizes that drastically unequal countries cannot simply be lumped together in a single category. How else, in the production of wheat, could the hand sickle of a Syrian farmer ever stand up to the combine harvester of a Canadian landowner?

Of course, the WTO has not taken this principle far enough or seriously enough, since the organization is based on the assumption that in the end free trade is equally beneficial to all. It is highly questionable, however, whether the WTO's basic idea of taking freedoms away from national states, and of giving extensive freedoms to transnational corporations, will give the weaker countries greater opportunity to develop, rather than carry them to the edge of a precipice. History shows that the great majority of industrial countries, including Britain and the United States, supported free trade only once they had established a certain position of strength, and that previously they tried by means of subsidies, tariffs and other forms of state intervention to protect themselves against stronger nations.[42] Today free trade is being pressed upon developing countries; they must not allow themselves the protectionist period of grace that the industrial countries enjoyed in their earlier phase. If the WTO were mainly concerned about the equal development of weaker economies, 'special and differential treatment' would for some time be the rule and not the exception (see Chapter 6).

Disadvantage under the cloak of equality is especially hard to swallow when we consider that the stronger countries, as a result of their colonial past, bear some of the historical responsibility for the poor starting point of the weaker countries. It is hard to consider it just that positions of unilateral advantage, which were built up without the consent of the disadvantaged, have become established and will persist into the future. The Rio Declaration of 1992, the final act of the UN Conference on Environment and Development, states: 'In view of the different contributions to global environmental degradation, States have common but differentiated responsibilities.'[43] And indeed this principle has become a pillar in the architecture of international cooperation on the environment. In the climate talks, for example, only the industrial countries are expected in the first phase to undertake to reduce emissions and to bear financial burdens (see Chapter 6). Two rules of fairness appear to lie behind this: (1) the strong should take on burdens corresponding to the advantages they unfairly appropriated in the past; and (2) the strong should also shoulder more of the costs than the weak in solving common problems.[44]

Ecological debt

To what extent should the rich countries today assume responsibility for what happened in the past? The principle of differentiated responsibilities in environmental policy is the first sign that the legal significance of past actions for the present has basically been recognized. For, even if it was not intended as such, what looks like a diplomatic concession may be read as a confession that over the last few centuries the North has accumulated ecological debts to the South, by consuming parts of the environment that the South now lacks for its development.[45] This has an economic and an ecological aspect. Economically speaking, a multitude of resources – from Bolivian silver through Kenyan coffee to Jamaican bauxite – were taken to the North in colonial times without the payment of a reasonable price. Sometimes nothing at all was paid for them, often too little, and in no case was the fair economic price calculated – not to speak of the ecosystemic value of the natural goods. Ecologically speaking, a disproportionately high share of resources was extracted from the ecosystems of the South, and this left behind enormous damage. Of course, 'ecological rucksacks' (see Chapter 2) also have a historical dimension; hunting activity, plantations or mines have reshaped nature more than the resulting products show us. Global common goods – the atmosphere, virgin forest – have been exploited to such a degree that today an equal share is no longer available to the disadvantaged. Against this background, the usual perception turns into its opposite: the North is not the creditor of the South, but the South is the creditor of the North.

Now, there may be an inclination to write off the financial debts of the South against the ecological debts of the North. That is politically understandable, but it is still a false path. For not only would it be foolhardy to quantify the damage suffered by the South in the colonial and neocolonial periods; the relations between the perpetrators and their actions and victims are too obscure to establish specific rights to compensation. It is also hard to determine who would owe how much compensation to whom for which damages – partly because the debts go back many generations. So, the attractiveness of the concept of ecological debt lies not in any account-book precision but in its political significance. To be sure, it is not possible to penalize the descendants of those who had no idea of the damaging effects of their actions, but some responsibility can be ascribed to them for the consequences.[46] Today's generation is for good and for ill the inheritor of past generations. And, just as it enjoys without hesitation its inherited privileges and wealth, it should also bear the burden of its inherited debts and responsibilities. It is part of the institution of inheritance that both the assets and the liabilities have to be accepted, and generations are ranked historically according to how they deal with both. For this reason, too, the industrial countries are not equal among equals; they have to make greater advance concessions than others to fairness. Indeed, cutting back on resource consumption (see Chapter 5) and on economic dominance (see Chapter 6) is the most important switch that can be made in the direction of a world of greater fairness.

Notes

1   Beck 2000.
2   Held 2003.

3 Beck 2004: 38.
4 As Scheffler 2001 and Nussbaum 1996 have argued in detail.
5 Walzer 1983; Miller 2004.
6 Schmid 1998.
7 Kesselring 2003.
8 Pogge 2002: 169.
9 Höffe 1989: 56.
10 Ritsert 1997: 8.
11 Rawls 1972: 7.
12 Fraser and Honneth 1998.
13 Taylor 1992: 26.
14 Krebs 2002.
15 Rawls 1972: 227.
16 Kesselring 2003: 72.
17 Ignatieff 2001: 5.
18 Steiner and Alston 1996.
19 Shue 1980: 23.
20 Gadgil and Guha 1995.
21 Roy 1999.
22 Quoted [and retranslated] from Human Rights Research and Education Centre, n.d., Article 2.
23 O'Neill 2000.
24 Pogge 2002.
25 Shue 1980: 52ff.
26 Ibid.: 118.
27 McNeill 2003: 30.
28 Miller 2004.
29 Meyer 2000.
30 Rawls 1999: 117.
31 Müller-Plantenberg 2002; Pogge 2002: 23.
32 Höffe 1989: 306.
33 Sen 1999.
34 O'Neill 2000: 136.
35 Latouche 2004: 141.
36 Altvater 1992; Hornborg 2001; Giljum and Eisenmenger 2003.
37 World Bank 2002b.
38 Paulitsch et al. 2004: 13.
39 Ritter 1994: 66.
40 Perna 1998; Roozen and van der Hoff 2003.
41 www.thebodyshopinternational.com; EFTA 2002: 25.
42 Chang 2002.
43 UNCED 1992, Principle 7.
44 Shue 1999.
45 Martinez-Alier et al. 2003.
46 Shue 1999.

5
Fair Wealth

The road to socialism passes through the bicycle.

Ivan Illich, 1974

Civilizations, however unassailable in their power and impressive in their glitter they may sometimes appear, rest upon special conditions that do not hold everywhere or for all time. Roman civilization, for example, was dependent upon food imports from the periphery of the Mediterranean, and the civilization of Middle China upon the supply and consumption of water in the Yangtse delta region. Things are no different with the Euro-Atlantic civilization of the nineteenth and twentieth centuries. Historians have advanced a whole range of factors to explain its dominance over the rest of the world,[1] but the latest research places special emphasis on the role of access to resources. Thus, whereas China's level of development until 1750 was roughly comparable to England's, the latter's decisive breakthrough during the following century was due to its shaking off resource fetters, particularly the limited availability of land.[2] There was not enough to supply wood and wool for newly emergent industries as well as food for the workers; take-off could really begin only when coal replaced wood and agricultural imports from North America filled the food gap. In other words, the rise of the Euro-Atlantic industrial culture was largely due to access to two major resources: fossil fuels from the earth's crust, and biotic raw materials from the (former) colonies. Without the mobilization of resources from the depths of geological time and the expanses of geographical space, industrial civilization as we know it today would not have taken shape.

Against this background, it becomes clear that Europe's self-aggrandizing bonfire of resources cannot be repeated, especially not in those many parts of the world where the population level is incomparably greater. For the two resources that enabled Europe's special role are simply no longer available: fossil fuels destabilize the climate and in any case are running low, and there are no longer any overseas colonies to provide biotic raw materials. Newly developing countries have to buy raw materials at fairly high prices or else turn parts of their own territory into *de facto* colonies – as we can see happening in Brazil or India. Anyone who, despite all the productivity advances in its wake, wishes simply to imitate the development path of industrial civilization does not reckon with the fact that resources are no longer so easy or cheap to come by. The strategists of catching-up development, who still occupy the commanding positions in economics and politics, are prone to a tragic confusion: they think that in the twenty-first century it is still possible to succeed with the utopias of the nineteenth. In reality, quite apart from the likely harm it will cause, any economic advance today has to face resource limits that are incompatible with the traditional models of production and consumption. It is impossible to imagine, for example, how everyone in the world could have access to a private car, an air-conditioned bungalow or a meat-rich diet. Prosperity for the few will therefore be the unintended consequence of actual industrial develop-ment, precisely because the democratization of resource-intensive prosperity runs up against the economically or ecologically insurmount-able limits of scarcity. Since the conditions that led to the Euro-Atlantic model of prosperity cannot be transferred to the rest of the world, it is structurally not capable of justice – or only at the price of making the planet inhospitable.

Hence the dilemma of justice in the age of biophysical limits: on the one hand, other peoples and societies fix their sights on the equality and dignity contained in the Euro-Atlantic model of prosperity, so that the exit from poverty and marginality is conceived as entry into industrial civilization; on the other hand, justice cannot be attained at the consumption level of the Northern economies, since the finite character of the biosphere prohibits measuring equality by the living standards of the North.

Contraction and convergence

Hypotheses are shorthand for a complex reality: they reduce a dense tangle of events to a simple but comprehensible schema. In order to picture which development paths might bring the world to a greater level of resource justice, it may be useful to employ the hypothesis of 'contraction and convergence' that developed out of research on future climate policy.[3] It concentrates on two development paths: one for the industrial countries, one for the developing countries.

Equality – at what level?
In the 'contraction and convergence' model for the future, the world's nations adjust their use of resources so that in half a century from now they no longer overstretch the absorption and regeneration capacity of the biosphere. Since no nation has the right to a disproportionate share of the global environment, each one tries – though with individual variations – to achieve the common goal of material and energy consumption compatible with the demands of other countries, while remaining within the load-bearing capacities of the biosphere. In the end, there is no justification for any other distribution of globally important resources; the right of all nations to a self-defined and equal development permits each nation only to make claims that are socially and ecologically sustainable at a global level. This is what the argument

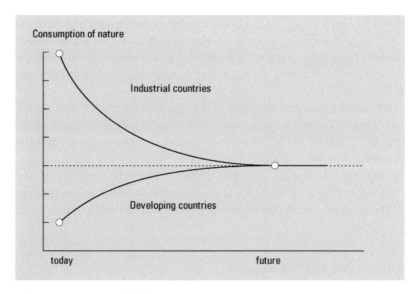

Figure 5.1 A future model: contraction and convergence. The industrial countries reduce their use of resources more sharply than the developing countries expand theirs. In the future all countries will meet in a common time corridor, which will be within the load capacity of the biosphere.
Source: Our own projection.

inspired by Kant comes down to: institutional patterns of resource consumption should be considered unjust if they rest upon rules which cannot in principle be adopted by all other nations (see Chapter 4).

This image of the future requires that the industrial countries contract – that is, that they reduce their consumption of resources. For it strictly follows from the above premises that the overconsumers should first of all step down from their excessively high level. Resource justice in the world crucially depends on whether the industrial countries are capable of retreating from overconsumption of the global environment. The example of greenhouse gases may serve to illustrate the path of shrinking resource consumption. By the middle of the century, the overconsumers must reduce by 80 to 90 per cent the strain they put on the atmosphere by burning fossil fuels, in order to do justice to the precepts of both ecology and fairness.[4] Since fossil energy at present accounts for the bulk of resource budgets in the rich countries, it has proved useful to speak of a 'Factor 10':[5] which means that by mid-century these countries will have to manage on resources ten times lower than the consumption levels of 1990 – unless viable technologies for the disposal of CO_2 can be developed in the meantime. We should remember that the consumer class in the countries of the South is placed under the same responsibility. The Factor 10 formula simply defines the order of magnitude; lower or even higher targets may be set in individual cases. Although Factor 10 refers to fossil resources, the aim is also to reduce consumption of biotic resources; the cuts may turn out be less drastic, but the limited areas of land suggest that restrictions will have to apply here too.

The developing countries, for their part, appear in the model as tracing an upward curve in resource consumption. First, poorer countries have an unquestionable right to attain at least the 'dignity line' of resource consumption which should apply to all citizens of the world. Without access to kerosene or biogas, without an energy and transport infrastructure, it is hard to satisfy even the basic needs of human life. Moreover, each country will try to achieve different images and forms of a prosperous society – an ambition that in turn requires access to resources such as energy, materials and land. But the upward movement cannot lead to an exponential curve; it should follow a linear path and tend towards convergence with the industrial countries in a common 'target corridor'. For the ascent ends at an upper line of ecological sustainability for all; natural limits set the framework for justice. The future model of 'contraction and convergence' thus combines ecology and justice. It begins with the insight that environmental space is finite, and it ends with a fair sharing of the environment by the citizens of the world.

Well-being and resource consumption

Of course, such a model does not sit well with the present-day economic dynamic. It contradicts two basic assumptions of the growth economy: (1) the widespread idea that economic development is bound up with high resource consumption, which implies that the industrial countries will remain on their high plateau while the developing countries struggle to reach it; and (2) the idea that human well-being grows at the same rate as resource consumption, so that the richest society is the one in which the aim of the economy – material well-being – is achieved in the most exemplary manner. Both assumptions sometimes attain the dignity of myth; they belong among the pre-analytic beliefs held as a matter of course in economic institutions. In common with most myths, however,

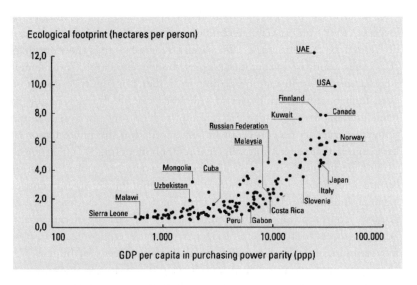

Figure 5.2 *Per capita* ecological footprint in comparison with *per capita* gross domestic product (2003). Starting with a GDP of $1,000 *per capita,* a rising ecological footprint becomes visible. Even with a high GDP of $50,000 *per capita,* however, there is a sizeable spread in resource consumption – between 4 and 10 hectares *per capita.*

Source: Our own presentation. Footprint statistics: WWF 2006. GDP data: World Bank 2006, additional information from Statistics Finland 2006.

they stand in a tense relationship with reality. On closer examination, the supposed links become looser and the underlying assumptions turn out to be suspect.

To see the first assumption in a clearer light, it is enough to place side by side the economic performance of a large number of countries (measured by *per capita* GDP) and their resource expenditure (measured by the *per capita* ecological footprint). Figure 5.2 allows us to draw the following two conclusions. First, a rough and extensive correlation may be drawn between resource consumption and wealth, since all industrial countries display a footprint greater than 4 hectares per person, whereas all less developed countries with an annual income of less than US$1,000 display a footprint below 2 hectares per person and, in most cases, below 1 hectare per person. This confirms the assumption, in as much as we can speak of a lower and upper threshold: there is no escape from poverty below a minimum use of resources, and high income is largely obtainable only through high use of resources. Second, there is nevertheless a considerable scattering of resource consumption above and below the income curve. Among the rich countries, the United States or the United Arab Emirates take more than twice as much in resources as Western Europe or Japan. A similar elasticity is apparent in countries with a middle income level: Gabon has roughly the same *per capita* GDP as Malaysia, yet it consumes only half as many resources; and Costa Rica, with a comparative average GDP as Peru, leaves a footprint almost twice as large. There is only a loose correlation, then, between economic development and resource use; even under present conditions, countries have considerable leeway – if they use geography, politics and intelligence – to achieve economic results with a reduced expenditure of resources.

As to the correlation between resource consumption and well-being, similar trends are evident, despite the differences, in developing countries and industrial countries. For more than a decade the United Nations Development Programme has been using indicators such as life expectancy, literacy levels and health standards to measure the 'human development' of various countries. If the aggregated Human Development Index is compared with resource consumption (Figure 5.3), then it becomes clear that development can increase up to an upper-middle level of human well-being (approx. 0.75) without a growth in the size of the ecological footprint; Georgia, for example, consumes two-thirds fewer resources than Turkmenistan, at the same level of development. Only in

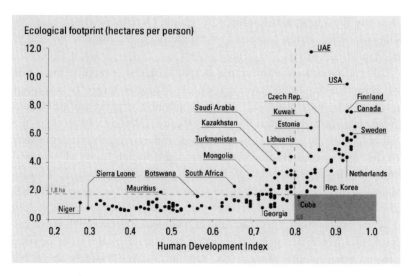

Figure 5.3 *Per capita* **ecological footprint in comparison with Human Development Index (2003).** Increased development up to an upper-middle level of human welfare (0.75) is possible without an increased ecological footprint. A clear spread begins at a high level of development (0.8), however, and most countries with an index above 0.9 leave a footprint of at least 4 hectares *per capita*. Only one country, Cuba, matches a high human development index (0.82) while remaining under the globally replicable level of 1.8 hectares per person.

Source: Our own presentation. Footprint statistics: WWF 2006. HDI data: UNDP 2005.

the case of countries that already have a high level of development (starting at 0.8) does a clear spread appear. But there are quite a few countries which, with low resource consumption, display a higher level of human well-being than countries with high resource consumption – and vice versa. The Netherlands or South Korea, for instance, have achieved higher well-being than the resource-intensive economies of Sweden or the Czech Republic – not to speak of Finland or even Kuwait. Just like income, human well-being is only loosely coupled with resource consumption.

There is also only a loose correlation between human well-being and income. Here too, from a bird's eye view, human well-being is correlated with economic achievement, but on closer examination this applies only up to a certain threshold. For example, people in Kerala, China or Sri Lanka have a significantly higher life expectancy than the populations with much more money to spend in Gabon, Brazil or Namibia, or even the African-American population in the United States.[6] This confirms a view of the industrial countries according to which well-being has by no means advanced in step with national income. In 1993, American citizens had more than twice as much disposable income as in 1957, but this did not make them twice as happy. Rather, it is their appreciation that seems to have changed: whereas in 1957 35 per cent of people interviewed said that they were very happy, the comparable figure in 1992 was down to 32 per cent.[7] Above a certain point, subjective well-being no longer has much to do with income level; income *differences* or the sense of social belonging do, however, play a larger role. Furthermore, rising national income no longer generally leads to an increase in disposable income, since all manner of social costs – from environmental damage through spending on the police to rent increases and hospital charges – tend to rise more steeply than personal disposable income.[8] Even if the economy is growing, citizens do not necessarily acquire more purchasing power. So, measures of welfare that deduct systemic costs from national income regularly suggest that since the late 1970s real well-being in the industrial countries has not grown as the same rate as national income and may even have stagnated.[9]

From all this we may conclude that quality of life has only a limited amount to do with standard of living. This paradox is due to the fact that human well-being has many dimensions, whereas an understanding of it as geared to material growth takes seriously only the money dimension. To put this in quasi-economic terms, we may say that well-being is based on the cultivation of money capital, natural capital and social capital; it encompasses communal as well as private wealth. If the 'commonwealth'– that is, urban safety, nature, social cohesion and institutional justice – is allowed to go to rack and ruin for the sake of increased private riches, the result is the destruction, not the creation, of value.

It is therefore misguided to look for greater well-being only through the maximization of money capital. At least it is misguided if this decisively affects natural or social capital, the other sources of well-being. Rather the optimal production of well-being – to continue with this language for a while – requires efficient use of money capital (hence, neither too much nor too little), in successful synergy with natural and social capital. A type of prosperity would then be regarded as truly efficient if – at the same level of contentment – it managed with the smallest possible use of money capital; if, that is, it was capable of extracting the maximum well-being from a given monetary income. There is much to suggest that only a 'consumption-efficient' prosperity of this kind is able to deliver justice worldwide; no one has yet credibly argued that resource-light prosperity, for either the developing or the industrial countries, can be permanently achieved with an exponential growth of money income. Hence the demand for justice in a finite world is always bound up with the search for other forms of prosperity that will increase natural and social capital and make the increase of money capital serve this end.

Cutting back on high consumption

As things stand, the transnational consumer class takes a disproportionately large part of the global environment (see Chapter 2). Precisely in the age when the load on nature is reaching its limits, the existential rights of economically weaker groups of people, as well as the opportunities for all nations to enjoy equal development, are coming under pressure (see Chapter 4). Justice thus demands a retreat from over-appropriation of the environment. At the same time, one-sided appropriation of natural resources is conjuring up all manner of conflicts, huge international rivalries and often unnoticed local struggles (see Chapter 3). In the name of greater security from destabilization and violence, a scaling down of demands on the biosphere has therefore become part of today's agenda: resource-light economics contributes to a policy of world peace. Against this background, a very long-term project is taking shape: the transnational high-consumption economy has to be restructured in such a way that eventually it will rarely need to use the earth as a mine or a rubbish tip.

The trio of efficiency, consistency and sufficiency

How can the transition from a resource-guzzling to a resource-light and naturally sustainable economy be achieved? Over the last thirty years, a host of engineers, managers, activists and scientists have been busily investigating the challenges of such a transition. What can be extracted from all their endeavours adds up to a conceptual trio: efficiency, consistency and sufficiency.

First, with regard to efficient resource consumption, the idea is to reduce the use of materials and energy per unit of goods and services, through improved technology and organization, recycling and waste avoidance. There are plenty of examples: washing-machines that save on water and electricity, lightweight motor vehicles, frequency-controlled industrial motors, high-efficiency power stations, recyclable products such as newspapers or chairs. Resource-efficient initiatives concentrate on the design of products for greater durability and repeated use, on the reduction of energy and material flows in the production process, and on corporate strategies to promote the extended use of products more than physical sales.[10]

But the efficiency strategy has an Achilles heel: it may score major successes in cutting the use of particular resources, and therefore the expenditure of materials and energy per unit of output, but it does not prevent greater overall consumption. For the sum of all savings may be eaten up and overcompensated by global growth in demand for goods and services. In fact, that is what has been happening. And so, although the efficiency strategy has the greatest potential as the first step on the road to sustainability,[11] it reaches its limits as soon as the increased production of goods and consumption of resources outweigh the total savings.

With regard to consistency, the key question is the compatibility of nature and technology. The principle is that industrial metabolic processes must not disturb natural cycles; the two should as far as possible complement or even reinforce each other. Where this is not possible, substances damaging to nature should be placed in a fail-safe technical circuit of their own or − if that is not successful − taken out of service altogether.[12] In fact, in intelligent systems there is no waste, only products. Mushroom cultures grow in the residue from beer production, and electric power stations also generate waste heat that can be used in other locations. An economy can be organized in such a way that − abstracting from the inevitable entropy − the waste from one activity is used as raw material for the next.[13] In this it is less important to reduce energy consumptions and material flows than to manage them in an ecologically sound manner. Solar-generated hydrogen, for instance, might make it possible in the long term to have an energy supply that does not damage the atmosphere. There is a similar potential in bionics, a technology which takes nature as a model to be imitated.[14]

The consistency strategy is not a panacea either. Cars with hydrogen fuel cells, for example, may not pollute the atmosphere, but they need and use land or infrastructure that is available only within certain limits. The fuel cells have to be produced and maintained, and the hydrogen stored and transported. Not all waste can become raw material for new products. There are even natural substances such as carbon dioxide or liquid manure which, in high quantities, cause ecological problems.[15] And up to now information technologies have resulted in larger, not smaller, consumption of matter and energy, as the predicted savings on transport, business travel, paper use, and so on have turned out to be deficits. Consistency, too, can facilitate only aspects of sustainability.

Sufficiency, on the other hand, raises the question of what is enough, of what is good for the economy and patterns of life. The etymology gives us a clue: the Latin *sufficere*, composed of *sub* and *facere*, means in its transitive use 'laying the ground', and in its intransitive use 'to be disposable, to be enough, to be able or capable'.[16] The point of sufficiency, then, is not to fall victim to excess and overstretch, but to take only as much as is beneficial for the well-being of individuals and the whole. Whereas – to borrow from Paul Hawken – efficiency requires us to do things right, sufficiency calls for the right things to be done. For it is doubtful whether the expectations raised in the age of resource abundance can be sustained in the age of resource saving. Strawberries in winter, four by fours in city traffic, hot water on tap day and night: such comforts bring little but cost a great deal. A resource-light economy would be better advised, therefore, to adjust itself to a middle level of achievements. The question 'How much is enough?' cannot be avoided.[17] Since it is necessary to change our behaviour and the way we relate to goods and services, eco-sufficiency is closely connected with what has been known since antiquity as the due measure, the good life, the art of living. And it may well be that the reasons for eco-sufficiency also stem from that wise ancient maxim, 'Nothing in excess'. We can therefore think only of a two-track transition to a sustainable economy: through the reinvention of technology and through an orientation to the quality of life rather than the quantity of goods.

All in all, then, three paths to sustainability are as indispensable as they are irreplaceable. Each has its own importance and its own limits. Efficiency is a basic ecological strategy with a high initial potential and lasting significance; one should never forgo using materials and energy as efficiently as possible. But efficiency alone cannot satisfy the growing requirements, nor neutralize the growing burdens on nature. Sufficiency, like efficiency, is a currently essential strategy for careful handling of the natural foundations of life. Whereas efficiency ensures the rational use of resources, sufficiency stands for their sparing consumption. Consistency strategies make possible economic operations within the limits of natural sustainability and are therefore essential for the survival of an ever-growing humanity. Efficiency and sufficiency bridge the time until sustainable technologies will be functionally mature, sufficiency relieving the pressure to produce results that presently rests on efficiency strategies. But, even if the expectations associated with consistency are one day fulfilled, efficiency and sufficiency will not lose their importance. For nine billion human beings will have to treat with care the limited ecosystems on which they depend, and to share them out equitably. And that will require efficiency as well as sufficiency – that is, the question of what is enough and what is good for us.

The possibilities of this trio of sustainability strategies are clear in the fields of energy and transport. In both of these there are important personal components, but they essentially involve state-organized infrastructure and their development is even today influenced by public investment and detailed legislation. Which power stations are built, how electricity grids and road or rail networks will look, what is done about water and sewage: all these are matters for government policy, though also influenced by the economy. And in turn these decisions have an impact on the decisions of households and economic players.

The example of energy
For the economies of the globalized North, the transition from a fossil to a solar energy base is the central challenge of the twenty-first century. Without a massive retreat from the use of fossil fuels, global warming will develop into an assault on the life chances of part of humanity, intensify security threats and the risks of war, and expose energy consumers everywhere to higher and higher scarcity prices. Only a resolute turn to renewable energies can both prevent this evolution and offer secure supplies. The changeover will have to pass through the three strategies discussed in the previous section: that is, a rational use of energy, moves to solar, wind and biological sources, and more careful demand for energy services.

Intelligence will be needed to raise the efficiency of energy use, as there is hidden scope at every level of the chain from production to consumption. To use this potential is an imperative of economic and technological reason. But the energy economy must redefine its objectives if there is really to be an 'efficiency revolution'.[18] Whereas for more than a century oil or electricity corporations have seen their business as

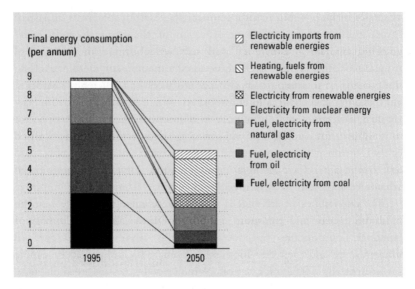

Figure 5.4 Germany's energy supply in 2050. To be sustainable, Germany's energy consumption must be lowered by approx. 50 per cent by the year 2050. Coal, oil and natural gas would then provide only two-fifths of the supply, with the main emphasis on natural gas. Just under 60 per cent of energy would derive from renewable sources.
Source: Fischedick et al. 2000: 122.

supply, they are now obliged to earn their money as much by avoiding waste. Instead of increasing demand, they will have to learn to keep it flat. This change of perspective means that the rational conversion and use of energy must take priority over its production. For customers the purchase of kilowatt hours is only a means to a certain end: power or warmth. Energy-saving buildings, vehicles and appliances, together with modern management and far-sighted vision, could skilfully remove the need for a lot of fuel yet offer the same utility values. It is also becoming easier to provide the remaining energy requirement mainly from renewable sources. In the end, the energy provider of the future will also take responsibility for the potential external damages due to its product, such as noxious emissions or nuclear waste. In return, the provider should expect the state to provide a suitable framework within which it can satisfy the social demand for the avoidance of unnecessary energy use and external costs. According to some scenarios for the year 2050,[19] if the rational use of energy took worldwide precedence, primary energy consumption could be held constant despite a threefold increase in global GNP.

If consistency is made a further priority, the global discharge of greenhouse gases could even be reduced dramatically. Greater sustainability of energy flows would mean, however, the use of naturally regenerating sources such as wind, water, sun and biomass. Solar collectors and solar cells for the production of heat and current directly use the sun's rays; wind and water power are indirectly derived from solar energy; heat pumps draw on heat from the surrounding air, water and soil; and geothermic power stations use the energy stored in the earth.[20] Already smart machines and systems are available which can convert what nature supplies into electricity, heat or motor fuels. Of course, regenerative energies cannot be had at zero ecological cost: biomass costs land area, wind power disturbs landscapes, and the production of efficiency technologies costs both energy and materials. However, these environmental effects are radically lower than those of traditional energies – even if they indicate that energy from renewable sources must also be used carefully and thriftily.[21]

Even with an optimum deployment of renewable energies, consumption will have to be reduced appreciably. For a system is all the more easily adjustable to the requirements of sustainability if its energy requirements are lower. If, as Figure 5.4 shows, the target for a country like Germany is to use 50 per cent less primary energy by the year 2050, efficiency and sufficiency will have to work hard together. They complement each other in many different ways, and there are flexible transitions in which an eco-efficient technology together with corresponding human behaviour can lead to the desired result. Good examples are room heat (only a combination of building insulation and considerate heat or ventilation behaviour gives a satisfactory result) and organic farming (only the deliberate buying of organic food makes it possible for resource-efficient agriculture to survive without the use of oil or chemicals). Quantitative limits on the use of fossil fuels, as envisaged in the system for trading pollution licences in Europe, might also enable competing corporations to contribute to the common good of climate security. If a change in values and perceptions also spreads more widely, so that success is measured in terms of solar facades, fresh food consumption, low car-use cities and general caution in the deployment of 'energy slaves', then further possibilities open up for a retreat from the fossil energy economy.

The example of transport

The introduction of combustion engines in the last third of the nineteenth century led to the rapid growth of transport over ever-greater distances – and with ever-greater energy consumption. The high rates of growth have continued to the present day. And, unlike in some sectors of industry, there is here no reversal of the trend in energy consumption and CO_2 emissions, even if in some countries, as a result of higher oil prices, individual car journeys and associated emissions have recently been declining. On a world scale, mobility is still a key stumbling block on the road to 'energy disarmament'. This concerns the vehicles as well as the nature of the transport system. Cars need roads, and roads attract more cars to drive longer distances, which then require the building of more roads. This vicious circle moulds spatial structures and gradually makes motorized movement a necessity for everyone. The same is true of air travel; larger and larger aircraft cover ever-longer distances at an ever cheaper price, partly because the price of kerosene does not contain environmental costs. But an economic and existential model that rests upon distance-intensive spatial structures is hard to generalize at world level, as the expenditure on land and materials would be too great.

The way to a more sustainable transport system again begins with greater resource efficiency. Numerous technological improvements to all vehicles, from mopeds to jet aircraft, could potentially cut down on fuel use, materials, noise pollution and noxious emissions. More economical ways of driving, together with reorganization of freight and passenger transport, are helping to achieve the necessary mobility with the least expenditure. Further opportunities arise out of new energy sources, such as bio-fuels or (in the future) regeneratively produced hydrogen.

Another strategic approach is to shift freight and passengers on to less harmful, and therefore more sustainable, means of transport. One thinks here of journeys by rail instead of on motorways, goods transport by rail or inland waterway instead of on lorries and trucks, or city transport on buses and trams (or, locally, the use of body power through cycling or walking) instead of by private car. Of course, this will have to be compatible with the requirements of everyday life – which is possible only if public transport is better adapted to passengers' needs, and if future price instruments ensure that polluting forms of transport are not subsidized at the expense of sustainable forms.

The third strategic approach, the avoidance of travel, again refers to the sufficiency perspective. For the consumer, such initiatives as car sharing (with the slogan 'Use, Don't Own') offer the opportunity to downgrade the private transport option, to save costs, but to keep access to a car for special situations. At the level of enterprises, a new attentiveness to regional supply and marketing would shorten freight conveyance times and therefore the general costs of transport: beer from Bavaria instead of Mexico – not exactly a major interference with the quality of life. At the level of German local politics, the widespread publicity for a 'town/region of short journeys' is meant to suggest that the spatial proximity of important places makes transport unnecessary. Instead of covering ever greater distances with ever faster transport, the idea is to build structures that will cut down on the need for moving around.[22]

As in the energy sector, however, the inclinations of road users and the dominance of supply thinking, together with the associated interests of power and profit, stand in the way of a radical reversal. All too many people gain from the expansion of transport, even if it is at the expense of the general welfare and of people without a car such as children, trainees, housewives and old people. Car firms and construction companies, factory outlets and leisure parks make money out of expansion, but no one is likely to make a huge return on demand-reducing investment. In general, the interests of money capital are able to articulate themselves more effectively than those of social or natural capital; prudence is not a lucrative business. This also explains why energy firms prefer to build new power stations than to trim down their customers' energy needs. The generation of megawatts sets a lot of money in motion, for the benefit of a few large players; 'negawatts', though representing a saving, tap only scattered money for the benefit of many small players. It is this structure of interests that slows the transition to an ecological service economy, in which money flows not in order to sell the greatest amount of goods, but to sell services such as heat, cooling or mobility and only to a limited extent actual goods.

Ecological leapfrogging

Two main obstacles stand in the way of greater resource justice in the world: the resource-intensive models of prosperity in the North, and the drive in the global South to copy those models. Skyscrapers in Shanghai, motorways in India, shopping malls in Morocco: historically outmoded types of construction, technology and marketing are spreading around the globe. Yet they embody the hope of escaping from poverty and powerlessness, and of one day gaining so much prosperity and respect that neither the country nor its people will any longer feel ashamed of their inferiority. The challenge of sustainable development is precisely to achieve this equalizing justice without endangering the biosphere.

Such development will aim both to ensure a livelihood for all citizens and to maintain and renew the country's resource base. It is not a shortage of workers which hinders this, but rather (apart from money) a shortage of nature. Human beings are generally plentiful in the South; development which systematically replaces labour with energy-intensive and material-intensive technology is therefore a false direction for society which allows the army of the superfluous to keep growing. The point is to get a larger number of hands and brains to work, instead of exchanging them for more and more kilowatt hours and megabytes. Moreover, in many parts of nature, there is less to go round than there was a century ago. More and more often economic progress is blocked not by a shortage of fishing boats but by a shortage of fish, not by poorly performing pumps but by the sinking of groundwater, not by a lack of chainsaws but by the disappearance of forest.[23] In this situation, a heavy industrial, machine-intensive and resource-squandering mode of development makes less sense than in nineteenth-century Europe. The only economic forms which offer a real promise of social progress are those which embrace a great number of people and at the same time deal circumspectly with material and biological resources.

This development path contains a historic opportunity: the countries of the South, as never before, have a chance to outwit the industrial countries. Since dependence on fossil fuels is driving the industrial countries into a dead end, countries in the South that were long regarded as backward could take the lead. They could wager on bold ecological 'leapfrogging' over the false paths of the industrial countries and, for that matter, move directly to modern renewable energies, perhaps investing earlier and more consistently than the Northern economies in solar energy. They could very soon find themselves with patterns of sustainability that the rich nations have not yet reached at all.[24] There are some signs that this is already happening. China, despite its high resource consumption in many sectors, is a leading seller of wireless telephony and solar heating systems – which signifies massive savings of copper and coal. Perhaps so-called underdevelopment will end up turning into an advantage?

Newly developing countries, in particular, face crucial decisions concerning energy, transport, sewage and communications systems.[25] In these key policy areas, many countries of the South are still in a position to opt for infrastructure that will put them on a resource-saving and low-emission path of development. Modern rail and coach systems, road lanes friendly to pedestrians and cyclists, decentralized energy production, water-processing circuits, well-adapted housing, regional food provision and concentrated housing estates can set a country on the road to cleaner, more cost-effective and equitable patterns of production and consumption.

Decentralized electricity generation
A minimum of energy is part of the welfare minimum. Yet roughly one-third of the world's population – two billion people – have available to them only what they can find in their immediate surroundings: wood, cow dung, branches, agricultural waste. This corrodes in three ways the lives of the poor. It means smoke in the home, as well as hardship and loss of time especially for women; it produces a constant energy shortage for homes and small trades; and it leads to repeated plundering of bushland and forest, which is a silent catastrophe since the layer of vegetation is gradually worn away under the pressure of more and more people. One of the main tasks in the alleviation of poverty and protection of the environment is therefore to facilitate access to renewable energies, thereby creating jobs and regenerating nature.[26] Another is the electrification of rural areas, which promotes health and education by providing energy for clinics, schools and water treatment stations.

This challenge, almost like a squaring of the circle, can be met only if a basic technological and political choice is made today. The electricity supply, which in the North but also in the South mostly rests on fossil fuels and a centralized, oligarchic organization, must be decentralized and put on a regenerative basis, with participation from the local population. Figure 5.5 shows what would be the economic and social import of such a choice. In the industrial countries, electrical energy is overwhelmingly supplied direct from high-output power stations along high-voltage networks to the centres of consumption. From there, individual consumers are supplied via the various voltage levels. The power flow is thus essentially vertical. In a mainly decentralized supply system, by contrast, a considerable part of the current is generated in small, modular output units, whose priority it is to supply a large number of small consumers. As an emergency back-up, there may also be a connection to a higher-level integrated network.

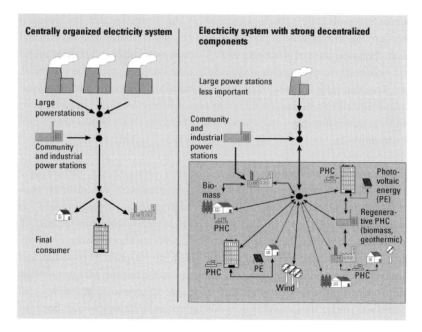

Figure 5.5 Comparative structure of central and decentralized energy supply. In a centrally organized system, most of the electrical energy is fed from high-performance large power stations into a high-voltage grid and passed down to the consumption centres. In a decentralized system, a considerable portion of electricity is generated in small, modular units (for example, power-heat coupling (PHC) or photovoltaic energy (PE)) and supplied directly to the consumer. A connection to the higher grid exists only to guarantee the supply. Source: Our own presentation.

Since the decentralized system generates more current close to consumers, it can be adjusted to local economic and natural conditions. Power generation becomes a local economic activity, and energy consumers increasingly become energy producers. The investment in technology is thus also socially meaningful: small power stations, regional raw materials and local supply networks require the involvement of the population, strengthen local competence and in any event have a greater affinity than central structures with democracy. They create more jobs, as a large number of systems have to be built and looked after; they enable planning for immediate needs and promote short construction schedules; and they give those involved a better understanding of the wider significance for society. The direct costs of a large system (50 to 200 megawatts) in the area of the central grid are still smaller than those of many small ones, but the latter have a greater usefulness for the national economy. By creating a mass market and facilitating the entry of new participants, they set in motion an upward trend in the economy.

Renewable energies will be the foundation of the decentralized supply system. Fossil materials usually need long lines of communication, which in turn create long value chains;[27] most jobs and most profits then arise far from the consumers. But a shift to a renewable raw materials base can change this logic, as photovoltaics, wind power, small hydroelectric stations and biomass have shorter lines of communication. In fact, this is true not only of the raw materials but often also of the conversion technologies associated with them. Labour and income are strengthened at local and regional levels, because the money circulates within a smaller geographical space. From the point of view of an Indonesian farmer, it would be real leapfrogging to have an energy-efficient cooker, a solar pump or a biogas system: all these technologies make living easier and spare the natural environment, and their sources – sunshine and biomass – are accessible everywhere.[28] The industrial model of squandering nature instead of giving people work would be turned on its head, because labour would be needed and raw materials would be saved.

Nevertheless, the trend towards central supply structures remains almost unbroken. The counterforces are too strong: bureaucratic inertia and the interests of corporations and the transnational consumer class in the South. Brazil offers a good case study of what can go wrong. In the last few decades Brazil built up an energy supply structure that is extremely centralized for the size of the country and its low population density. It supplies the economic centres in the Southeast with energy from large hydroelectric stations and a number of thermal power stations, while leaving the hinterland and poorer layers of the population neglected.[29] Here there is a low level of electrification, and what exists is highly prone to interruption. This division within the country is not unique but seems to be typical of newly industrializing countries. Energy choices are taken mainly by economists and engineers, who pay scant regard to the needs of the majority. Indeed, the experts happily gamble on large-scale projects like atomic and coal-fired power stations, because they raise the national pride, secure profits and prestige for investors and engineers, and can be combined with military interests. Only very recently have there been some diffident attempts to promote renewable energies.[30]

Yet public interest in a non-conventional energy supply has been growing in many countries. This may be seen in certain obligations that were undertaken under the intergovernmental 'Renewables' process, initiated in Bonn in 2004. Egypt, for example, is pursuing ambitious targets for hydroelectric power and wind and solar power stations, while the Philippines, the world's largest user of geothermic energy, wants to become the leading producer of wind energy and an exporter of solar cells. A number of Caribbean states have announced that they plan to follow Brazil in producing ethanol fuel from sugar cane, as a replacement for some of their expensive oil imports.

Mobility without car dependence

How much transport does a society need for its well-being? The trivial but momentous answer is: neither too little nor too much. As with energy, water and other natural materials, there is a minimum threshold for transport below which few chances exist of raising living standards. Presumably this is the case in all societies whose average travel *per capita* is less than 2,000 kilometres a year: that is, most countries in the South. They will therefore have to develop their transport systems. But how? This too requires a choice of direction.

A country with a low degree of motorization faces an alternative: either it can promote a system based on high motorization for a minority, or it can opt for more restrained motorization for as many people as possible. Many countries strive to reach Northern levels of car ownership, but these are unattainable because the ecological as well as the social and economic costs will prove too high. At some point things will get stuck: either the fuel imports will become unaffordable or the land for roads will run out or the weaker sections of society will not have sufficient purchasing power.

The option of high mobility for a minority increases motorization from above, creates new inequalities and leaves the non-motorized worse off.[31] In the cities of the South, most people continue to move around with rickshaws or bicycles, on foot or by bus. A growth of car transport would restrict their freedom of movement more and more: their lives would be degraded by greater insecurity and air pollution; they would be increasingly forced off the streets; and they would have to cope with ever greater distances in the urban area. Thus, in India 90 per cent of the cars are located in the six largest cities. China's cities, once a cyclist's paradise, are choking in a smog from mopeds, cars and taxis, which often take up more than half of the road surface to move less than 10 per cent of the population. Whether in Delhi or Nairobi, it is pedestrians who suffer the most fatal accidents – followed by people on motor rickshaws and bicycles. In many ways, then, greater speed for the relatively few leads to less speed for ordinary people; the mobility of some dramatically increases the immobility of others.

A sustainable strategy will therefore opt for a different structure of transport growth, concentrating on where it will bring the greatest advantage to society. This means, for example, extending roads to remote areas so that teachers and doctors can reach people, and farm produce can be supplied to local markets, instead of building motorways and ring roads demanded by the car-owning upper classes. Or it means giving priority not to wide roads that might reduce jams for car owners in big cities, but to the social and economic mobility requirements of the great majority – through the introduction of smart public transportation systems. There will still be a place for lorries, of course, but not so much to deliver consumer goods from the harbours to the big cities as to transport inexpensive health, education and production goods to outlying regions. Anyone who wishes to improve living conditions for the broad masses should not adopt the value preferences of the affluent countries: 'We'll build roads where heavy transport already makes them necessary', or, as the World Bank's neoliberal planners argue, 'We'll fund roads where car and lorry drivers are able to pay for them.' That is not the way to sustainable mobility. A real attempt to achieve it will require simple, cost-effective systems in which footpaths, non-motorized locomotion and public transport develop hand in hand.[32] They can count on far wider popular acceptance than in the transport-spoiled lands of prosperity.

There is a good maxim: first walk, then bike, then ride. Instead of being regarded as antediluvian, walking and cycling should be continued and encouraged. This requires the improvement of safety for the weakest people on the road, by creating special bicycle routes and planning integrated cities where non-motorized transport is not excluded but becomes a central concern.[33] Since not every journey can be done on foot or with a bicycle, there is a need for a well-equipped public transport system that everyone can afford. Here the financial straits of many developing countries actually offer an opportunity. One form of mass transportation, whose popularity is growing all over the world, is the 'rapid bus transit', a model of which exists in Curitiba, Brazil. This is not simply an express bus but a special transport system which, among other things, has its own lanes that offer the same transport capacity as an underground but at much lower cost.[34]

Curitiba's exemplary system, which has since been taken up by many other cities, reminds us that the triumphal march of the car and the decline of public transport are by no means an inevitable trend but the result of specific cost structures, subsidies and state-built infrastructure. This is also true of automobile construction itself. Let it be noted: the point is to correct the false path represented by the car, not to forgo the many useful and necessary applications of automobile transport. But the highly industrialized countries have invented cars which move 1,000 to 1,500 kg of material to transport a person's weight of 70 to 90 kg. This is due not to some law of nature but to a combination of indifference towards natural wealth, the marketing of cars as a fun product for the well-off, a love of speed, and massive subsidies for the deployment of resources. For a doctor or commercial traveller to have access to scattered communities in areas with a low population density, what is needed is not a 'varnished bulldog' type of sports utility vehicle capable of performing at several hundred kilowatts and a speed of 180 km/h or more, but vehicles running on a tenth of the energy consumption, capable of a modest 100 km/h and a performance level of 30 kilowatts. A carefully motorized, resource-light fleet of cars could do wonders in raising mobility, without causing the same drag-mark that vehicles from the North's prodigal industries leave behind. Of course, automobile corporations will make light, slow and economic cars for countries in the South only if governments take action to promote them by building appropriate infrastructures and creating a legal and economic framework that favours them over other models.

But there are major obstacles to such 'leapfrogging' ecological innovations: namely, the desire of the rich to have high-performance prestige cars, the profit considerations of automobile companies seeking to offload their top models in new markets, and the desire of politicians to influence voters by building more roads. The combined effect of these three factors may be observed in China – a country whose growth dynamic is bound up with the export interests of large automobile corporations, and which has been heading towards individual motorization through the reduction of import tariffs and a breakneck programme of road and motorway construction. China is thus spoiling its future prospects for sustainable mobility. And it is saddling itself with the kind of scarcely affordable long-term maintenance costs that already weigh on the highly motorized countries.

Regenerative agriculture

The leap forward in the agriculture of the South is a leap over and beyond methods that countries which have adopted industrial principles regard as 'conventional'. But, just as the development path of nineteenth-century industrialization was a historical exception based upon long-distance trade and fossil energies, so is this true also of the industrialization of agriculture. For only the shipping of guano (bird excrement containing phosphorus and nitrogen) from Peru in the middle of the nineteenth century, followed by the industrial production of synthetic fertilizer, compelled farmers to turn away from natural cycles and a balance between agriculture and pastoral farming.[35] At the same time, the great demand for labour in industry and the cities gave rise to increasingly capital-intensive and resource-intensive production in agriculture, which would make it possible to release the necessary manpower. Today, however, the countries of the South find themselves in a fundamentally different situation: they have a surplus of labour on the land and a great interest in reducing migration flows to the cities.

Furthermore, industrial agriculture – in both North and South – has manoeuvred itself into an ecological and social dead end. It uses huge quantities of fertilizer and pesticide, as well as water and energy, mainly for highly technological large-scale production and the factory farming of animals for cheap food. This results in soil erosion and declining fertility, in the pollution of groundwater, lakes and seas, and in a decrease in agro-biodiversity that is only worsened by the introduction of genetically engineered plants and animals. Industrial agriculture is thus the point where a number of pressing ecological problems intersect. In the South it is also the point where social problems intersect, as it is the main cause of food supply shortages in many countries and means that people who used to be employed in agriculture can no longer find work anywhere (see Chapter 3).

The ecological and social consequences of industrial agriculture are especially hard for poor people living in the countryside. Their livelihood usually depends not only on cultivated crops or animal breeding but also on wild plants and animals that can be gathered, hunted or fished on common land. In Bangladesh, one study found, the rural population derives at least 40 per cent of its food by weight and the greatest part of its nutritive requirements from land or lakes that are not farmed.[36] The basic assumption behind monoculture – that specialization in a single crop is the most productive form of agriculture – suffers from shortness of vision. For, even if it increases yields, the resulting soil erosion, reduced fertility, environmental pollution and water shortage wipe out much of the food growing in the wild. This is why less food is available as a result of monoculture, even though individual yields per crop may at first be larger.

In contrast to industrial forms, the aims of regenerative agriculture are to use natural and social resources more sparingly, to increase output in sustainable ways, to gear it mainly to self-provision and local markets, to develop new and rehabilitate older agricultural techniques in an ecological spirit, and to adapt to natural ecosystems. This presupposes a new way of thinking. It is necessary to free ourselves from the ideas behind the industrial on-tap economy, so that use is made of species diversity and natural cycles and circuits, and so that people rather than machines are recognized as the most important means of production.

Methods of regenerative agriculture involve the following essential principles: simultaneous growing of several crops alongside one another in a single field (as mixed crops and through intercropping, for example), so as to offer a habitat for natural enemies of pests and to stimulate the biotic activity of the soil; crop rotation to regenerate the fertility of the soil and to break the life cycles of pests; mixed use of land for agriculture and forest, together with the planting of crops under trees to keep pests away and to stabilize soil humidity and the microclimate; and, finally, the integration of agriculture, animal farming and, where possible, fishing, to obtain sufficient biomass and to return both organic and natural nutrients to the cycles of matter.[37]

There have already been good experiences with regenerative agriculture in the South. Jules Pretty and Rachel Hine have evaluated 208 agrarian projects in 53 countries to counter food shortages in the most environmentally friendly ways.[38] Here is one example. In Bangladesh farmers sowed their seeds for decades with hybrid seeds and chemicals, in accordance with the precepts of the 'Green Revolution' advocated by their government and the World Bank. Through massive use of pesticides and mineral fertilizer they initially succeeded in raising yields, but these later fell again as the soil and water became contaminated and exhausted. The turning point came with the disastrous floods of 1988, which neither seeds nor chemicals were able to withstand. There was no capital to buy any more, and so the farmers in question decided to try new directions. Where they had previously grown only one crop (for example, sugar cane), they now have a lush mixed cultivation on small plots. Either simultaneously or in rotation, they produce such vegetables as onions, garlic, potatoes, radishes, lentils, gourds and sweet potatoes; sugar cane is planted in between the rows or patches of other crops. To avoid buying mineral fertilizer, they scatter nitrogen-producing legumes, okra shoots, water hyacinths – which used to be thought of as an aggressive weed – banana leaves, rice straw or cow dung in among the plants. In the tropical climate, the organisms in the soil soon manage to form humus. Not only in Bangladesh but also in China and Vietnam, the wet rice fields also serve for aquaculture: fish and prawns are produced among the rice plants for their protein content. The fish in turn devour the larvae of mosquitoes and other disease-bearing insects, helping to reduce the danger of epidemics. Dykes built around the fields are put to use as vegetable patches.[39]

It is crucially important that agriculture here makes better use of the regular cycles of nature, because it adapts to the local climate and soil and nurtures species diversity. It is therefore more cost-efficient than industrial agriculture, especially in low-wage regions: labour-intensive units operating on relatively small plots of land permit considerable savings in comparison with outside methods involving machinery, mineral fertilizer and pesticides. Since the ecosystem survives intact and species diversity is preserved, poor people in particular can continue to practise hunting and gathering as sources of food and income. And the avoidance in principle of harmful pollutants means that the economy does not have to pay the heavy costs associated with them.

Further costs can be avoided if the multiplication of seeds is not entrusted to (foreign) corporations but kept inside the country. Women have handed down countless techniques for handling and exchanging seeds, and these make possible the cost-free nurture of agro-biodiversity. Local non-commercial organizations can also play a role: for example, the Seed Wealth Centre in Bangladesh, which collects hundreds of local plant and tree seeds and makes them available to farmers for the improvement of their stock.

Well-adapted agriculture will not only regenerate pasture and farmland but also assist the restoration of wetland, forest and river bank or lakeside biotopes, which are indispensable for the storing of water and the formation of groundwater. Also important is the recycling of urban sewage. This requires real 'leapfrogging' over modern organic methods in the North, which up to now have not systematically employed treated sewage in agriculture. The following division of urban sewage suggests itself: yellow water (urine), which contains the highest quantity of nutrients, can be drained off and processed into high-grade fertilizer; brown water (faeces) can be either composted and used to improve the soil or employed in the generation of energy in biogas plants; relatively uncontaminated grey water (from sources such as bathing, washing or dishwashing) can be lightly purified through biological treatment and made available for irrigation. Separate treatment of industrial effluent may well also be necessary; special decentralized plants would filter out toxic substances originating in a factory or hospital, so that the water could then be used again.[40] The systematic association of agricultural production with sewage management would save on scarce water resources and reduce the contamination of lakes, rivers and groundwater (Figure 5.6).

Finally, regenerative farming as a whole shows a positive energy balance, whereas industrialized agriculture – if properly computed – invests more energy than it produces.[41] This too makes it clear that, for the countries of the South, the leap forward for agriculture lies not with industrialization but with better adaptation to local conditions, to improve both their own self-provision and their exchange relations with other countries. For where is all the extra energy to come from, and how is it to be paid for, when fossil fuels start to run out? Labour-intensive and energy-saving production would enable a reversal of the role played by agriculture in the economy. It could become a branch of the future, as a central source of energy supply. By supplying biomass and growing raw materials for biofuels, it would in the medium term – also in the North – take over some of the functions that industry has performed until now. The countries of the South have a historic opportunity to become the spearhead of this development and to make their farmers the 'oil sheikhs' of the twenty-first century. However, the provision of energy would not have to compete with food production, or with the cause of agricultural and natural conservation; on average a maximum of 3 per cent of the global land surface should be the maximum for this purpose.[42] Besides, sustainable crop growing can succeed only with the methods of regenerative mixed-culture farming geared mainly to the regional market – otherwise the vegetation-rich regions of the South threaten to degenerate into impoverished monocultural 'gas stations' of the world market.

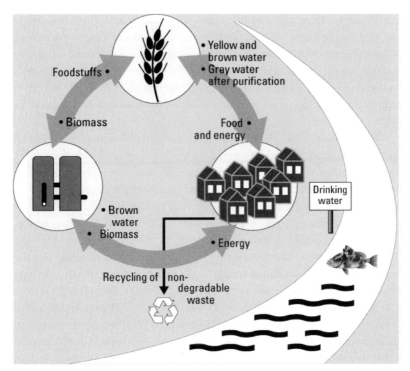

Figure 5.6 Integration of agriculture, sewage disposal and energy supply. The association of agriculture with urban sewage management and energy production from biomass will close a material cycle and save scarce water resources. Source: Our own presentation.

The World Bank – an agency of the fossil age?

It is scarcely an exaggeration to say that in many countries multilateral finance institutions appear as agencies of the fossil age. For a considerable time the World Bank has seen its constitutional task as being to help overcome poverty, mainly through the promotion of growth, and especially since the 1990s to produce in the countries of the South the infrastructural conditions for the inflow of private investment capital from abroad. Motorway infrastructure, for example, may in the short run serve these objectives, but by opening up new regions to juggernauts and private cars it tends to push the whole country into full-scale motorization. This can be seen in many countries where international financial institutions such as the World Bank have appeared as a third major player alongside the national government and the automobile industry. Huge loans are advanced to support road building in particular, as in the case of China's 30,000-kilometre National Trunk Highway System, which is planned to link 95 cities by the year 2008, or India's 14,000-kilometre National Highway Development Project, which is supposed to run along the coasts and on a North–South and East–West axis.

The promotion of growth through a fossil-fuel-oriented policy is all the more disastrous because infrastructural investments leave their mark downstream on the economic structure and continue to have an effect for decades to come. They set the country on a certain development path for the rest of the century, by closing ever tighter the time window in which sustainable options could have been chosen. This diagnosis applies to much more than just transport projects. In the energy sector, too, the World Bank and other multilateral lenders are concentrating on the expansion of fossil-produced energy – as a far greater priority than energy efficiency or the development of renewable sources. Between 1992 (the year of the Earth Summit in Rio) and 2004, the World Bank group approved loans totalling 11 billion dollars for 128 projects related to oil, gas and coal extraction in 45 countries. Of these projects, 52 are directed at the export of fossil fuels on the world market, mostly to the industrial countries. According to the *Extractive Industries Review*, the World Bank invested 94 per cent of its energy portfolio for the year 2003 in fossil energies, and only 6 per cent in renewable energies.[43]

This is remarkable, because one would like to think that the World Bank, as an institution of the United Nations, felt a special obligation with regard to the agreements on sustainable development in general and climate change in particular that the UN Conference on Environment and Development reached in Rio, as well as the 2002 World Summit in Johannesburg. Of course, there can be no talk of that. Despite many attempts at reform – for example, in its action plan for the 'Renewables 2004' conference, the World Bank undertook to do more to promote renewable energies – multilateral financial institutions are still in reality among the forces impelling fossil fuel development, not only under the pressure of donor nations in the North, but increasingly also under the pressure of newly industrializing countries in the South. Thus, billions of dollars of public money are being invested in such a way that prosperity combined with justice will soon cease to be the horizon and become the mirage of global society.

This is all too clearly visible in farming policy. The triumphal march of industrial agriculture – publicized for farmers and public opinion as the 'Green Revolution' – was driven by the World Bank and the International Monetary Fund in association with other international institutions. The 'Green Revolution' replaced the farmer's input of labour, water, vegetable and animal fertilizer and home-grown seeds with industrial products which jointly and severally consume far more energy than the farmer's production methods and accordingly release far more toxic emissions. While generating larger harvests in the short run, and thus contributing to poverty reduction for a time, it made cultivators dependent on annual purchases of seeds, fertilizer, pesticide and insecticide, and forced a changeover to monocultures. To encourage this, the World Bank gave loans to large agricultural corporations for the (initially cost-free) dissemination of hybrid seeds and accompanying chemicals in developing countries, and funded water projects for industrial agribusiness.[44] Here too a course has been set, and it cannot easily be changed once the diversity of plant species is on the decline and large-scale monocultural structures are in place.

A leap by the countries of the South into a post-fossil-fuel economy may at first sometimes require further investment, which will prove profitable only on the basis of its long-term benefit to the national society. The financial institutions of the twenty-first century have a responsibility to assist this leap. It is high time that the World Bank and other donors reconsidered their role in promoting infrastructures and technologies, and realized that, in a world of limited resources, it is possible in the long term to reduce poverty and to achieve justice only within the framework of a resource-light economy.

Notes

1 Landes 1998.
2 Pomeranz 2000; 2002.
3 Meyer 2000.
4 WBGU 2003b: 6 argues for a reduction of approximately 80 per cent.
5 BUND/Misereor 1996.
6 Sen 1999.
7 See Lane 2000, which also provides a survey of similar studies.
8 Ayres 1998: 105ff.
9 A summary of these studies may be found in Diefenbacher 2001: 133ff.
10 Weizsäcker, Lovins and Lovins 1997; Fussler 1997; Hawken, Lovins and Lovins 1999; Hennicke and Seifried 2000.

11   Jochem 2003.
12   Braungart and McDonough 2003.
13   Pauli 1999.
14   Gleich 2001.
15   Bringezu 2004: 113.
16   Georges 1880; Werner 1989.
17   Segal 1999; Sachs et al. 2002; Linz 2004.
18   Weizsäcker, Lovins and Lovins 1997.
19   Lovins and Hennicke 1999.
20   Fischedick et al. 2000.
21   On the development of regenerative energies for Germany, see DLR/ ifeu/WI 2004.
22   An introduction to ecological transport policy may be found in Petersen and Schallaböck 1995.
23   Hawken, Lovins and Lovins 1999.
24   Colombo 2002; Goldemberg 2003.
25   A number of the following arguments are developed in Dalkmann et al. 2004.
26   Goldemberg and Johansson 1995.
27   Scheer 1999.
28   Khosla 2003.
29   Oliviera 1998.
30   For an overview, see Dalkmann et al. 2004.
31   Whitelegg and Haq 2003.
32   GTZ and Kaltheier 2001.
33   Mohan and Tiwari 2000.
34   Zimmermann 2002.
35   Radkau 2000: 223.
36   Mazhar and Akhter 2000.
37   Altieri 2004.
38   Pretty and Hine 2001.
39   Ibid.: 126ff.
40   Dalkmann et al. 2004.
41   Thomas and Vögel 1993.
42   WGBU 2004: 4.
43   Fritsche and Matthes 2003.
44   Barker 2002: 250ff.

6
Agreements for Fairness and Ecology

Law must never be adapted to politics, but always politics to the law.

Immanuel Kant, 1797

A quarter of a century ago, before all the talk of 'globalization', a German chancellor with unerring insight summed up the political consequences of the worldwide interdependence that had sprung up around him. All foreign policy – Willy Brandt said, borrowing a term from Carl Friedrich von Weizsäcker – is from now on nothing other than global domestic policy. That is how Brandt characterized the position of politics in the postmodern age. After the withdrawal of economics and culture, or considerable parts of it, from the national state, domestic policy can no longer be separated from foreign policy. The internal affairs of a country are now influenced in many ways by transnational force fields. And, conversely, external policy can no longer be differentiated so clearly from internal policy, since internal affairs, even if regulated within Europe (one thinks of energy policy or agricultural subsidies), increasingly display external effects. Under these circumstances, the distinction between global and local is superimposed on the one between external and internal. With the demand for a global domestic policy, Willy Brandt drew the logical conclusion from this shift: it is not the national welfare but the common good of global society which is the framework for an enlightened foreign policy. Brandt thus placed himself in a line going back to Kant's project of a cosmo-politan world society, in *On Perpetual Peace* (1795). For Kant, a viable global order was one in which states would cease behaving as rivals interested only in their own power advantages; instead, power relations would give way to cooperative relations, and the rights of citizens would be placed higher than the interests of their states.

There is worldwide controversy over what such a global domestic policy would look like and which principles it would obey. Globalizers stand against critics of globalization, Davos against Porto Alegre, and both have been pushed into the background in the last few years by one-sided action against terrorism. In the face of the unilateral – or, in less diplomatic language, high-handed – security policy of the United States, there may be some common ground between the two positions, in so far as both globalizers and critics of globalization, in opposing the Washington unilateralists, rely on the supremacy of law and multilateral cooperation.

The differences are greater than the common ground, however. Without generalizing too much, we may say that two concepts of globalization are today in conflict with each other. Market-driven globalization is interested in turning the whole world into a single economic space; transnationally active corporations are supposed to compete globally with one another, to increase wealth and prosperity in the world as efficiently as possible. This conception, which may be traced back to free-trade ideas in eighteenth-century England, has marked international politics especially since the 1980s. On the other side, the conception of a politically driven globalization sees the world not as an economic arena but as a community in which people, nations and societies coexist with one another; this community should develop institutions committed to the common good, and that requires constant weighing of the values of democracy, ecology and economic utility. The roots of this conception go back to theories of the *polis*, and later the *cosmopolis*, in Greek antiquity, and to the European Enlightenment. To sum up the difference, we may say that advocates of politically driven globalization look at the world and see a society that has a market, whereas advocates of market-driven globalization look at the world and see a society that *is* a market.

In the preceding chapters we have offered contributions to the empirical and theoretical study of global resource justice. For the idea of resource justice draws together the two challenges that the world will have to face in the future: the achievement of greater justice, and protection of the biosphere. This raises three key questions. First, how can institutions of transnational governance help to shape access to natural resources in such a way that basic livelihood rights are guaranteed for all of the world's citizens? Second, how should such institutions be designed to give all nations the opportunity for freely chosen and equal development? And, third, how can institutions of 'global governance' support the transition to patterns of production and consumption that are capable of sustaining justice? With these questions we turn in this chapter to some important areas of international environmental and economic policy that have recently been at the centre of disputes about the architecture of global institutions.

Among the arenas for these disputes have been the international environmental regime and the World Trade Organization. But the players on the international stage are also becoming the focus of attention again: transnational corporations as trailblazers and profiteers of globalization; the players of civil society as purveyors of ideas and boosters of a global society capable of facing the future; and, not least, the European Union as a possible but still indecisive promoter of such a development. However, only part of this controversy is visible at the global level. Changes at the top remain rather toothless if they are not accompanied with, or indeed challenged by, changes from below. It is above all the many varied initiatives for ecology and justice at local, regional and national level which are impelling trends towards greater resource justice: the movement of rubber gatherers in the virgin forest of Amazonia, the tree protection movement in India, employers' initiatives to develop less resource-intensive economic models, consumers' campaigns for fair trade, and the numerous members of human rights groups and environmental associations. They are all part of the great effort to make global society capable of facing the future. In the end, it also includes the many millions of people who, through their own action and as voters, exert an influence on the course of events.

Equity in the greenhouse

The burning of coal, oil, gas and wood releases carbon dioxide (CO_2) as a by-product. This is partly absorbed by vegetation and the sea, but is partly accumulated in the earth's atmosphere. If excessive amounts of it concentrate there, they function as an additional layer of insulation and keep too much of the sun's heat on earth. Not all countries and certainly not all people release equal quantities of greenhouse gases; these are correlated with the distribution of power on the globe. The relationship between atmospheric pollution and economic prosperity is unambiguous (see Chapter 2): the richer and more powerful a society is, the greater (with slight variations) are its carbon dioxide emissions; for the possibility of using the planet's mantle of life as a rubbish tip represents a source of economic power. Whoever strives to gain a greater share of economic power will therefore insist on having a greater share of atmospheric pollution. This is the root of the distribution conflict over the limited resource of the earth's atmosphere. Yet demands on the atmosphere not only create power but also intensify the lack of power. Global warming brings pollution effects which are unevenly distributed across the earth and may push economically weak regions and people to the limits of survival – or beyond. To take just one example, as many as 100 million people or more live below the 88 centimetres which, according to climate experts, is the possible amount by which sea levels may rise.[1]

Molecules and human rights

The tug-of-war over development and emissions condensed into two interrelated agreements under international law: the United Nations Framework Convention on Climate Change (1992) and the Kyoto Protocol (1997). Whereas the first set a framework for scientific and political cooperation, the second went considerably further and established legally binding minimum obligations for industrial countries.[2] The central idea of the Framework Convention, as specified in Article 2, is that there is a common duty to 'prevent dangerous anthropogenic interference with the climate system', essentially understood as the dumping of carbon dioxide and other gases. The international community thus gave some foretaste of what governance might mean in the transnational space: since emissions know no frontiers, there is a need for multilateral decisions; and, since the atmosphere is a common good, there can be only shared sovereignty over it.

Of course, the problems were only beginning, and since then waves of controversy have rolled through the world of science, journalism and politics. How much climate change can be attributed to anthropogenic influences? What degree of global warming is acceptable? When can interference with the climate system become dangerous, and for whom? A lot depends on the answers to these questions. They determine the upper emission limits that global society should set, and therefore also how much space is left on earth for the oil, gas and coal economy.

What increase in global mean temperatures is tolerable – and for whom? Lurking behind this key question are basic issues to do with the coexistence of people and nations on earth. Only one would often look in vain for some recognition of this in the public debate on the climate, where social blindness tends to be the prevailing feature. There are reasons why this is so. The damaging effects of climate change do not hit everyone; they affect the poor more than the rich, who can therefore allow themselves a higher threshold of tolerance (see Chapter 2).

Specialist studies agree that the countries of the South, especially rural groups with little purchasing power who directly depend upon nature, will come to feel the destabilizing effects of global warming much more abruptly than the industrial countries and urban populations.[3] Whereas the transnational consumer class is partly responsible for climate change, large sections of the world's majority pick up the bill. For example, rising temperatures threaten the economic security and the culture of Inuit people living in Arctic regions of Canada. Hunters disappear on the hunt as traditional routes across the ice are no longer able to take the load; food supplies go off because the permafrost breaks up; igloos lose their insulating property when the snow melts and freezes again. And, in the end, the de-icing of the shores leads to a draining away of freshwater and, with it, of the fishing populations in the Arctic Ocean.

The dangers are greatest for the most vulnerable. Excessive burning of fossil resources is undermining the integrity of their habitat, as harvest yields decline and prices rise as a result. Slum areas become prone to devastating mudslides, and diseases seek out those with the least physical and economic strength to resist. In any event, whole countries in the South have prepared themselves for major economic losses. The risks are concentrated on the socially weak and powerless; the integrity of their habitats is being undermined by the excessive burning of fossil fuels in richer areas.

Nor is this only what is in store for the future. Global warming has already begun, and it is being caused by industrial countries. In accordance with the 'polluter pays' principle, the industrial countries therefore have a responsibility today to compensate the non-polluters for the damage. There is already a need to strengthen basic healthcare, to build dykes, and to resettle people living in areas threatened by high water levels. Up to now the industrial countries have refused to discuss giving such assistance for adaptation to climate change. Only in the follow-on talks after Kyoto in 2000 and 2001 did the G-77 group of countries (plus China) grasp the opportunity to make their agreement dependent on additional aid payments. In fact, the Marrakesh accord of 2003 established three new funds that are supposed mainly to support adjustment projects and other measures in the South.[4] But only one of these funds can count on a modest but secure income, from contributions to projects under Kyoto's Clean Development Mechanism. For the other two, any binding commitment is still in the lap of the gods.

Compensatory payments are necessary, but they leave the causes of pollution untouched. Cuts in fossil fuel use are imperative not only to protect the atmosphere but also to protect human rights (see Chapter 4). Since the Bill of Rights was won during England's 'Glorious Revolution', freedom from physical harm has been the core of the basic legal canon that states have an obligation to guarantee. Yet millions of people are in the process of losing this core of civil rights: food and water, fertile soil, a home and an infection-free environment. Climate change represents an assault on the economic, social and cultural rights of large population groups. Only here the threat of physical harm comes not from the state but from the cumulative long-range effects of energy consumption in the prosperous parts of the world. The need for low-emission economies in the South and the North is therefore far more than a question of an appeal to morality; it is a core demand of cosmopolitan politics.

User rights to the atmosphere

Nearly all participants in the climate negotiations suppress the fact that limits on greenhouse gases involve a choice between human rights and prosperity rights. The task of keeping temperature rises below two degrees appears too great – and too threatening to the interests of those who profit from current levels of consumption. According to expert calculations, it is already necessary to reduce carbon dioxide emissions by 45 to 60 per cent between now and the year 2050.[5] The Kyoto Protocol, with its commitment by industrial countries to an average of 5.2 per cent between 1990 and 2012, falls well behind this target. And, because of various loopholes, the actual reductions are even smaller. The agreement is inadequate because until now the industrial countries – first of all the United States, the leading source of emissions, which is outside the treaty altogether – have been unwilling to change. But it is also inadequate because the newly developing countries have so far escaped without limitations. Things cannot remain so. For total emissions only in the countries of the South would exceed the capacity of the atmosphere to absorb them, even if every industrial country were to vanish with a wave of the wand.[6] Without the newly industrializing countries, in particular, global climate protection is doomed to failure.

This is precisely what makes fairness an inherent necessity,[7] since the countries of the South will refuse to cooperate so long as they fear that it will simply enshrine global inequality. They are afraid that the North is pulling up behind it the ladder on which other nations seek to achieve a high standard of living. To save the climate at the price of perpetual inferiority is not an option for them. They refuse to pull the chestnuts out of the fire for the North if that means that they have to continue burning themselves. Why should countries like China, Brazil or India get involved in an agreement that would allow them fewer emissions than the industrial countries for an indeterminate period? The conclusion is inescapable: global climate protection will be just pie in the sky without fairness between North and South. Ecology without equity is as impossible as equity without ecology.

There is reason to expand this point, however. Already in 1992, under the climate Framework Convention signed in Rio, the international community was supposed to take measures 'to protect the climate system ... on the basis of equity and in accordance with their common but differentiated responsibilities and respective capabilities' (Article 3.1). At the time, the countries of the South succeeded in making the industrial countries lead the way, since they were responsible for most of the present and past emissions. The countries of the South could remain free to increase their emissions, so as to 'satisfy their social and developmental needs'. For the same reasons, the Kyoto Protocol merely enjoins the industrial countries to implement minimum thresholds. However, at Kyoto the definition of targets for individual countries was redolent of a bazaar, with nothing planned about it. The key factors were bargaining skill, political power, obstinacy and chutzpah.[8]

If newly developing and poor countries are to come on board after the Kyoto Protocol period, fair rules must be negotiated for the distribution of emission rights. Disturbances due to overburdening of the atmosphere will sooner or later affect everyone. Obviously the atmosphere belongs to all, not some; it is a global common good. So, who in future should still emit greenhouse gases, and in what quantities? In accordance with which principles should the 'cake' be fairly divided?

This question has been hotly debated for some time.[9] Some have suggested a 'grandfathering principle' based on historical development and customary right: first come, first served. But this rule, which would mean accepting the currently unjust distribution of emissions and imposing the same minimum obligations on all, would set in stone the global prosperity gulf and could hardly be described as fair. Somewhat better is the principle that countries should reduce emissions in accordance with their respective capabilities. Economically strong countries would then bear the main burden – regardless of how frugal and efficient they were with energy. This may be a fair proposal but it does not make ecological sense, for it would offer rich countries no inducement to use energy more efficiently. A third principle, which involves allocating minimum obligations in accordance with historical responsibilities, corresponds to the rule that the wrongdoer should carry the can. The size of the obligation would then obey the 'polluter pays' principle: each state should undertake to reduce emissions by an amount proportional to its historical contribution to climate change. This would cost industrial countries the most. Brazil tabled such a proposal in 1997 at the international climate talks, and since then the theme of 'ecological debt' has been on the agenda of environmental diplomacy.[10] But it is doubtful how much responsibility can be demanded for actions that were committed in ignorance of the consequences (see Chapter 4).

The so-called *per capita* approach should be judged differently.[11] It is based on the idea that a global common good belongs not to all countries but to all human beings, and therefore on the equal right of all citizens to have access to the atmosphere. This model, which has its roots in the Universal Declaration of Human Rights, can be seen emerging in recent negotiations on climate policy. Thus, in the Marrakesh accord on implementation of the Kyoto Protocol, the parties agreed that measures would be taken in their respective countries to level out *per capita* differences between industrial and developing countries.[12] Indian prime minister Vajpayee declared at the 2002 climate summit in New Delhi that 'we do not believe that the ethos of democracy can support any norm other than equal *per capita* rights to global environment resources'.[13] And French president Jacques Chirac, both at the 2000 climate summit in The Hague and before the European Parliament, gave his support to this approach.[14]

The aim of equalizing *per capita* emissions first requires greater reductions on the part of the industrial countries. It is therefore a compromise between demands that the industrial countries be held liable for emissions earlier in history and their own demand that the *status quo* should be taken as the starting point. It fulfils the minimum condition of equitable distribution: that is, not to intensify but to mitigate existing inequalities. If this is combined with the 'emission trading' that will be discussed below, income from the selling of extra emission rights could even help to reduce the global cleavage between rich and poor.

In 2005 negotiations will begin over the post-2013 set of commitments under the Kyoto Protocol. The industrial countries will have to accept drastic reductions, but the countries of the South must also take on phased obligations. Fair and workable distinctions will also have to be drawn between countries as different from each other as Burkina Faso and South Korea;[15] the former should be permitted some increases in emissions, while the latter should commit itself to limits. There is no other way to preserve both the existential rights of the poor and the freedoms of the nations of the South.

A per capita *cheque*
The principle of equal *per capita* rights to the atmosphere along with the use of emission trading will reduce inequality among nations. But there is not yet any attention to the unequal access to resources within countries, where gross differences persist between population groups in relation to welfare and emission levels (see Chapter 2). Moreover, states are today no longer the only addressees of international law; individual resource users may also be recognized as bearers of rights, which, if necessary, may be asserted in opposition to governments.

How to ensure that individuals or groups become beneficiaries of international laws is a new and important area of study. In the traditional model of intergovernmental agreements, there is no guarantee that a government will distribute on a *per capita* basis the funds due to it under a system of international emission trading. It is not only in despotic regimes that many other interests than those of the sovereign people have an influence on decisions. A policy geared to transnational justice must therefore closely examine, alongside distribution between and within countries, the just distribution of atmospheric remunerative payments among the population or to institutions serving the public good.

How is this to be achieved? The existing literature gives scarcely any answer – indeed, in most cases the question is never even asked. One of the few exceptions is Peter Barnes's idea of a 'sky trust', which he conceives along the lines of the Alaska Permanent Fund (APF). This administers part of Alaska's oil revenue, so that a long-term investment strategy can convert the state's finite oil wealth into a steady source of income.[16] Since the early 1980s, some of the yearly income from interest – more than $1,000 *per capita* – has been paid out to Alaska's inhabitants as a dividend. The APF is thus one of the rare examples in which every citizen has a direct economic stake in a public good.

Similarly, Barnes's 'sky trust' might administer on behalf of all citizens the emission rights internationally awarded to each country. Mineral or oil corporations, for example, would have to acquire emission rights from their government in order to continue emitting carbon dioxide, and if the demand for these rights within the country was not sufficiently high some of them might be sold to other countries or foreign corporations. The climate trust would then distribute the income once a year to the citizens, who would thus directly benefit from the emission rights awarded to their country. However, the benefit would not fall equally to all, since the climate trust would also operate a redistributive mechanism whereby, through an increase in final consumption prices, citizens with a higher demand for emission-intensive products and services would pay out more than they received from the dividends. They would thus become net payers: the higher prices they were charged would pay for the corporate purchase of emission rights – and hence for the dividends to citizens. On the other hand, anyone leading a low-emission lifestyle would stand to gain, since the dividends from the climate trust would make them better off than before. Climate-friendly behaviour – whether conscious or unconscious, intentional or unintentional – would be directly reflected in the finance budget. For money would actually flow, from those who overused the public good of the 'atmosphere' to those who made more considerate demands on it.[17]

A climate trust of this kind would help greatly to gain public recognition for the idea that, despite different emission levels, all citzens have an equal *per capita* right to the atmosphere. In the medium term, the European emission trading system might be reshaped and expanded along these lines. The European Union has a chance here to set up, at first internally, a model of climate democracy that might possibly serve as an example to other countries or even the rest of the world. Nor can we exclude a breakthrough in cosmopolitan awareness precisely at the level of climate policy. New institutions such as a climate trust, which allows everyone to share in the fees for use of a public good, might create a common interest out of being, along with millions of others, a joint owner of the atmosphere.

Fairness and diversity

Two different environmental crises are troubling contemporary humanity: one concerns fossil resources, the other living resources. The two are closely bound up with each other, but they are different in origin and character. The fossil crisis stems from the accelerated transfer of solid, liquid and gaseous substances from the earth's crust into the atmosphere by means of industrial technology. The living resources crisis, on the other hand, is attributable to the excessive pressure that human beings place on the biosphere, thereby weakening or even destroying whole natural systems large and small, a process which may reach the point where humanity itself is under threat. One danger coming from over-loaded ecosystems is the lower probable yield of vital products such as grains, milk, meat, wood, crude fibres or water. The other is that eco-systems will have a reduced capacity to sustain life by purifying the air and water, decomposing and recomposing nutrients, or regenerating the topsoil. Whereas the fossil crisis is the hottest issue in the North, the living resources crisis is at the centre of attention in the South.[18]

The reason for this difference is simple: the South is more affected than the North, in both its monetary and its subsistence economies, by the decline of living systems. Quite a few countries rely quite heavily on harvesting freely available ecosystems. After all, agriculture, forestry and fishing still account for half of all jobs worldwide, and as much as two-thirds in sub-Saharan Africa, South or East Asia and the Pacific region. A quarter of all countries do more business in crops, timber and fish than in industrial goods.[19] Finally, two out of three poor people in the South live in rural areas. A considerable portion of them get their food, their clothing or housing material and their medicines directly from natural surroundings. Intact ecosystems are indispensable precisely in places where little purchasing power is available – both for people's subsistence and for the earning of money.

Against this background, two conflicts over justice have arisen in the last two decades. The first concerns fairness between different countries in the use of biological resources; the second relates to fairness between state and industry on the one hand and local communities on the other. As in climate policy, the biodiversity justice conflict between North and South goes back to an underlying asymmetry: the South has greater diversity in ecosystems, species and genes (Table 6.1), whereas the demand for natural goods as well as the genetic engineering industry are mainly located in the North. The issue in dispute is who has access to the biological resources and under what conditions. It concerns the tradi-tional patterns of economic exchange as well as the power claims of the industrial countries, for the tussle over biological resources also reflects the struggle of the newly developing and peripheral countries to equal development rights.

Table 6.1 Plant diversity in selected countries

Country	Plant varieties	Of which, varieties present only there	Plant varieties per 1000 km²
Australia	15,638	14,074	2.0
Brazil	56,215	n.a.	6.6
Brunei	6,000	n.a.	1,040.8
Canada	3,270	147	0.3
China	32,200	18,000	3.4
Colombia	51,220	15,000	45.0
Congo DR	11,007	1,100	4.7
Costa Rica	12,119	950	238.1
France	4,630	133	10.0
Germany	2,682	6	7.5
Guatemala	8,681	1,171	79.7
Indonesia	29,375	17,500	15.3
Malaysia	15,500	3,600	46.6
Mexico	26,071	12,500	13.2
USA	19,473	4,036	2.1

Source: Our own compilation, based on Groombridge and Jenkins 2002.

A similar asymmetry may be observed within countries, and it gives rise to justice conflicts over people's livelihood and human rights. The domestic middle and upper layer, often in harmony with transnational economic interests, has its eyes fixed on the commercial use of wood, seafood, farmland, water supplies and genetic wealth, whereas local communities look on the same natural goods as their communal property or, at any rate, as their subsistence base. To whom does biodiversity belong? Conflict between the desire for prosperity and the needs of existence is scarcely anywhere as present as in the realm of living resources.

Sovereignty as protection

The UN Conference on Environment and Development, held in Rio de Janeiro in 1992, adopted a Convention on Biological Diversity (CBD),[20] which is still today the most important platform for international cooperation in the domain of living resources. Nearly every country in the world has ratified the Convention – with the exception of the USA.

Alarmed by reports of the shrinking natural wealth, the governments of the time reached an agreement that committed all parties to preserve biodiversity and use it in sustainable ways, and to share equitably the resulting benefits.[21] Although the CBD focuses on the diversity of ecosystems, species and genes, the negotiations mostly concentrated on access to plant genetic material and the profits obtainable from it.[22] Countries initially turned their attention less to the wealth of nature than to the wealth that corporations and governments hoped to make out of using genetic resources. Although in recent years the contracting parties have also tried to reach agreement on macro-ecosystems such as oceans and forests and on species diversity, lines of divide have opened up over the issue of plant genetic resources.

It is only in the last few decades that information contained in the genetic make-up of living creatures has been perceived as a new kind of resource. In contrast to traditional breeding, science and industry now aim to reprogramme organisms with outside genes so as to achieve the maximum results. This discovery of genetic material as a resource for life industries has opened a new round in the history of resource conflicts between North and South. Is it permissible to acquire any genetic material from other countries? Who should own the profits resulting from use of this material? A dispute is welling up between industrial and developing countries over the legitimate ownership and use of plant genes (see Chapter 3).

The idea of genetic resources as a 'global commons' was contrary to the interests of powerful players, and so it retreated more and more into the background and no longer featured in the Rio biodiversity Convention. Access to biological diversity was no longer to be free. Many countries, however, especially in the South, successfully insisted on their right to regulate the use of genetic resources within their sovereign territory; they no longer wanted to be cost-free suppliers of raw materials, but sought to tap new sources of income by sharing in the use of plant genetic resources.

The CBD's recognition of national sovereignty over genetic resources strengthened the position of countries with a high level of biodiversity *vis-à-vis* those seeking to gain access to it. But these rights went together with an obligation 'to facilitate access to genetic resources for environ-mentally sound uses by other Contracting Parties and not to impose restrictions that run counter to the objectives of this Convention' (Article 15.2). Sovereignty thus underwent a limitation, which played to the interests of biotech industries. Of course, amid the continual clash of interests, agreement has been reached only on certain 'guidelines' concerning the shape of legislation on equal benefits, which can then be got round in various ways (see Chapter 3). But even such weak agreement is not unimportant as a counterweight to the other assault stemming from the World Trade Organization, which aims to establish worldwide intellectual property rights (see Chapter 6).

Rights of local communities

Mostly, however, the protectors of areas with high biodiversity are not governments but traditional communities and indigenous peoples. They are not a negligible quantity, since 300 million of the earth's inhabitants are estimated to belong to indigenous peoples – about the equivalent of the population of the United States. If one adds local communities with traditional lifestyles, as the biodiversity Convention does,[23] then the total figure is almost as large as that of the transnational consumer class, which is culturally as well as economically its counterpart.

Local and indigenous communities are in many ways bound up with the biological resources in their surroundings, which not only provide food and material for medicine, clothing and housing but also play a major role in the spiritual life of the community.[24] Just as the culture of traditional communities cannot be separated from nature, so conversely are seed varieties, cultivated plants, livestock and vegetation marked by the passage of these communities through history. Cultures, then, also impress their seal upon nature. Biological diversity and cultural diversity have to a considerable degree developed in tandem;[25] the two dimensions are yoked to each other for better or worse. Cultures lose their hold when there is a loss of species diversity, and the erosion of cultures also impoverishes the world of plants and animals. Traditional communities are usually the best preservers of biodiversity. So, the protection of biological diversity is much more than just a question of natural conservation; it also has to do with the capacity of local communities to survive, and hence with cultural pluralism and participatory rights.

At the same time, this leads to conflict within nations. Precisely in species-rich countries like Brazil, India, Indonesia or Mexico, there is a long history of disputes between local communities and the colonial or central state. The issue has been and still is the survival capacity of indigenous and traditional communities, their land rights, autonomy and cultural freedom. Again and again the sovereign majesty of the state, often in league with domestic or foreign industry eager to make profits from the forests, fishing grounds or mineral wealth, has collided with the interest of local communities in living space, resource security and cultural survival. Natural goods rarely exist in a no man's land, so the protection of nature cannot escape the question: natural diversity for whom? From the point of view of self-provision, the answer is that local communities live on biodiversity and therefore have priority rights to local natural resources. This is also good news as far as natural conservation is concerned. All experiences indicate that biodiversity cannot be preserved against local communities, but only with them.[26] More participation and more cultural freedom – in short, more equity – again turn out to be the precondition for environmental protection.

This interplay of self-determination and natural diversity conservation was to some extent taken up in the biodiversity Convention. Article 8j, in particular, urges the contracting governments to 'respect, preserve and maintain knowledge, innovations and practices of indigenous and local communities embodying traditional lifestyles relevant for the conservation and sustainable use of biological diversity'; it also provides for 'equitable sharing of the benefits arising from the utilization of knowledge' concerning biological diversity. At the same time, the Convention stresses that indigenous and traditional communities are part of the solution, not the problem. States were supposed to give up part of their sovereignty rights – although subsequently there has been no binding international agreement on how this should be done. Some countries – for example, Costa Rica, the Philippines and certain Andean states – have already passed legislation in which local communities are guaranteed a say in the granting of access and use rights to third parties.

From the point of view of biodiversity, the existing genetic pool for agricultural crops is a legacy of centuries of cultural achievement. It is embedded in the technical and spiritual competence of local communities to use and preserve the diversity of forms of life. Traditional knowledge is indeed often the soil from which diversity springs. But the knowledge of indigenous communities frequently serves bioprospectors in their search for useful, and therefore exploitable, properties of plants; it has been the inspiration for many a marketable medicine or cosmetic, without receiving due recognition of its share in their development. For this reason, the Convention envisages that traditional communities should profit from equal access and benefit sharing.

One sign of the new strength of local communities was the model law adopted by African heads of government in the year 2000, which was supposed to offer a framework for implementation of the Convention on Biological Diversity.[27] The rights of local communities to their resources are there defined as '*a priori* rights', placed higher than rights serving only private interests. Any access of third parties to plant genetic resources requires the consent of the community affected, and, in the event that such access is likely to harm the cultural and/or natural legacy of the local community, it may be prohibited or restricted in various ways. The document attaches considerable importance to the equal inclusion of women in decision making, on the grounds that they are often the bearers of special knowledge about the use of natural resources yet customarily have little influence on policy formation.[28] It also places the state under an obligation to transfer to local communities at least a half of the goods accumulated through benefit sharing. Notwithstanding these points, the right of communities to use resources in accordance with their traditional practices remains inalienable.

The African model law adopts a position that is set out in the Convention and has found acceptance much more widely: namely, that the protection of biological diversity and the greater self-determination of local communities belong together. Species diversity strengthens the poor, and the poor strengthen species diversity. Of course, a greater degree of elementary democracy is the decisive condition for this equation to work. Resource rights of local communities can be built into national legislation as well as into international law, so that governments and corporations have a legal obligation to engage in talks about fair access and equitable sharing of the benefits. The preamble of the International Pact on Economic, Social and Cultural Rights already stipulates: 'All peoples may, for their own ends, freely dispose of their natural wealth and resources ... based upon the principle of mutual benefit, and international law. In no case may a people be deprived of its own means of subsistence.'[29]

Fair trade instead of free trade

The one who can lay down the rules has power – and the one who has power can lay down the rules. In many cases international economic institutions are built in accordance with this political feedback loop: the World Bank and the International Monetary Fund, for instance, but also the World Trade Organization (WTO) founded in 1994. With some exceptions the feedback loop strengthens both of the asymmetries that are driving the world in its disastrous direction: that is, the inequality between rich and poor and the inequality between man and biosphere. But, since power and regulatory system stand in a positive feedback relationship with each other, dangers easily appear as material constraints; the impression arises that there is no alternative to the *status quo*. A revision of the rules for global institutions is therefore the centrepiece of a politically guided globalization.

Since the late 1990s, debate on the future of globalization has mainly concentrated on the WTO. As the successor to the General Agreement on Trade and Tariffs (GATT), which in the post-war years gave considerable impetus to world trade through mutually agreed tariff cuts, the WTO has established itself as the main organizational framework for the transnational economy. But it does not simply get on with the business of enforcing market non-discrimination, which is supposed to create a level playing field for all domestic and foreign goods; it wants to implement this principle more fundamentally, to apply it more comprehensively, and to impose it everywhere in the world. The reason for this is that not only customs barriers but also subsidies, technical regulations and environmental or social standards are now regarded as unjustifiable obstacles to open market access. This way, public policy loses its capacity to shape society to a much greater degree. Moreover, the non-discrimination principle is now being applied beyond industry, to encompass agricultural goods, services and intellectual property rights – all economic activities, it would seem. This creates serious problems precisely in the case of services and agricultural goods that are central to livelihood security. And, finally, the sphere of application of the WTO's basic principle is being extended to the whole planet. Not only the old GATT signatories but every country in the world is invited to join, on condition that it binds itself under international law to implement the WTO's open markets programme. The countries of the South and East, in particular, are thus confronted with a new international context for their development. In this light the transition from GATT to WTO appears as a turning point in the history of world trade.

Moreover, the WTO also occupies a dominant position in the architecture of the international order. As an organization not under the aegis of the United Nations, it overshadows such important UN institutions as the International Labour Organization, the World Health

Organization, the UN Environment Programme and the UN Development Programme; it can therefore push to the sidelines UN objectives relating to social rights, health, environmental protection or development. The WTO is the only international institution endowed with a dispute settlement mechanism that has powers of sanction, with the result that its rules permeate policy areas far beyond the economy. Whether at environmental or social summits, the law of open markets always hangs like a sword of Damocles above the efforts to reach agreement on what is good for the world. The goal of trade without frontiers has thus been pushing itself to the top of the ladder of public values; an ear is given to other values only if they do not conflict with the hierarchy. In the last decade, this superiority of economic over non-economic values generated a tendency to identify the newly forming global society with its economic order. And, since economic rules now dominate social rules at world level, the WTO may be regarded as the actually existing world government. The institution of the WTO embodies the interim victory of free trade as the guiding principle of the emergent global society. Or, to borrow a formulation of Karl Polanyi's, the WTO stands for the construction at world level of a market society, not only a market economy.

To be sure, a multilateral system of economic negotiations can have great advantages for weaker countries, since they would otherwise have to face the even more vigorous imposition of bilateral trade agreements and be unable to exert any influence as a group.[30] It is easy to imagine how the United States and Burkina Faso, for example, would then shape up against each other. So, the WTO has a function. But it will have to be reinvented if it is to become the guarantor of a fair system of world trade capable of facing up to the future. The founding treaty of the WTO states that its objective is to raise living standards, especially in the South, but it is by no means certain that the spread of trade is the only or even the main way of achieving this.[31] In the view of many experts, legal security, education and a legitimate government are more important factors. Yet the WTO has a chronic tendency to confuse the means with the end, the spread of trade with economic prosperity. The rule of the means over the end becomes still more dramatic when the goals of 'environmental sustainability' and 'human rights' are brushed aside in favour of 'living standards'. Trade liberalization cannot be considered a panacea: it is one of many means, which has to be carefully considered and applied at the right time in the right dosage. A world trade system can face the challenge of the future only if, at the same time as seeking prosperity, it pursues the regeneration of nature and the securing of human rights. A reorientation of the WTO will therefore involve displacing trade liberalization from the centre of economic cooperation. Instead, multilateral trade policies should focus on balancing the interests of different countries and economic structures, and on shaping trade flows in accordance with efficiency, fairness and ecology.

Development rights before market access
To treat unlike as like can be the acme of injustice (see Chapter 4). From the beginning, the WTO has been in danger of falling into this trap of false equality. How, in a world of dramatic inequalities, could the same level playing field be built for all players? The idea of having the same rules everywhere for the world market fascinates liberal minds, but it makes them myopic about the enormous differences among players in respect of starting position and capacities. Since formally equal rules disadvantage the weak, fairness is required to ensure that the disadvantaged are given advantages.

On closer examination, therefore, the principle of non-discrimination against foreign producers turns out to be discriminatory towards developing countries. Equal treatment initially appears a good and just thing, as surely a nation which allows one country to sell goods to it at lower tariffs should extend the same favour to all other countries; this 'most favoured nation' principle seems to ensure that the most competitive supplier will win, whatever its nationality. Competitive advantages, however, can for the most part be achieved by companies from industrial nations with a high level of productivity. Reciprocal opening of markets therefore often means for countries in the South nothing other than forced access for the products of industrial countries. The principle of non-discrimination becomes an underhand advantage for the strong. The same is true of the principle that comparable products from abroad should not be worse placed than those from the country itself. For, since comparability here refers only to the product itself but not to the conditions under which it has been produced, an initially just principle turns into a disadvantage for the weak – and the careful. As a result, North American beef producers are allowed to use growth-promoting hormones and to market their steaks without restriction in countries that produce a less plentiful but healthier product.[32] What began as equal treatment ends with an advantage of foreign over domestic suppliers.

Furthermore, foreign suppliers are often like economic nomads, who glide between production locations escaping taxes and social or environmental charges and demanding special conditions for themselves. In contrast, domestic producers are very largely tied to their own country and community. Unlike their transnational competitors, they are neither able nor willing to change production locations as and when they wish.

On the basis of these experiences, the countries of the South have for more than forty years been demanding 'special and differential treatment' according to their individual economic capacities. On the one hand, this would allow the industrial countries to make it easier for selective products from the South to gain access to the markets of the North; on the other hand, the countries of the South would be permitted to treat selected imports unequally, so that they did not have to leave their domestic companies at the total mercy of highly efficient competitors in the North.

Up to now special and differential treatment has remained at a highly modest level,[33] although since 1979 the industrial countries have been able to grant the South special conditions. Indeed, the opening of markets in a context of preferential treatment, whose aim is precisely to avoid a basis of reciprocity, is regularly used as a bargaining chip to induce concessions on another matter from the country in question. During the Uruguay Round of negotiations, this sometimes went so far that the industrial countries demanded preferential treatment for themselves,[34] and in the Doha round that opened in November 2001 the principle of special and differential treatment was once more neglected. Although it was held out as a promise to lure the countries of the South back into negotiations, not much mention has since been made of it in the game of political poker.[35] This indifference has led to a situation where, indeed, the poor countries of the South are worse off under the present trade regime than they were in the age of GATT.

In the sobering history of preferential treatment, it became clear how the asymmetry of power works its effects behind the rhetoric of equal rights. In the practice of free trade, then, some are freer than others. For example, a liberalized world market theoretically implies the free movement of goods, capital and people, but in reality there is movement mainly for capital and goods flowing from the North to the South, but much less for goods and people trying to get from the South to the North. The industrial countries prove hesitant, if not positively hostile, when it comes to dismantling barriers to the free movement of labour.

Marrakesh – where the WTO was founded – is designed for goods, but Schengen – where it was agreed to reject refugees on Europe's frontiers – is designed for people. Meanwhile the South has done far more than the North to liberalize trade. Whereas the industrial countries have largely enforced free access to the markets of developing countries, exports in the reverse direction continue to be kept at bay through tariffs and non-tariff barriers. Double standards apply everywhere in the actual practice of free trade: the North orders the South to open its markets but is itself a long way from doing the same. No sign of special and differential treatment, except in the sense that the power imbalance has so far ensured a bisection of free trade in favour of the strong.

In any event, the principle of free trade is not enough to give the countries of the South greater opportunities for stable economic and social development. To be sure, in recent decades scarcely any country has achieved lasting development without an opening to the world market, but nor has any achieved it only on that basis.[36] It is generally doubtful whether a country's economic success has to do mainly with the openness of its markets; often it is internal conditions such as the rule of law, social policy or the active participation of citizens which tip the balance. Besides, none of the industrial countries followed the recipe of open markets during the period of its rise – on the contrary, they all tried to protect their still undeveloped economy from the superior competition abroad. The chances of equal development for the weaker countries, in the face of global market regulation, today depend on whether they have enough room to shape their own legal and social order and their own economic policy.[37]

To put it more bluntly, a trade order that regards an increase in development opportunities as important will make special and differential treatment the starting point. Countries need an independent political space – not as the exception but as the rule.[38] Multilateral trade rules that make governments incapable of looking after their country's welfare are counterproductive, since the whole point of such rules is to make international trade secure and to keep transaction costs low, not to hinder the development of societies. Since citizens of different countries have different ideas about labour rights, social policy, the environment or food quality, it is advisable to frame trade rules not with a view to uniformity but for the productive coexistence of different economic and social models.[39] WTO policy could move in that direction if two principles were established. First, rules should be made retroactive when market access has already gone too far; this could help weaker countries to introduce mechanisms such as tariffs or import quotas to protect the existential rights of their population. Second, WTO agreements should not apply to all countries; negotiations can by all means be multilateral, but not every rule should be unconditionally adopted by all. Instead, member states might agree to the opening of markets at different tempos, according to the position from which they start out;[40] competition among economic systems could then take account of different social and ecological interests. These would all be steps on the road to a world trade organization which, instead of flattening out diversity in favour of global uniformity, brings the different national economies into a fruitful and dependable relationship with one another.

Human rights before market access

The bedrock of the United Nations is a commitment by member states to respect human rights. Without this, it would be nothing more than a confederation that could not claim any global social legitimacy. Human rights are the supreme legal right, not only nationally but internationally. It is therefore all the more astonishing to find no reference to them either in the WTO founding agreement of 1994 or in the practice of the WTO's court of arbitration.[41] The WTO operates in a legal framework in which the basic law of the United Nations plays no role. Nevertheless, it cannot escape the obligations that arise out of the human rights canon, as in the end this has universal validity. The UN Charter leaves no room for misunderstanding: 'In the event of a conflict between the obligations of the Members of the United Nations under the present Charter and their obligations under any other international agreement, their obligations under the present Charter shall prevail' (Article 103). For human rights have an absolute character: they apply under all circumstances and can be neither bargained away nor sacrificed to economic utility. They are not subordinate even to a democratic majority decision, still less to a cost-benefit analysis. Human rights take precedence over all other moral, political or economic claims.[42]

Foodstuffs, for example, have a human rights reference; they are not a commodity like any other. They are indispensable for the preservation of physical existence, and in the countries of the South are also an indispensable source of income for the majority. After all, an average of 56 per cent of the population is economically active in agriculture – a figure which rises as high as 90 per cent in a country such as Rwanda or

Burkina Faso.[43] An attack on the production and supply of food may therefore mean a severe attack on the basis of life for large numbers of people. The right to food, however, is indisputably one of the fundamental human rights (Article 25); it sets a standard for the availability and distribution of food within an economic system.[44]

International trade regulations have a visible effect on which food is available to whom and in what quantity. Yet the WTO Agreement on Agriculture treats food and agricultural products as any other commodity, regulating their import and export with special reference to North–South trade. Exports are important as far as food security is concerned: either too few or too many can threaten the existence of large groups of people. If the South is prevented from exporting to markets in the North, not enough money comes in for the purposes of a redistributive policy. But, if exports account for too large a share of agricultural output, this may undermine self-provision (see Chapter 3). On the other hand, fluctuations on the import side are also important: a shortage of inexpensive import options may intensify a food crisis, but too many imports may also affect food security from the point of view of prices and volumes.

The countries of the South were initially pleased when the WTO Agreement for the first time brought the agricultural sector into a regulatory framework. In particular, they expected to obtain greater benefits from world trade as a result of improved access to the markets of industrial countries. But up to now these hopes have been disappointed. Tariffs in rich countries have remained at such a high level that little has changed: for example, US tariffs on sugar were set at 244 per cent of the import price and on groundnuts at 174 per cent, while EU tariffs on beef and wheat were fixed at 213 and 168 per cent respectively.[45] Moreover, the industrial countries are allowed to maintain so-called 'peak tariffs' on especially sensitive goods – often the very ones such as beef or sugar in which countries of the South have a competitive advantage[46] – and to engage in 'escalation' by increasing tariff levels to match the degree of product processing. Thus, green coffee is allowed free entry into the EU, whereas roasted or freeze-dried coffee is subject to high tariffs. The South is still mainly a supplier of raw materials, and measures such as these prevent it from switching to more profitable processing activities.[47]

Conversely, a growing export orientation may well make the plight of small farmers more precarious, as well as intensifying the environmental crisis in agriculture. For it often favours large landowners over small, strengthens corporations rather than small businesses, leads to monoculture instead of species diversity, and steers public funds to export infrastructure rather than local provision (see Chapter 3). An export promotion policy may therefore soon conflict with a policy of food security.[48] Indeed, the very imperative of food security runs counter to the pressure on farmers to make short-term profits by concentrating on cash crops. Brazil is a good example of this. It is true that its income from agricultural exports more than doubled between 1991 and 2001, from $7.9 billion to $16 billion. But the preference for export companies, as well as the import pressure resulting from open markets, led to the closing down of traditional cooperatives and small farms. The trading profits were concentrated in the hands of big industrial producers – at the expense of small traditional ones. But this also worsened the general food situation, so that between 1980 and 2002 rice production fell by a quarter and manioc by a third.[49] The story is similar in the Indian state of Kerala, where large areas of forest and rice fields were converted in the 1990s into rubber, coconut and coffee plantations, while fishing companies with export interests fought over coastal waters with local fishermen.[50] As export agriculture eats its way through large tracts of fertile land, food production and the small farmers themselves are left to their fate.

Meanwhile, many countries in the South have been forced to open their markets wide to imports from the North, usually in the context of IMF or World Bank structural adjustment programmes. Often the lowering of import tariffs preceded and went beyond the measures demanded in the WTO Agreement on Agriculture.[51] As a result, the markets of the South have been flooded with products from the North, at prices kept down through government subsidies in the North. Agriculture in the OECD countries is currently supported to the tune of more than $300 billion a year – six times more than the figure for official development aid.[52] These subsidies have led more than once to price collapses on the world market, which may please consumers but land producers in dire straits. In India accelerated imports of edible oil products drove countless producers of sunflower, coconut and palm oil from the market; in Ghana stockbreeders and butchers cannot withstand cheap imports of meat from Europe; and in Mexico maize farmers have been driven to the wall by subsidized exports from the United States. Imports that undercut domestic prices reduce consumption costs for urban dwellers but undermine the livelihoods of countless people engaged in agriculture and food production (see Chapter 3).

In sum, too few exports make a country poor, while too many agricultural exports enrich a minority and push the majority to the sidelines. In a period of crisis, too few imports may threaten the food situation, while too many, too cheap and too sudden imports may ruin a country's domestic food trade. Each of these situations depends on various factors, but each also points up the same problem: deregulation of agricultural markets can seriously affect people's livelihood rights. But, if farmers are squeezed out, if less food is produced, if whole sectors of the economy are ruined and large tracts of land are impoverished, it is scarcely possible to argue that free markets increase the general well-being. Once food security and human lives are on the line, the free agricultural market turns into a threat to human rights.

The General Agreement on Trade in Services (GATS) poses similar problems to those of the Agreement on Agriculture. Introduced in 1994, at the time when the WTO was founded, it initially did no more than underwrite the *status quo* in the cross-frontier trade in services,[53] but since the year 2000 member states have been engaged in further talks to liberalize services. Of course, the relevance of a liberalization of services for social and economic human rights is not immediately apparent. But the core of the agreement is the obligation for countries to treat foreign suppliers of services in the same way as domestic suppliers – that is, as in the case of goods, to ensure free competition. A brief look at the list of potential services makes clear what is involved. For it is not, as one might think, a question only of insurance and finance, but rather of tourism and transport, education and culture, the construction trade and hospitals, company management and environmental services – nor is that all, by any means.[54] If full liberalization came about, government offices would have to put out to international tender the running of a hospital or a city's water supply, and appoint a domestic supplier only if it offered better terms than a foreign corporation. But the GATS does not stop at the mere opening of markets; even the conditions under which a service is performed in a given country must not lead to a competitive advantage or be changed over the course of time. It goes without saying that this considerably restricts the freedom of action for governments – for example, with regard to regulations concerning health, the environment or social policy. Altogether, then, the Agreement is designed to privatize publicly provided services and to make them and other service sectors accessible to foreign corporations. The GATS is therefore not only a trade agreement but also, in effect, an investment agreement; it clips the wings of the state and offers transnational corporations a licence to invest in central areas of life.

Affordable basic services such as water, energy, health and education are vitally important to sections of the population with little purchasing power, but the GATS takes no heed of that. Liberalization may therefore clash directly with the existential rights of the poor, as private suppliers are guided by considerations of profit and tend to concentrate on fee-paying strata of the population. This can deprive poor or sick people of the basic provision to which everyone should be entitled. Higher prices have the effect of excluding people. A good example of this is the struggle over water in Cochabamba, Bolivia, where the US Bechtel corporation bought up supply rights and raised prices by 200 per cent in the year 2002 alone. After protest actions verging on civil war, the government was forced to cancel the sale to Bechtel.[55] But similar protests against the restriction of access to water or electricity have taken place in many towns in the South (see Chapter 3). Moreover, the major new powers that private suppliers have acquired under the GATS agreement undermine the capacity of the state to guarantee social and economic human rights. Up to a point governments have a duty to ensure the right of all to drinking water, housing and healthcare, if necessary through subsidies or legislation that help vulnerable groups to enjoy their rights. The least that is required is a minimum level of supply, independent of market prices. But such practices are at odds with unregulated competition. Full implementation of the WTO's agreement would sharpen social polarization, as corporations (especially transnationals) and affluent upper and middle classes could expect to enjoy higher profits and improved services, while low-income groups would be exposed to further ill effects.

The WTO agreements on trade in agriculture and services, as well as on intellectual property rights (TRIPS), are intended to open up more sectors of life to the transnational economy, especially in the South. Goods and services that have until now been produced mainly through economic activity linked to the community are to be handed over to corporations globally competing for consumers and investors. Seeds, for example, are usually obtainable within the subsistence economy, as are many food staples such as rice, millet or milk. Since time immemorial, drinks or foodstuffs have been available through the markets of the regional economy. And water pipes, schools or health clinics have usually been sustained by the communal economy, whether in the form of special associations or public institutions. All three types of economy – self-providing, regional and communal – have two features in common: they mostly follow social-cultural norms rather than the dictates of the accumulation of capital; and their activity is steered and supervised at a local, or at most national, level. If corporations oriented to the world market gain unhindered access to them, as the WTO's mission requires, these small-scale forms of economy linked to the community will come under ever more intense pressure. Commercialization is sinking deeper roots – a wider range of goods and services is now subject to profit norms – and the control of economic activity is shifting from local-national to global level. The plurality of economic forms is dramatically reduced when the global competitive economy asserts its supremacy over subsistence economies, local markets or the public sector.

Admittedly the types of economy linked to communities are often shot through with repression and poverty, but as a rule they afford a basic livelihood to most people on the periphery of the world market. In their mix of non-monetary, custom-based and tax-supported performance, they offer a living to poorer sections of society, sometimes even a decent and dignified living. The liberalization of life-supporting economic sectors and basic services hands weaker groups over to the distant laws of the world market and increases their economic insecurity. This hits women especially hard, as cheap mass-produced goods, expulsion from the land and rising prices of craft materials wipe out their anyway small earning capacity.[56]

Such consequences are not unknown even to the champions of free international markets. But, as in the World Bank's kind of enlightened free trade theory, they plead for social cushioning and a far-sighted government. In this they are guided by a 'philosophy of history' assumption that poverty is a temporary phenomenon that will sooner or later yield to the general upward movement of the economy; the present victims are the price to be paid for success in the future. In this view, then, the poor must suffer today so that poverty can be overcome tomorrow; what counts is the aggregate welfare, not individual rights. So, when economic experts speak of rising welfare, they usually have in mind the general welfare rather than the fate of particular groups, who may in fact be exposing themselves to even greater disadvantage. From the point of view of justice, however, inequality is most admissible when the least advantaged are better off as a result of it (see Chapter 4). Human rights, in particular, are absolute rights of persons or groups living here and now; they cannot be sacrificed to the greater good of society, present or future.

In this light, food and basic services are not suitable candidates for trade liberalization. To protect the economic, social and cultural human rights of countless citizens in the southern hemisphere, it is necessary to redefine the logic of the World Trade Organization so that agricultural products and services are not in thrall to the regime of free trade. Multilateral agreements are indispensable, but they must aim at the political equality of differently positioned national economies. The motto might be: trade through mutual interest, not through freedom from regulation. To move in this direction, the agricultural sector of the countries of the South might first be exempted from WTO obligations, and then subsequently, on the basis of positive lists for each sector of agriculture, individual decisions could be made as to whether it should be opened up for the world market.[57] Restrictive measures such as quotas or higher tariffs could be permitted if they served to guarantee the right to food. A special case could be made for a mechanism that allowed any country to give temporary protection if imports of a product suddenly increased, or if its price sharply fell.

A similar procedure would apply to the trade in services. Perhaps the logic of open markets makes some sense in the insurance business, in tourism, construction and transport, but certainly not in the supply of water, education or health. Services important to life itself should accordingly be excluded from talks on liberalization. How these services are used depends entirely on the traditions and political will in each country, but in any event it is advisable in negotiations to start from a narrow definition of services, one which regulates only the cross-frontier trade in services but not their provision within each country. This would mean little GATS interference in internal affairs: national governments would retain their competence intact and could even lay down social, environmental and economic standards for the supply of services. Then a world agreement on trade could concentrate on its core task, which is to guarantee the plurality of economic forms and to make the institutional diversity of countries mutually compatible.

Environmental rights before market access
In lengthy and conflict-ridden negotiations over the last half-century, the countries of the world have developed legal orders that are supposed to

give form and dependability to global society. Specialists in international law place the multiplicity of regulations and agreements into several groups under the general heading 'international regime'. The oldest of these groups, the human rights regime, consists of the basic legal declarations contained in the International Bill of Rights. The environmental regime comprises several hundred agreements, the most prominent of which are the conventions on climate protection and biodiversity. The world trade regime contains the WTO agreements, in addition to various regional and bilateral accords. The chaos in the construction of an overarching 'global governance' stems from the fact that the three regimes are scarcely compatible with one another; they do not obey the same logic, and their agreements and norms embody conflicting values. A zone of conflict has arisen not only between the world trade regime and human rights, but also between the world trade regime and environmental rights.

World trade policy strives to remove barriers to economic activity, whereas agreements on the environment and human rights seek rather to limit harmful, dangerous or degrading economic activity. Or, world trade law puts its weight behind a market operating as much as possible without state intervention, whereas the other legal regimes react to market failure by protecting public goods or making them available in sufficient quantity. Or, the WTO looks to competition to ensure the most effective use of natural and other resources and to enable further cost-efficient expansion, whereas the environmental agreements start from the long-term limits of natural resources and see them as a brake on continued expansion. Finally, a world trade policy that seeks to maximize comparative cost advantages implies the greatest possible shifting of ecological costs on to others, whereas environmental agreements aim at the most extensive internationalization of such costs through legislation and taxation.[58]

The preamble to the WTO Agreement does state that the goal of 'sustainable development' should qualify 'the raising of living standards' and 'the expansion of production', and that trade relations should 'allow for the optimal use of the world's resources in accordance with the objective of sustainable development'. The GATT, for its part, under the special provisions of Article XX, permits governments to introduce trade restrictions if there is a threat to the health of plants, animals or humans of if the consumption of exhaustible natural resources has to be cut back. When we look back at ten years of negotiations in the WTO, however, it is evident that the words in the preamble have had a largely rhetorical character. The broad spectrum of trade policy has never been systematically reviewed with reference to 'sustainable development', although the Appellate Body has invoked it in some of its rulings. In the institutional structure of the WTO, environmental issues are discussed by the special Trade and Environment Committee, but of course the main concern there has been with the effects of conservation measures on free competition, and much less with the effects of free competition on the environment.[59] The countries of the South, in particular, have resisted environmental regulation, fearing that it would cause their comparative advantages on the world market to melt away.[60] Locked out of important markets in the industrial countries, despite any number of promises to the contrary, they have anyway not wished to let themselves in for additional barriers in the name of environmental protection. Meanwhile the industrial countries have been rather eager to keep their own part of the world clean, and to curb environmental pollution in the South, in so far as it is not against their economic interests. But they have been, and still are, a long way from questioning the consumption levels of their own industry and export sectors. All in all, a coalition between Southern and Northern protagonists of growth has operated against an ecological turn in the economy, blithely assuming that growth is a precondition before there can be talk of environmental protection. 'Mutual support of trade and environment' has been the standard formula, without any effort to identify the conditions for such synergy.

In general, WTO negotiations display a rather antediluvian conception of environmental policy; the idea is more to contain pollution through laws and technology than to reorient production to a better use of resources. But what is necessary is not only to reduce pollution at the end of a given production process but to introduce resource-saving innovations at the design stage. Environmental policy may appear obstructive, and therefore displease the countries of the South in particular, because it implies the luxury and extra cost of additional production requirements. But things look different if we are talking of integrated rather than additive protection of the environment. Then it becomes a question of production and consumption that can manage with fewer natural resources, entailing fewer costs to companies and, in the medium term, also to society. Such an approach has many attractions for the countries of the South: it saves on costs, gives people work and offers lasting relief from the growing shortage of nature. It also directs attention to the high consumption of the environment in the industrial countries, for in the end the export of one laptop demands more resources than the import of a textile cargo. With an integrated environmental policy that favours resource savings, countries in the South that introduce leapfrogging forms of resource-light production and consumption could soon be especially well placed to reap comparative advantages *vis-à-vis* their resource-intensive trading partners.

Instead, we might say that Marrakesh has defeated Rio, and that a hierarchy has become apparent in the relationship between economic and environmental agreements. Or, not to beat about the bush, neither the climate nor the biodiversity Convention really counts for the World Trade Organization. Environmental agreements might just as well have been written on a different planet. To be sure, people have been debating for years the relationship between the two kinds of agreement, but the main issue has been whether trade restrictions – for which provision is made in, for example, the agreements on species protection and biological security – are compatible with the WTO's principle of free trade. Far more pressing, however, is the question of what kind of transnational trade policy is needed to advance the goals of the environmental conventions. That is said to lie outside the competence of the WTO. Yet the WTO framework of rules can massively obstruct efforts to set the world economy on a path that would cherish climate protection as well as biodiversity.

First, there are regulations which contradict the environmental agreements: for example, the Agreement on Trade-Related Aspects of Intellectual Property Rights (TRIPS), in so far as it concerns the patenting of forms of life, is in blatant conflict with the Convention on Biological Diversity. The TRIPS agreement recognizes neither the principle of state sovereignty over natural resources nor the special role of indigenous groups and traditional communities; it therefore calls into question the principle of equal access and benefit sharing. This is not the least of the reasons why it has been accused of 'legalizing biopiracy' (see Chapter 3).[61] Furthermore, as in the precedent of the 'Green Revolution', the patenting of certain plant genes leads to the elimination of other strains and hence to a further loss of crop diversity. The supremacy of the WTO scares many governments away from adjusting markets to environmental goals. Thus, although the biodiversity Convention urges governments to protect forests, fishing grounds, wetlands and watercourses, it is not easy to see how that could be done without regulation and reorientation of the transnational timber industry, fishing economy and *a fortiori* agricultural production chains. The fear is that emphatic moves in that direction would collide with WTO rules. Similarly, in the case of the climate Convention, trade measures in favour of climate-friendly goods could be interpreted as discrimination against energy-intensive products. The same applies to a whole swathe of instruments such as taxes, tariffs, subsidies and production standards, which are necessary for any serious course towards a low-emission economy.[62]

Nor is it clear how a breakthrough to a fair and environmentally sustainable world trade regime could be set in train. At best the relationship of forces is shifting slightly in favour of the 'Group of 20' countries under the leadership of India and Brazil, which at and since the ministerial conference in Cancún in 2003 has wrested some concessions from Europe and the United States over access to Northern markets. Easier exports for the South create greater fairness, but they do not go outside the free trade regime. Less skewed access to markets may put an end to the most blatant injustices, but this scarcely helps to reorient world trade towards protection of the biosphere and of social and economic human rights.

Reinventing the WTO

Such a reorientation cannot dispense with a reinvention of the world trade regime. The public debate has thrown up three partly compatible, partly competing approaches to that end: the approach of global minimum standards, the approach of national policy space, and the approach of the separation of powers.

Global standards on the environment and human rights have the advantage of fitting well with the logic of free trade. It is argued that they lay the basis on which the promise of free trade can be fulfilled: namely, that the best will have their nose in front. Therefore, the WTO tells us, protectionism at a country's borders must be removed, not only to prevent governments from protecting their industries, but also to stop plunderers and exploiters from gaining crucial competitive advantages. Competition, in this model, is beneficial to the common good only if the playing field has no slope favouring those who pass their costs on to others. Why, of all people, should an unscrupulous sweatshop owner, a lawbreaker or a squanderer of resources have better competitive opportunities? Only through the most thorough internationalization of external costs can competition bring about a general increase in welfare. What is more, it may then even be that competition among countries and locations will work in favour of environmental and human rights.[63]

One way of approaching this objective is to set up one or more trade licensing agencies;[64] there is already a model for this in the institutions of Fair Trade or environmental labelling. Whether it is a question of fair trade in coffee or ecological trade in wood, the basic functions are the same: a certifying body sets standards, a company applies for a certificate, an agency checks the conditions of production and marketing, and if the results are positive the company is authorized to engage in international trade. The procedure has been tried out many times on a small scale – from the Transfair label to the Forest Stewardship certificate, though up to now participation has been voluntary (see Chapter 4). A world trade organization that sees itself as a driving force for fairness and ecology will gradually make such procedures compulsory for all sectors of the economy and all regions. For, as with any other right, certain responsibilities come with the right of companies to conduct transnational economic relations. Global standards are nothing more than a way of helping to pin down this responsibility.

The weak points in the global standards approach are diversity and self-determination. To enforce standards worldwide, for Vietnam and Colombia alike, for small export firms and global corporations, is to impose a uniformity that contradicts the diversity of the real world; the more that standardization goes beyond a minimum threshold, the more difficult it becomes to do justice to different situations. Besides, there is an inevitable tension between global norms and the democratic self-government of a society. It is therefore important that the second conceptual approach should expand the room for manoeuvre of individual states in world trade. Circumstances and priorities differ from country to country, so flexibility and, above all, democratic legitimacy can only really be catered for at a national level. Societies must be in a position to express their collective preferences – otherwise no democratic will to reorient economic processes can assert itself. National states must therefore have the power to make their own decisions, and that means pruning the authority of the WTO. In other words, protectionism is indispensable – in the South as well as the North – when it is a question of protecting social and environmental rights.

It is possible to imagine a new empowerment of individual governments in a number of stages. First, there could be considerable expansion of Article XX of GATT, which permits state intervention in exceptional circumstances. National governments might be allowed to steer trade policy if this helped to achieve the goals of a multilateral social or environmental treaty.[65] But a more fundamental idea would be to promote, under the heading 'deglobalization', the right of every country to direct its own independent form of development;[66] free trade would then be replaced with a network of trade agreements. Such a strategy would set the course for a domestic orientation of the economy, moving away from export orientation as the supposedly royal road to the alleviation of poverty. This attaches greater importance to a country's own capacities than to its export potential, on the grounds that it cannot act independently and pursue its own development path unless it can first of all rely upon a domestic economic base. A still more pronounced alternative to contemporary globalization comes from the theorists of 'localization',[67] who advocate an empowerment of national states up to and including the reversal of priorities. In order to protect the local/national economy on a world scale, this strategy seeks to prioritize local industry and agriculture in economic policy and regards international trade as a residual quantity. It is easy to see how, in these two positions, there is a shift in the basic idea of how world trade should be conceived: that is, it appears not as a globally integrated economic arena but as a system coordinating a multiplicity of national economies.

The third conceptual approach seeks to circumscribe the WTO's supremacy at a constitutional level. The idea here is to ensure the coexistence of such different values as economic power, ecology and human rights within the world economy, and to strike a balance among the relevant international institutions. Neither of these is present today, since the World Trade Organization claims the sole right to solve conflicts concerning trade matters. It has the strictest and most effective dispute settlement mechanism that has ever existed under international law, and unlike other arbitral authorities it has real powers of sanction. The inferior party can be punished with retaliatory trade measures. Consequently, there is no independent adjudication in the event of a conflict between trade law and human, social or environmental rights, nor is there a clear separation of legislative, executive and judicial powers; all functions are united under the roof of the WTO. The primal democratic principle of the separation of powers, invented for the sake of mutual checks and balances, plays no role at the international level. But each society, and especially global society, is permeated with conflicts among different values, interests and institutions. It is absolutely essential to create a neutral body to regulate these conflicts – otherwise the dominance of trade law will be more or less enshrined. In this model, the most important step is to confine the WTO's Dispute Settlement Mechanism to trade issues in the narrow sense. As soon as environmental, social or human rights enter the dispute, it must be transferred to the jurisdiction of a neutral body such as the International Court of Justice or the International Court of Arbitration, or else a new commercial tribunal must be set up.[68] Even in trade conflicts, the search for a resolution should not take place only within the framework of the WTO Agreement but should also have recourse to other multilateral accords. It is high time that the WTO itself should include a reference to human rights and international treaties such as the environmental agreement, so that individual countries can demand properly motivated exemptions from WTO rules.[69] All in all, there needs to be an extensive transfer of dispute settlement powers away from the WTO, in order to ensure the impartiality of final rulings.

Civil duties for corporations

In the age of great discoveries in the sixteenth century, when the European states began to draw their rulers' net across the planet, trading houses immediately followed the explorers, and private entrepreneurs set about making a profit from the gold fever and the spice trade. The first transnational company was actually founded in Amsterdam in 1602: the famous United East India Company. Soon trading ships were plying the oceans alongside armed naval vessels, and economic plunder joined with state power as the twin foundation of centuries of colonial rule. Eventually the erstwhile conquerors gave up their political domination in the South after long struggles for national independence. But the activities of transnational corporations have since grown four times over. At present there are a good 60,000 TNCs around the globe, with a total of some 870,000 subsidiaries. Not only do they employ a workforce of 53 million; they also control millions of local suppliers and service firms.[70]

Transnational corporations are today more than ever global players, since the globalization of economic relations is taking place primarily among and within companies. Two-thirds of world trade is carried out by TNCs, more than half of it entirely among their scattered production locations. Some TNCs have reached such proportions that even medium-sized states look small beside them. A comparison between gross national product and corporate turnover shows that, of the hundred largest economies in the world, only 49 are still national; all the others are corporate. Wal-Mart, for example, the world's largest company, recorded a turnover of $218 billion in 2002, while in the same year the combined GNP of the fifty least developed countries came to $207 billion.[71]

At the end of 2002, foreign investments worldwide amounted to a total of more than $7.1 thousand billion,[72] with the bulk of it concentrated in a few rich countries. A third of total investments was to be found in the countries of the South, but 90 per cent of this was confined to the nine frontrunners in the race to catch up industrially, first and foremost China. The remaining countries lie on the margins of transnational economic activity. If all the countries of the South are taken together, the share of foreign investments in their GNP – an indicator of dependence – rose from 13 per cent in 1980 to more than 30 per cent in the year 2000.[73]

A good part of the foreign investments were and are there to construct global production systems, especially in high-tech industries such as electronics and semiconductors and in labour-intensive consumer goods industries such as textiles and footwear.[74] In high-tech industry, subsidiaries in newly developing countries usually take over the production of selected components, while research and design remain in the industrial countries. In consumer goods industries, on the other hand, the whole production process is often handed over with certain specifications to local firms, and the transnational corporation retains control of marketing, brand and image.

Whether to reduce poverty and unemployment or to attain growth, prosperity and votes, governments everywhere court the favour of the transnationals. The doors are opened especially wide to them in the South, in the hope that they will provide the initial spark for the domestic economy and a transfer of modern technology. Countries there cannot usually lure them with a business environment of modern supply firms or favourable infrastructure. Rather, their location advantages are low wages, tax breaks and poor social standards. Nearly 4,300 intergovernmental agreements to protect investment and avoid double taxation ensure that corporations can safely spread their global business network;[75] they are more like charters than genuine accords. Only in rare cases is it the aim of these agreements to steer investments or companies in the interests of the host country.

Nevertheless, it is not so easy to draw up a balance sheet of the activity of TNCs in the South: the data are too contradictory, the situations too diverse. With regard to income and the physical quality of life, one study ascribes an unambiguously positive influence to the transnational corporations,[76] while another study using the same methodology but a larger data base comes to exactly opposite conclusions.[77] Their role in relation to jobs is also ambivalent. On the one hand, they create millions of new jobs by opening new production plants and signing contracts with suppliers. Women, in particular, are commonly regarded as the big winners from the global division of labour: for example, of the 1.5 million new jobs created over twenty years in two free trade zones in Bangladesh, 90 per cent were for women.[78] On the other hand, the change in local economic structures entails the loss of jobs elsewhere, so that many studies conclude that on the whole transnational corporations destroy more jobs than they create.[79] By no means always, but often enough, the quality of the jobs leaves a lot to be desired: there are many reports of wretched working conditions, unpaid overtime, repression and drastic punishment for even minor infringements of the rules. Most important of all, women's jobs are often very insecure, as they tend to be dismissed when they marry or become pregnant. The picture is equally murky in relation to the environment. Especially in areas where there is little or no state authority, TNCs often keep higher standards than local companies as they are geared to international technological and quality levels. But corporations active in the extraction of raw materials tend to have a bad record on the environment.[80] Roads used by timber companies destroy living space, oil leaks pollute large areas, water taken by drinks producers lowers the groundwater level, and the industrial growing of bananas drives farmers from the land.

The dramatic rise in foreign investment over the past twenty years has not gone together with the development of a legal framework to guarantee basic conditions of public welfare. Transnational corporations are able to get round national regulations. They search the globe for the most favourable locations with the lowest production costs – which also means that they are able to reduce their costs or pass them on to the general public. TNCs are veritable 'externalization machines',[81] for they have the power and scope to avoid taxes and the costs of maintaining social or environmental standards, and even to demand subsidies for themselves, by migrating – or threatening to migrate – from one location to another. In areas of the South or East where weak, corrupt governments do not fulfil their regulatory tasks, many corporations use their muscle to keep standards low[82] or to exploit raw materials and labour on the cheap.[83] Not a few foreign investments are directed to what are in effect law-free zones. So, the political shaping of transnational economic relations cannot limit itself to the reorientation of trade in goods and services; it must also include rules for trans-border investment.

Beyond the balance sheet

In the last few decades, people directly affected as well as civil society groups have made ever more vocal demands that TNCs should be held to minimum social and ecological standards. Such demands are certainly nothing new. In 1948 the Havana Charter envisaged the taxation of foreign investments – but it was never adopted. In 1972 the United Nations Conference on Trade and Development (UNCTAD) called for the introduction of rules to govern the behaviour of transnational companies. In 1974 a United Nations Centre on Transnational Corporations (UNCTC) was founded. And in 1976 the UN Economic and Social Council (ECOSOC) declared the development of standards its priority goal – but only cited a few rudimentary points.[84]

Then the mood changed in the middle of the 1980s. The above-mentioned initiatives were called off and the UNCTC was closed down (in 1992). TNCs were soon being treated more as responsible negotiating partners than as players to be called to account.[85] In 1994, in the framework of the North American Free Trade Agreement (NAFTA), corporations acquired extensive rights in relation to governments, without picking up any duties for the common good. At the end of the 1990s inconclusive negotiations took place in the OECD for an accord on the protection of investments (MAI), and at the same time various countries with a powerful market position wanted to introduce a similar agreement within the WTO and at a bilateral level.

Of course, the rejection of binding rules of conduct was not the end of the matter. Since the 1990s people and organizations directly affected, rather than politicians working from the top down, have taken a series of new initiatives. Employers' associations and civil society groups, management advisers and financial service providers have developed codes of conduct to help companies put their business on a sustainable footing. A respectable number have inscribed the motto 'corporate social responsibility' on their banners and voluntarily undertaken to observe the relevant code of conduct.[86] They have various reasons for doing this: to translate their company's values into concrete action; to strengthen the image of a socially and ecologically responsible corporation; to respond to pressure from the media and civil society; and, hopefully, to ensure that governments do not introduce binding rules instead of voluntary standards.[87] In many cases, they can thereby also reduce energy or material costs and develop innovations.

International institutions have launched a number of initiatives of their own. The best known of these is the Global Compact, which UN Secretary-General Kofi Annan and various corporations launched in 2000 as a partnership between the United Nations and private business, and which today has more than a thousand signatories.[88] Also in 2000 the OECD issued a set of guidelines for transnational corporations which is both more concrete and more comprehensive than the Global Compact. The OECD member states and (currently) eight other countries undertook to develop so-called national contact offices, to which individuals, non-governmental organizations and governments can lodge complaints about the practices of a transnational corporation.[89]

Four points may be underlined in this connection.[90] Some of these initiatives seek to involve the greatest possible number of individuals and groups affected by a corporation (so-called 'stakeholders') in its decisions. Whereas a company's shareholders are mainly interested in the maximum profits, those positively and negatively affected by its activity will ideally also take into account the general welfare.[91] Some corporations have already developed networks to involve large numbers of players in their decisions: Mondragón Cooperatives of Spain Basque Country, for example, has established a network of approximately a thousand contact centres, which make it possible for stakeholders to become quite extensively involved; and the Swedish supermarket chain KF is actually controlled through consumers' cooperatives.[92]

Since the Rio Earth Summit in 1992, a number of environmental management systems have sprung up through initiatives at local, regional, national and international level, with further inputs from civil society groups, international institutions and financial service providers. Their goal is to shape production processes in such a way that they make the most economical and efficient use of resources and waste products. Some of these systems – stretching from suppliers of raw materials through producers of semi-finished products to final consumers – seek to draw in as many players as possible along the company's product chain. They offer training programmes for managers, develop pilot projects or seek to support the spread of good practices through an organized exchange of information.[93] Examples are the 'ISO 14001 Standard' and the Eco-Management and Audit Scheme (EMAS). Up to now there are scarcely any management systems which focus on social improvements.

Networking and public attention are required to make voluntary codes of conduct effective. Thus, the Global Reporting Initiative is trying to bring transparency into corporate reports in accordance with various ecological, social and economic criteria. The Extractive Industries Transparency Initiative concentrates on the transparency of payments for raw materials from countries in the South. The Forest Stewardship Council reports on timber products from sustainable forestry. And the Rugmark label identifies rugs and carpets from the South that have been produced without child labour.[94]

Finally, many independent initiatives have been monitoring the behaviour of corporations and their implementation of voluntary standards: AccountAbility, Social Accountability International and Social Observatory are just three of these. Their activities are complemented by the services of management consultants and by share indices or sustainability indicators on the stock exchange: for example, the Dow Jones Sustainability Index or the German Natur Aktien Index. They all aim not only to ensure the public transparency of corporations but also to help them make improvements in response to criticism and feedback.[95]

How much can voluntary standards achieve?

Voluntary standards have the unquestionable advantage that corporations and directly affected groups can develop them with a technical know-how not usually available to other institutions.[96] They are therefore an essential laboratory for good practices and the development of production standards. They stimulate public debate about corporate responsibility, show how enterprises can be made more transparent, contribute to the spread of good practice, enrich thinking about alternative corporate strategies, and improve the flow of information among companies, political decision makers and the public. If the previously mentioned four elements are working together – that is, integration of stakeholders into decision-making processes, application of management systems, improvement of transparency and independent monitoring – then codes of conduct are an effective means to draw one step closer to resource justice in the world economy.

It is nevertheless advisable not to place too many hopes on voluntary obligations and good practice. For their effectiveness stands or falls with the number of participating companies and the scale of the objectives – two factors which are in an inverse relationship: the more demanding the objectives, the less enthusiastic the participation. Moreover, companies often take on obligations in response to public pressure. But only a few end products are liable to attract public attention, and they are precisely the ones for which public pressure is most to be feared. Consumers have no knowledge of most intermediate products or raw materials, and up to now few transnational corporations have effectively included in their voluntary obligations the legion of supply firms and raw materials producers that assist them in the stages prior to production.[97]

Companies will first set themselves the obligations that come most easily. They will tend to concentrate on anything that has a media impact: for example, environmental reports or a public declaration of rules of conduct and standards to be observed. More than half of managers surveyed by an independent consultancy agreed that the environmentalism of their company was merely 'greenwash' for public appearances.[98] A study by the World Economic Forum concluded that just under half of the world's top corporations produce reports on responsible management.[99] Yet, of the hundred largest TNCs operating in the countries of the South, considerably less than half produce such a report, and fewer than ten have one independently checked.[100] Moreover, the reports are highly variable in both quality and depth: for example, whereas Ricoh analyses and publishes the environmental impact of its products, at all stages from production through application to disposal, most corporations report only on effects directly associated with the production process.[101]

Against this background, codes of conduct and voluntary minimum standards can have only limited effect. They are most suited to harvest the 'low-hanging fruits' of direct cost savings that can be reached without too much financial investment.[102] The central question is therefore how the wealth of constructive initiatives can be placed on a basis from which they can develop and spread into the economy. For, if they win through economically, the pioneers will not reap a competitive advantage. And, if they win through politically, it will become accepted that the duty to make a profit for shareholders must be made compatible with the duty of ethical management towards society.

In reality, the balance sheets of ecologically and socially progressive companies consistently show they are no less successful because of their sense of responsibility; they even have a better record on the stock exchange than do most companies with a more traditional conception of management.[103] It is an outdated idea that ecologically and socially aware management must lead to economically worse results. Anyway, by now a growing minority of shareholders are willing to prefer companies that take ecological and social criteria as seriously as economic factors; and to invest their money in accordance with an ethical–ecological evaluation of various companies.[104] Regulation of the duty of companies to file reports is also developing in this direction.[105]

Responsibility to world society

A number of proposals have recently been published for an internationally binding legal framework to cover the activity of transnational corporations.[106] The international environmental organization Friends of the Earth argued at the World Summit on Sustainable Development for a framework convention on corporate responsibility, and in fact the international community did decide there 'actively to promote corporate responsibility and accountability ... including through the full elaboration and effective implementation of intergovernmental agreements and measures'. Admittedly these intergovernmental agreements have been a long time coming, but there is a further initiative from the United Nations that is well worth taking up. In August 2003 a subcommittee of the UN Commission on Human Rights published the 'UN Norms on the Responsibility of Transnational Corporations and Other Business Enterprises with Regard to Human Rights'. This is based upon a number of legal sources: the human rights conventions, the agreement within the International Labour Organization on the rights of workers and indigenous peoples, and the Rio Declaration on Environment and Development. Together with the running commentary, the UN norms constitute the most comprehensive catalogue to date of international rules of conduct for transnational corporations.[107]

It would seem that an international convention on corporate responsibility must rest upon four pillars: the duty of information and transparency; the recognition of certain standards in human, labour and environmental rights; adherence to fair and balanced relations within international production systems; and accountability before the law.

On the first pillar: unobtainable data, obscure product components, hidden money flows and sometimes even the legal cover of commercial secrecy form a protective wall for shady businesses. But transparency is the precondition for control of power, a principle of democracy valid in relation not only to governments but also to companies. In its absence, citizens (or consumers) are not taken seriously in their role as bearers of sovereignty. Information about products and production processes, the publication of evaluation reports, the visibility of subsidies, fiscal conditions and cash payments to governments: all this may be described as the civil duty of companies. The spirit of the Åarhus agreement on freedom of information and public involvement in environmental matters – which came into force in the EU in October 2001[108] – should be generalized and made applicable to corporate activities.

As to the second pillar, universal human, labour and environmental rights hang in the air if there are not also matching duties. Traditionally governments have been regarded as the guarantors of universal rights, but with the transition from a community of states to a global community responsibility should also attach to non-governmental players, especially transnational corporations (see Chapter 4). In the age of globalization their rights have grown enormously, and a matching consolidation of their duties is long overdue. These may include an obligation to allow no complicity with human rights violations; to check one's own operations for their effects on economic, social and cultural human rights; and to obtain the prior consent of indigenous peoples for any activity on their territories. As far as labour rights are concerned, in accordance with the code of the International Labour Organization, the main points are non-discrimination, a legal minimum wage, safety at work and freedom of assembly. Environmental rights have the principles of prevention and harm avoidance at their heart; they should be observed even if they mean a short-term loss for capital. Prevention also means that technologies, processes and materials should be appropriately checked before they are put on the market, the responsibility for this falling on the producer, not the purchaser.

In many respects, the situation with the third pillar in today's globalized economy is akin to the experience of industrialization in nineteenth-century Europe. In that earlier age, after a period of naked exploitation, it became accepted that it would be in the interests of the state and the economy to have clear rules governing the relationship between workers and employers. The prohibition of child labour, the limits on working hours, an insurance system for illness and unemployment, health and safety standards and a legal minimum wage eventually became the core of a system that could be described as a social market economy.

In today's global production chains, however, power is often so unequally distributed that the weakest links face a system of crass exploitation. Profits and power increase as one approaches the stage of final production and marketing, while they decrease as one approaches suppliers of raw materials and subcontractors. The framing of non-exploitative exchange relations within global production chains is one of the responsibilities incumbent on transnational corporations; they have a duty to plan the secure integration of supply firms and contractual partners into their business and to provide for a balanced sharing of profits. A multiplicity of fair trade initiatives offer some precedent here, and they all show how the interests of profit and justice can be made compatible. Companies are urged to sign with commercial partners long-term contracts and mission statements that make it easier to agree on fair prices, investment aid, interim payments and a shared say on business strategies. Suppliers, for their part, are expected to take a distance from the widespread practices of wage dumping and environmental pollution.[109] Transnational corporations thereby become able to design quality standards for the whole production chain.

On the fourth and final pillar, corporate accountability and compensation for damages, it is clear that evaluation and monitoring are essential for the implementation of a regulatory system; independent inspectors and a national or intergovernmental agency might undertake this task. It is also necessary to institutionalize legal proceedings, so that citizens and organizations are able to settle disputes and to take action against violations. Finally, the 'culprit pays' principle needs to be emphasized: that is, the principle that the party which causes damage is obliged to make restitution. This would go beyond any limited liability rule and ensure that top management can be held accountable. The prevention and liability principles might be combined with a duty to take out insurance, which would force companies to internalize risks in their pricing and offer an economic incentive for damage avoidance.

A convention on corporate responsibility would go a step further towards ending the imbalance between the legal status of companies and citizens. As 'juristic persons', companies are generally placed on the same footing as 'natural persons' – which puts the former at an advantage and the latter at a disadvantage. For companies enjoy personal rights such as property, the right to take legal action and the freedom of opinion, but have only limited liability and are much larger and live much longer than physical persons.[110] The idea that companies are accountable to society for their legally privileged status was already present at the birth of the United East India Company; in fact, it owed its trading licence to the English Crown, which in a special 'Charter' reserved the right to dispose of its property and trading profits. In the USA, too, during the period of its industrialization and its rise to become a world economic power, companies in many states were subject to a similar charter for more than a hundred years. It stipulated the conditions under which companies were allowed to produce, which public taxes and contributions they had to pay, how shareholders should have a say, and which land rights had to be acquired. Only if a company fulfilled its obligations was its licence to trade extended.[111] It really looks as if today's world should learn from its historical past, so that the social responsibility of property ownership can become a reality not only in one country but throughout the world.

Notes

1   IPCC 2001a.
2   UNFCCC 1998; Oberthür and Ott 1999.
3   For a survey of such studies, see Hare 2003.
4   Huq 2002.
5   WBGU 2003b.
6   Ott et al. 2004.
7   Athanasiou and Baer 2002: 74.
8   Oberthür and Ott 1999.
9   Grubb 1995; Agarwal and Narain 1991; Kaiser et al. 1991; and, for a current survey, Brouns 2004.
10 La Rovere et al. 2002; UNFCCC 1997.
11 Aslam 2002; Meyer 2000.
12 UNFCCC 2001.
13 Vajpayee 2002.
14 Lammi and Tynkkynnen 2001; European Parliament 1998.
15 A worked-out proposal may be found in Ott et al. 2004.
16 APFC 2001.
17 Barnes 2001: 72.
18 Sachs et al. 2002: 45.
19 WRI 2000: 4.
20 For an introduction, see Henne 1998.
21 BMU 1992.
22 McAfee 1998.

23   UNHCHR 2001.
24   UNEP 1999.
25   Posey 1999; Grim 2001.
26   Kothari et al. 1998.
27   OAU 2000.
28   Schäfer et al. 2002.
29   Consulted   at   www.univie.ac.at/RI/KONTERM/intlaw/konterm/
     vrkon_en/html/doku/pact1.htm#6.0.
30   For a survey of bilateral agreements, see www.bilaterals.org.
31   Rodrik 2001.
32   Ehring 2002: 938f.
33   Whalley 1999; CUTS 2003; Jawara and Kwa 2003. For a survey of special
     rules for the countries of the South, see UNDP 2003: 58ff.
34   Whalley 1999: 8.
35   IISD 2003; Stevens 2003: 3.
36   Rodrik 2001.
37   WCSDG 2004: 78ff.
38   UNDP 2003: 74.
39   Vogel 2000; UNDP 2003: 63ff.
40   IISD 2003; Stevens 2003.
41   Petersmann 2003: 18.
42   Normand 2000.
43   FAO 2001b: 8.
44   Gray 2003.
45   Khor 2003: 8.
46   UNDP 2003: 115f.
47   Ibid.: 116; Windfuhr 2003: 3.
48   For a survey see Madeley 2000, and, on experiences in India in the 1990s,
     Patnaik 2003.
49   FAO 1999; Cassel and Patel 2003.
50   Sharma 2003.
51   FAO 1999.
52   IATP 2003: 5; A SEED Europe 2003: 3; UNDP 2003: 123.
53   Senti 2001: 13.
54   WTO 2002a: 2.
55   Mayer et al. 2002.
56   WCSDG 2004: 47.
57   IISD 2003: 2; UNDP 2003: 138.
58   Santarius et al. 2003.
59   Ibid.
60   Eglin 1998; Tarasofsky 1999.
61   Shiva 2002: 91.
62   For a more detailed discussion, see Charnovitz 2003; Buck and Verheyen
     2001.
63   Vogel 2000.

64 Monbiot 2003: 217ff.
65 Proposals in this direction may be found in Helm 1995: 123ff.; Biermann 1999.
66 Bello 2002.
67 Hines 2004.
68 Guruswamy 1998; Neumann 2001: 575ff.; IFG 2002: 235f.
69 Santarius et al. 2003.
70 UNCTAD 2003.
71 World Bank 2003 and Wal-Mart 2002.
72 UNCTAD 2003.
73 Ibid.
74 WCSDG 2004: 33f.
75 UNCTAD 2003.
76 Meyer 1998.
77 Smith et al. 1999, also referred to in Meyer 2003.
78 Wichterich 2000.
79 Windfuhr 1993; Meyer 1998.
80 Spar 1998a and 1998b; Caruso et al. 2003; EIR 2003.
81 Mitchell 2002 describes this in the case of US corporations.
82 Porter 1999; Vogel 2000.
83 Forsythe 2000.
84 For greater detail, see Bendell 2004.
85 Richter 2002.
86 For an overview, see European Commission 2001a.
87 Arts 2003: 39.
88 Global Compact 2004; for a critical assessment, Hamm 2002; Weiss 2002; Martens 2004.
89 OECD 2000 and 2004; for a critical assessment, DNR 2003; Germanwatch 2003.
90 Kuhndt et al. 2003.
91 Turnbull 2002.
92 Ibid.; www.anglamark.com.
93 Buck, Helmchen and Moltke 2002.
94 Kuhndt et al. 2003.
95 Ibid. 2003.
96 Arts 2003: 39.
97 Porter 1999; Alberini and Segerson 2002.
98 Nima Hunter 2003.
99 WEF 2002.
100 KPMG 2002.
101 WRI 2003.
102 Gabel and Sinclair-Desgagné 2001.
103 Orlitzky, Schmidt and Rynes 2003.
104 Hoffmann and Scherhorn 2002.
105 See, for example, the EU guidelines 2003/51/EG, issued on 18 July 2003.

106 Bendell 2004.
107 Hillemanns 2003; Elliesen 2004.
108 UNECE 1998.
109 Porter 1999; Woodroffe 1999.
110 IFG 2002: 126ff.
111 Grossmann and Adams 1993.

7
What is Europe Worth?

In European affairs, anyone who does not believe in miracles is not a realist.

Walter Hallstein, 1964

Even someone who thinks Heraclitus is a rock formation will have heard of the famous saying left behind by the philosopher from Ephesus: 'War is the father of all things.' Though originally applied to the conflict of opposites in the cosmos, it contains a kernel of truth in the more familiar sense of the words. Wars speed up history, as the war in Iraq did in 2003. The American attack, both against Iraq and against morality and international law, proved to be a springboard for the quest for European identity. The old continent, previously conceived as no more than an economic area, had long been searching for a political identity. But, after the collapse of communism, there was no opportunity to redefine itself in relation to others, especially the US, which had emerged as Europe's 'big brother' in the period after the Second World War. The campaign in Iraq brought to an end this period of identity weakness. In contrast to the United States, Europe discovered itself as a power ready to endorse international law as the basis for a future world order resting on multilateral agreements and cooperation and seeking a peaceful equilibrium between cultures and nations. For a fleeting moment Europe discovered its cosmopolitan vocation.

It had scarcely found it, however, when a shrill discordance distorted the new-found unison of its voice. As a few West European and a series of East European governments gave their support to the war, Donald Rumsfeld, the American defence secretary, coined the term 'old Europe' – a description which, though intended to deride, was soon accepted with pride by many Europeans. Most of the nations of Europe were not represented by governments favourable to war. Moreover, Europeans took pleasure in the new interest that other parts of the world were taking in them, and in the realization that, for many people around the globe, Europe stands for a non-hegemonic model of world politics.

Make law not war

World politics has arrived at a parting of the ways. Will the international community be marked in future by unilateral supremacy or multilateral law? With the invasion of Iraq, Washington put into effect the conception that President George W. Bush had laid down in his National Security Strategy in September 2002, when he solemnly stated that he would neither enter into nor observe international obligations if they were contrary to the vital interests of the United States. The only global power thereby declared itself exempt from the letter and spirit of international law. In fact, this hegemonic unilateralism had already announced itself in the 1990s.[1] The Senate systematically withheld its assent to multilateral agreements, such as those on the banning of landmines or the creation of an international criminal court, and refused to ratify environmental agreements such as the Convention on Biological Diversity and the Kyoto Protocol – often enough after American diplomats had been the most energetic in watering them down first. But hegemonic unilateralism became a political programme only in answer to the terrorist attacks of 11 September 2001. Since then, fear of an invisible yet ubiquitous enemy has run through the foreign policy of the United States. The insistence on unilateral supremacy is born of the world power's need for complete freedom of action, in accordance with the motto: 'The strong man is strongest when alone.'

A majority of European countries responded with disappointment and indignation to the world power's ending of multilateralism. The European Union itself is quite a distinctive actor on the world stage, as independent national states have never before voluntarily agreed to hand over part of their sovereignty in this way to a supranational organization.[2] This came as the result of long and bloody wars, of a painful learning process by millions of people and their governments. At first the idea was to bind Germany economically so that it would never again launch a policy of conquest, but over the past fifty years the European states have built up a more and more dense system of cooperation.[3] Perhaps the most important basis for the success of such a complex project was the principle that the European Union should become a community in law.[4] In the case of a multitude of players and regulatory functions, opacity and arbitrariness can be prevented only if relations are placed on a legal foundation, so that inevitable conflicts are settled at a level above the interested parties. Dependability, transparency and contractual relations have proved to be binding agents of supranational cooperation. It has been possible to neutralize a long history of rivalry and force, without anyone losing out. The European states have learned that their power does not diminish but actually increases if they give up national sovereignty.[5] Multilateralism is by now part of their genetic code. No wonder, then, that Europe has been so allergic to America's high-handed way of dealing with transnational violence.

Furthermore, a majority of Europeans have a different notion of security. They shared with Americans the shock of violence, the sense of vulnerability, but they are less inclined to think that this new threat can be kept at bay through counter-violence. In their view, secret service surveillance and military operations are by no means the only instruments against terrorism; they have a sense that violence is socially learned and therefore stems from the experience and memory of humiliation and exclusion. The division of the world into rich and poor, powerful and powerless, recognized and unrecognized, is the real driving force for so much unrest and insecurity. Transnational terrorism is like a hydra that will keep growing new heads until one of its main sources – chronic debasement and disrespect – dries up; and, as the Iraqi experience shows, massive counter-violence seems to produce the exact opposite of pacification. Europeans can also see other global dangers such as climate change or migration pressure. They have understood that, in a world interwoven in so many ways, the need for security cannot be satisfied only for one side; the safety of some cannot be had without the safety of others. A planet that is safer for all its inhabitants can therefore only be a more equitable world; structures of fairness and justice are the foundation for long-term security and peace. In short, Europe tends more towards preventive justice than preventive warfare.

By virtue of its spiritual and historical premises, Europe can today offer the world a non-hegemonic model of coexistence in unity and diversity. Its theoretical tradition has given rise to the idea of cosmopolitan law, its history to an order based on peace and cooperation, its politics to a social and ecological framework for market economy, and its legal system to the precedence of citizens over states. What still keeps Europe from playing an independent role internationally is an outdated understanding of trans-Atlantic loyalty. It is a relic of the Cold War to believe that Europe's mission lies in standing shoulder to shoulder with the United States. Formerly the stability of the world hung on this attitude; today it is promoting instability. It is not evident how America's conception of the way forward – unilateralism, preventive use of force, market fundamentalism, exploitation of the environment – can serve the future of world society. Therefore, Europe has a responsibility in the new century to propose an alternative path in the global dialogue. America's incapacity for cosmopolitan leadership may be a historic opportunity for Europe. After colonialism, catastrophic wars and economic miracles, the time may have come when Europe, as a civilization based on successful coexistence, will attract the interest of the world.

For this to happen, of course, Europe must reposition itself on the stage of world politics; not much can be done in the role of 'economic giant, political dwarf'. Europe as standard-bearer for a cosmopolitan outline of global society, whose cornerstones would be cooperation, legality and environmental sustainability: this idea has the charm of being deeply rooted in European traditions, as well as being commensurate with the scale of the challenges today. Such a profile could shift, if not power relations, then the relations of attraction in the world. Europe might become a crystallising force for a democratic and ecological world society, and offer itself as an ally for any like-minded efforts elsewhere in the world, including in the United States. Recently American authors have been the first to advocate Europe's acceptance of this role.[6]

Kyoto – and what else?

At the level of states, apart from the USA, only Europe today has the symbolic and economic power to unleash the momentum for an alternative model of world politics. This is true also, and especially, of a policy for resource justice. The acceptance of issues in the international field requires a strong advocate, someone to lead the way.[7] Individual people, organizations and movements are indispensable for the development of ideas; they raise issues in the public mind and the world of politics, as the ecological movement did in the 1980s, and as the worldwide movement critical of globalization is trying to do at present. However, in an international system still geared to national states, there comes a point when a governmental player is necessary to champion ideas, to enlist fellow-combatants and to initiate concrete measures.[8]

Can Europe be such a player? Doubts are certainly in order, as Europe's make-up is presently unclear. The EU's leap from 15 to 25 members will eat up financial and personal resources and perhaps force it to concentrate on its own problems. Nor should one underestimate the effects on its capacity for political decision: the complex structure of the Union will not make it easier to agree and maintain common guidelines in foreign policy. Yet, if the European constitution is finally adopted, it may lead to more effective decision making and a greater continuity of personnel.[9]

In foreign affairs – to use the outmoded term of traditional diplomacy – it is anyway part of the agenda to design environmental policy as part of a global domestic policy. This would require seeing environmental policy itself in a new perspective. For forty years the main perspective was to improve the quality of life for EU citizens, but in the future environmental policy will have to be placed within a perspective of global society. Europe's citizens undoubtedly have clean seas and pesticide-free fruit close to their hearts, but in the rest of the world the vision of Europe as a shiny, well-cared-for island does not arouse much enthusiasm.

Beyond the quality of life, there are three important goals for world society. First, an ecological Europe is the precondition for a more just world: a deliberate, carefully considered retreat from overexploitation of the global environment would help to protect the existential rights of poor citizens in the world's rural peripheries and create space for the development of hitherto disadvantaged nations. Second, an ecological Europe is a laboratory for prosperity that is also capable of justice; types of economy that allow a good life with the least possible use of nature will be in great demand in the twenty-first century. Europe is therefore well advised to review its model of prosperity, in order to lead the way in the worldwide search for resource-light models of production and consumption. And third, an ecological Europe gives a new meaning to the demand for progress. The American way of life still dominates the imagination of large sections of the world's population. Technologies and lifestyles of a sustainable Europe have a demonstration effect; they offer examples of success more compatible with life and set up different goals as models.

In any event, the European Union can show some evidence of its credibility. In 1992, at the Johannesburg World Summit on Sustainable Development, it presented itself as a pioneering champion of the rights of the poor and the rights of the biosphere. Its diplomats campaigned for a halving by 2015 of the number of people without adequate access to energy and drinking water, for a worldwide expansion of renewable energies, and for the development of sustainable models of production and consumption in the industrial countries. The EU also fought for a reaffirmation of the principles of the 1992 conference in Rio, especially the precautionary principle and the case that the industrial countries should take the main responsibility for global protection of the environment. All this was by no means universally accepted: indeed, it involved an anti-hegemonic position, since the United States had shown up in Johannesburg as a world power bent on obstructing multilateral environmental policy. The EU revealed itself as a counterplayer to the USA. It went down fighting gloriously over renewable energies when the newly developing countries, committed to oil and coal, refused to lend it their support. But it kept the upper hand on the Rio principles, when the international community rejected Washington's attempt to turn back the clock of history by dismantling basic agreements reached in 1992.

On other diplomatic stages, too, the EU has been a bearer of hopes for a new global awareness of ecology. The Kyoto Protocol came into force seven years after it was signed – thanks to the insistence of the European Union[10] – and that is both a success for environmental policy and an anti-hegemonic success. Without Europe, this first world treaty on legally binding emission targets for greenhouse gases would not have happened. The same is true of follow-up work on the biodiversity convention and, above all, the biosafety protocol. Over the past fifteen years, Europe has established an independent global profile mainly through its environmental policy.

But there is still a big gap between reputation and reality. If it was only a question of intentions, the EU would not look bad in the field of environmental policy: the goal of sustainable development is firmly anchored in Article 2 of the EU Treaty[11] and Article 3 of its planned new constitution, and the EU has agreed a far-reaching and integrative strategy according to which environmental, social and economic interests are to be linked together at every level in the spirit of sustainability. The crux, as so often, lies in the implementation, because interests and power relations point in a different direction. The so-called Lisbon process, which is supposed to make Europe the most competitive economic area by the year 2010, has the upper hand over the Gothenburg process, which is supposed to gear institutions and behaviour to sustainability and to integrate environmental affairs into a number of special policies. The picture is therefore contradictory: rather forward-looking approaches in natural conservation, agricultural policy and climate protection contrast with omissions on transport, industrial policy, structural funds and prices policy.[12] True, the Union has championed the cause of prevention, but it has not yet managed to put the burden of proof on companies (for example, over the non-dangerous character of chemicals). And, although Europe sets itself up as a pioneer in the cause of climate protection, it is helpless to do anything about the spread of luxury sports utility vehicles or cheap flights.

So, opaqueness is one of the features of European environmental policy, but this also points to a political process in continuous change. Environmental policy is a permanent building site, where industry, environmental administration and civil society keep measuring their forces anew. This is not the worst basis from which to understand the ecological reshaping of Europe as part of a policy of global fairness. Thus, before Europe proceeds to humanitarian interventions and Marshall plans, it needs to reform itself in a cosmopolitan spirit. As we have seen in earlier chapters, it is vitally important to shift the resource base from fossil to renewable materials, because otherwise world society will know no peace and experience even deeper social divisions. A switch to ecological agriculture and food production is also indispensable, because otherwise the existential base of considerable sections of the world's population will crumble away. If Europeans already see themselves, by contrast with Americans, as citizens of the world, they should also be more receptive to the idea that an orderly retreat from overuse of the global environment would be a great cosmopolitan deed. Perhaps it is not too much to say that Europe must get involved in building global society as a resource-light solar civilization.

Farewell to Marrakesh
In this endeavour, Europeans will be guided by two insights: global justice necessarily implies an ecological economy in Europe; and this ecological transition must be embedded in a policy of equality within global society. Europe is comparatively well equipped to appear as an advocate for social and human rights, since it was here that the idea of the modern social state was born. As before in the nation-states of late nineteenth century, so today is the idea of solidarity fundamental for European society. The operation of the market, as enshrined in the EU's programmes, requires a counterweight in labour law and social legis-

lation; Europe is both an economic area and a space for social equalization. Thus, Europe has established redistributive mechanisms with the
help of its structural and cohesion funds, in order gradually to close the
economic gap among its members (first in southern Europe, now in the
East).

Human rights also rank high in Europe's scale of values. The European Convention on Human Rights and the European Court of Human
Rights have had an unequalled record since the 1950s,[13] both as regards
the substance and further development of the convention and in terms of
guaranteeing legal recourse for individual citizens and, when necessary,
upholding the rights of the individual against the will of his or her
national state. Here a good part of what is just beginning in transnational
space has already been accomplished: human rights take precedence over
the rights of nations, and no longer the other way around. Whereas
traditionally the idea of citizenship is tied to the nation-state, the rights of
European citizens are now additionally guaranteed by a supranational
body. So, Europe is currently preparing to achieve for 450 million
citizens a model of membership rooted in the recognition of individual
rights regardless of territory.[14] Of course, EU citizenship does not annul
citizenship in a particular nation: the two exist alongside each other.[15] As
may one day be true in global society, dual membership is becoming the
norm in Europe: citizens are the bearer of rights and duties, in a
territorial community and at the same time in a supra-territorial
community.

As far as the economy is concerned, the European Union finds
nothing alien in the idea of regarding its relations with the southern
hemisphere not only in market terms but also in those of a social
agreement. Since its foundation, it has applied special conditions to the
so-called ACP countries, essentially the former colonies in Africa, the
Caribbean and the Pacific. Granted unilateral advantages to create certain
opportunities for development, they were allowed to export their products duty-free to Europe and at the same time to raise taxes on imports
from Europe. Since the year 2000, however, the tune has changed in
the Cotonou agreement regulating this relationship. In keeping with the
WTO view of the world, the emphasis is now on freedom of
movement for corporations and their goods and services, not on
development opportunities for less-strong economies. And, as so often
under the WTO regime, the first experiences indicate a blockage of
economic development: milk imports from Europe, now duty-free, are

driving out domestic production in Jamaica; import bans on beans or chocolate from Cameroon are excluding poor producers from the world market.[16]

In general, one cannot say that the EU's profile in trade policy is as independent as the one it has developed in environmental policy. In the WTO negotiating process it appears more as a twin sister of the USA, occasionally having a family squabble but keeping up appearances with the outside world; on issues of trade with the countries of the South, Europe and America, for all their divergences, make common cause. At the ministerial talks of the WTO in Cancún, in September 2003, the European Union acted in pursuit of its own interests by taking advantage of the weakness of others. It came forward as the advocate of free trade, putting the countries of the South under pressure to open their markets to investment, but rejecting free access to its own markets for agricultural goods from the South. When, under these conditions, the countries of the South felt compelled to break off talks, they did so with the EU's policy in mind as much as that of the USA.[17] Besides, multilateral negotiations are only one arena for the assertion of economic interests. In bilateral agreements, too, the EU has not distinguished itself by its generosity; it has, for example, used its bargaining power to achieve access for European water corporations to the countries of the South, in return for vital commitments on development aid. In world trade policy, Europe's hegemonic ambitions are not an inch inferior to those of the United States. Without a clear turn, then, its policy on trade matters will continue to lag far behind its tradition on social and human rights.

If Europe is to be true to its mission, it must take an equal distance from the 'Washington consensus' and the 'Washington security agenda'.[18] The orthodoxy that has gripped the international financial and economic institutions since the 1980s, with its pat formulas for free trade, deregulation and privatization, does not sit well with Europe's claim to have reconciled competition and solidarity at the level of civilization. It would suit it far better to stand up for the model that is the core of how it understands itself: that is, the model of an eco-social market economy. Although the relevance and scope of this model in relation to markets without frontiers are today highly controversial issues, a basic cross-party consensus is taking shape over the perspective of European unity.[19] Why not also for global society? Europe is not needed to support and foster market-driven globalization. What the world expects from Europe are impulses for eco-social globalization.

A policy aimed at globalization of an eco-social market economy will take the basic rule of fairness as its supreme guideline: that is, decisions should be taken in such a way, and institutions structured in such a way, that the least advantaged in the world will not be worse off as a result (see Chapter 4). In any event, there is no worldwide social market economy if the wretched lives of the poor in the southern hemisphere are accepted as collateral damage of prosperity in the northern hemisphere. Furthermore, in a globalized world, no country and no continent can afford systematically to shift environmental and poverty risks on to other nations. To recognize the basic rule of fairness therefore means not to attach supreme importance to the economic competition among companies and nations. Neither in WTO negotiations nor in climate talks, neither in competition law nor in export promotion, can the competitive strength of the European Union be the only decisive argument. It must be complemented by a kind of human rights sustainability check. Will the poor layers of society in question be better or worse off? The core of the basic rule of fairness is not aid or redistribution but the avoidance of harm. Good global neighbourliness means putting the avoidance of harm before aid and redistribution – although it is just as difficult to achieve.

This provides us with a guiding principle for a European policy on justice. In all areas of world trade involving sensitive human rights issues, the free trade agreements should be converted into fair trade agreements. The sectors immediately significant for economic, social and cultural human rights include intellectual property rights and, above all, agriculture (see Chapter 6). In the past ten years, with energetic assistance from the European Union, a system of rules has been built up in these sectors that is geared to the interests of the powerful corporations and nations. In parts complete, in other parts still taking shape, this system represents a threat to large numbers of the least advantaged citizens of global society; it therefore cannot continue to exist under the criteria of a social market economy. A Europe that really values these criteria will direct international trade in these sectors through agreements that take into account the rights and development opportunities of economically weak populations.

A learning process and a change in the institutions of the European Union are required to achieve this. But they can come about only though greater democratic legitimation of community policy, not – as the planned new constitution threatened – through the uncoupling of trade policy from legitimation by member states and national parliaments. For only if decision making is open, transparent and participatory, and only if it balances the greatest possible number of heterogeneous interests, can we expect it to have results geared to the general welfare. Finally, no pact of any description between rich and poor countries will succeed without a strong element of financial equalization. The former colonial countries rightly expect reparations from the North for its unjustly gained advantages, and it is in the vital interests of the North – politically and economically – to prevent the gap in the world from growing too wide. But equalization should be mutually agreed and conducted, so that ecological guidelines can be built into it on both the donor and the recipient side. In short, money flows should be used as pacemakers for the transition to environmentally sustainable economies. A number of approaches have been suggested, but the basic idea is always the same: negative financial incentives will apply to material and energy turnover by heavy users, in order to stimulate the transition to resource-saving economies, while the amounts saved in this way will be invested among light users to facilitate ecological leapfrogging (see Chapter 5). There are a number of models for this. Overconsumption might be regulated through a 'global resource dividend';[20] heavy users would have to purchase special rights in the international emission trade;[21] and, in the case of global common goods such as airspace or the seas,[22] payment would include charges for the use and pollution of a resource that belongs to nobody and everybody. There are similar proposals for how the money might be used: revenue from taxes on resources should go into development funds; low users should gain from emission trading through the sale of emission rights; or a 'global Marshall plan' might help to fund eco-social development paths.[23] In each case, the money transfers are embedded in a social contract for the promotion of sustainable development.

Alliances for a fair future

It may be precisely Europe's brittle integration which enables the EU to play a role in pioneering global resource justice. Only a cosmopolitan opening in the context of global society will consolidate Europe's internal definition of itself.[24] From its inception the European Union rested on an idea larger than the geographical area: Jean Monnet, the spiritual father of a united Europe, was driven not least by the desire to make a 'contribution to a better world' (*une contribution à un monde meilleur*).

Europe's strength as a 'cooperative world power'[25] will have to consist in building alliances and forming networks. Transnational politics, in any case, is already developing in this direction, since geographical alliances, once held together by the fear of neighbouring countries, will increasingly be replaced by coalitions of like-minded states pursuing related goals. Of course, truly universal alliances are not yet in sight, and for the time being the strongest player and hegemon seems unwilling to cooperate. The only possible strategic answer to this, as the international legal success of the Kyoto Protocol demonstrates, is that other countries will, if necessary, proceed without the USA on vital issues – and keep the door open for it to come in later. Since there is little likelihood that Washington will turn to a policy of resource justice in the foreseeable future, a number of willing states must join together to regulate and solve a global problem. For it would be a misunderstanding of universalism to seek the solution only in global unanimity. As things stand, there is scarcely any other option than to pursue a strategy of 'universalism minus X'. Neither the convention to ban anti-personnel mines nor the creation of the International Criminal Court would have been possible if Europe and Canada had waited for the United States. In both cases, an alliance of Europe, Canada, Japan and many countries in the South proved strong enough to conclude valid agreements without the superpower.

The establishment of an international organization to promote renewable energies would be another worthwhile project of this kind. It would require only a handful of industrial countries to reallocate some of the financial resources presently going to EURATOM or the nuclear cooperation programme of the International Atomic Agency. In fact, statutes have already been worked out for an international renewable energy agency,[26] and in April 2003 the German Bundestag approved the founding of such an organization. Unfortunately, the conference on renewable energies organized by Germany in June 2004 did not serve to advance the cause – mainly because the courage was lacking to drive the nail home without the United States and Saudi Arabia.

In the multilayered transnational society of the twenty-first century, however, national states are no longer the only possible partners for the achievement of strategic goals. Players in civil society have invaded many areas of international politics and diplomacy in recent years, especially in relation to justice and the environment. Many of these new players are specialist associations that often help to shape international policy in a highly professional manner.[27] Along with states and business, civil society organizations are now the third category of players in international affairs. The rapid rise of non-governmental organizations (NGOs) in international policy began in the early 1990s, in the run-up to the Rio Earth Summit. The UN conferences on environment and development (Rio de Janeiro 1992), human rights (Vienna 1993), population (Cairo 1994), social development (Copenhagen 1995) and women (Beijing 1995) involved the participation of several thousand people from the heart of civil society.[28] Altogether, civil society organizations have lent a new quality to international relations since the Second World War.[29] Many of the interests represented by NGOs would have no voice at all without them: for example, the ocean coral reefs or the virgin forests of Tasmania. NGOs appear over and over again in their function as 'the conscience of society' offering a critical check on policies – including the policies of the European Union (at world trade conferences, for instance).

European strategies to promote resource justice acquire greater weight and social anchorage when they can rely on an alliance with major players from the civil societies of the North and South, such as Oxfam, Greenpeace, Friends of the Earth, Human Rights Watch, Amnesty International and Third World Network, to name but a few. Such connections are to be recommended, especially when governments are keen to strengthen their influence by means of research, persuasion and networking. Thus, without the Climate Action Network comprising some three hundred environmental organizations, founded in Germany in 1989 with help from Germany and Sweden,[30] there would have been neither the climate framework convention nor the Kyoto Protocol in its present form. An alliance of governments and civil society groups also played a major role in driving the campaigns for a landmine convention and the International Criminal Court. And, at the WTO interministerial conference at Cancún in September 2003, governments from the South actually asked civil society groups to enter into an alliance with them against unfair rules and free trade across frontiers.

A more extensive form of cooperation between NGOs and governments is the foundation of hybrid organizations that are neither NGOs nor intergovernmental organizations. An early example of this is the International Union for the Conservation of Nature (IUCN), which was founded in 1948 under the umbrella of UNESCO with a central secretariat in Switzerland. Membership in it is open not only to national and international NGOs but also to governments and state authorities – even to state institutions from countries that are not members. In this way the IUCN has gathered nearly a thousand members from some 140 countries. Another successful application of the IUCN model is the World Commission on Dams.[31] This body, formed with representatives from governments, industry and NGOs, has worked out proposals for ecological and social standards in the construction of large dams. Its success has been due to its independence, to the broad involvement of both supporters and critics of dams, and to the greatest possible transparency in its work.[32] It has come to provide an important example for the solution of international problems through 'global policy networks', in which all the important players in a particular field – governments, corporations and representatives of civil society – work together to find an acceptable resolution.[33] This clearly demonstrates that an energetic, non-hierarchical organizational structure can address complex problems of global governance.

Europe will have to choose. If it opts for preventive war to protect itself, it will set its sights on close cooperation with Washington and the market fundamentalists. If it wishes to pioneer a policy of preventive justice in the world, it will seek to build coalitions with like-minded countries and representative organizations in civil society. For it can only be good for the European project if every now and then Europeans look up from the everyday mêlée in Brussels and ask themselves how they want to be remembered by future generations at the end of the twenty-first century. Europe will not survive in the emerging global society through the numbers of its people but only through the force of its ideas. Brown, yellow and black faces will people tomorrow's transnational world; white Europeans will be scarcely more than 7 per cent of its population. Thus, the global society of the twenty-first century will certainly not be a European society – just as fifteenth-century Europe was not a Greco-Roman society. And yet, without the Greco-Roman legacy in law and culture, Europe as a civilization would have been poorer and even, perhaps, more barbaric. That is both a consolation and an encouragement. Why should Europe not become for global society what Rome once was for the Renaissance?

Notes

1 Habermas 2004.
2 Slaughter 2004; Rifkin 2004.

3   Nuscheler 2001; Hamm et al. 2002.
4   Pernice 2003.
5   Beck 2004: 262.
6   George 2003; Rifkin 2004.
7   Young and Osherenko 1995.
8   Beck 2002: 419.
9   Schaik and Egenhofer 2003.
10 Oberthür and Ott 1999.
11 European Commission 2001b.
12 For a critical evaluation of EU policy on sustainability, see EEB 2004.
13 Meyer-Ladewig 2003.
14 Rifkin 2004.
15 Preuss 1998.
16 For an initial overview of the Cotonou agreement, see Eurostep et al. 2004.
17 Narain 2003.
18 Held 2004.
19 Radermacher 2002.
20 Pogge 2003.
21 Oberthür and Ott 1999.
22 WBGU 2002.
23 Radermacher et al. 2004.
24 Beck 2004.
25 Messner 2001.
26 Eurosolar 2001; Scheer 2003.
27 Walk and Brunnengräber 2000.
28 Messner and Nuscheler 1996.
29 Hummer 2000: 49.
30 Waddell 2003.
31 See www.dams.org.
32 WRI et al. 2001.
33 See Reinicke et al. 2000; Streck 2002.

Bibliography

A SEED (Action for Solidarity, Equality, Environment and Development) Europe (2003): *The World Trade Organization's Agreement on Agriculture: a Fair Deal?*

ACI (Airports Council International) (2002): 'World Airport Ranking 2000', personal communication. Geneva.

Adriaanse, Albert von, Bringezu, Stefan, Hammond, Allan, Moriguchi, Yuicbi, Rodenburg, Ellen, Rogich, D., Schutz, Helmut (1998): *Stoffströme: Die materielle Basis von Industriegesellschaften*. Berlin, Basle, Boston.

Agarwal, Anil and Narain, Sunita (1991): *Global Warming in an Unequal World*. Centre for Science and Environment. New Delhi.

Aguliar, Lorena and Blanco, Monserrat (2004): 'Diversity Makes the Difference! Gender Considerations for Promoting an Equitable Access to and Fair Sharing of Benefits Arising from the Utilization of Biodiversity'. Paper prepared for the Seventh Meeting of the Conference to the Parties to the Convention of Biological Diversity. Gland.

Alberini, Anna and Segerson, Kathleen (2002): 'Assessing Voluntary Programs to Improve Environmental Quality', *Environmental and Resource Economics* 22: 157–84.

Alfarra, Amani (2004): *Modelling Water Resource Management in Lake Naivasha*. International Institute for Geo-Information Science and Earth Observation. Enschede.

al-Husseini, Sadad (2004): 'Why Higher Oil Prices Are Inevitable This Year, Rest of Decade', *Oil and Gas Journal* (2 August 2004): 14–18.

Altieri, Miguel A. (2004): 'Agroecology: Principles and Strategies for Designing Sustainable Farming Systems'. University of California, Berkeley. www.agroeco.org/doc/new_docs/Agroeco_principles.pdf (30 September 2004).

Altvater, Elmar (1992): *Der Preis des Wohlstands*. Munster.

Altvater, Elmar and Mahnkopf, Birgit (2002): *Globalisierung der Unsicherheit. Arbeit im Schatten, Schmutziges Geld und informelle Politik*. Munster.

Altvater, Elmar and Mahnkopf, Birgit (1996): *Grenzen der Globalisierung. Ökonomie, Ökologie und Politik in der Weltgesellschaft*. Munster.

Andersson, Jan Otto and Lindroth, Mattias (2001): 'Ecologically Unsustainable Trade', *Ecological Economics* 37: 113–22.

APFC (Alaska Permanent Fund Corporation) (2001): *An Alaskan's Guide to the Permanent Fund*. Juneau.

Arndt, Heinz W. (1987): *Economic Development. The History of an Idea.* Chicago.

Arrow, Kenneth et al. (1995): 'Economic Growth, Carrying Capacity, and the Environment', *Ecological Economics* 15, 2: 91–5.

Arts, Bas (2003): *Non-State Actors in Global Governance. Three Faces of Power.* Reprint from the Max-Planck-Projektgruppe Recht der Gemeinschaftsgüter. Preprint. Bonn.

Aslam, Amin (2002): 'Equal Per Capita Entitlements. A Key to Global Participation in Climate Change?', in Baumert, Kevin A. (ed.), *Building on the Kyoto Protocol: Options for Protecting the Climate.* Washington, pp. 175–201.

ASPO (Association for the Study of Peak Oil and Gas) (2004): *Newsletter* No. 44, August. Uppsala.

Athanasiou, Tom and Baer, Paul (2002): *Dead Heat. Global Justice and Global Warming.* New York.

Ayres, Robert U. (1998): *Turning Point. An End to the Growth Paradigm.* London.

Baccini, Peter and Brunner, Paul H. (1991): *The Metabolism of the Anthroposphere.* Berlin, Heidelberg, New York.

Barber, Benjamin R. (2003): *Fear's Empire: War, Terrorism and Democracy.* New York.

Barker, Debi (2002): 'Globalization and Industrial Agriculture', in Kimball, Andrew (ed.), *The Fatal Harvest Reader.* Washington, pp. 249–63.

Barlow, Maude and Clarke, Tony (2003): *Blue Gold. The Battle against Corporate Theft of the World's Water.* London.

Barnes, Peter (2001): *Who Owns the Sky? Our Common Assets and the Future of Capitalism.* Washington.

Barwa, Sharmishta and Rai, Shirin M. (2002): 'The Political Economy of Intellectual Property Rights: a Gender Perspective', in Newell, Peter, Rai, Shirin M. and Scott, Andrew (eds.), *Development and the Challenge of Globalisation.* London.

Beck, Ulrich (2004): *Der kosmopolitische Blick oder: Krieg ist Frieden.* Frankfurt/Main.

Beck, Ulrich (2002): *Macht und Gegenmacht im globalen Zeitalter.* Frankfurt/Main.

Beck, Ulrich (2000): *What Is Globalization?* Cambridge.

Beckman, David, Jasny, Michael, Wadewitz, Lissa and Wetzler, Andrew (2000): *Drawdown. Groundwater Mining on Black Mesa.* New York.

Bello, Walden (2002): *Deglobalization: Ideas for a New Economy.* London.

Bendell, Jem (2004): *Barricades and Boardrooms. A Contemporary History of the Corporate Accountability Movement.* Technology, Business and Society Programme, No. 13. Geneva.

Bentley, Matthew D. (2003): 'Sustainable Consumption: Ethics, National Indices and International Relations'. Dissertation: American Graduate School of International Relations and Diplomacy. Paris.

Bernhardt, Dörte (2005): 'Fiasco in Manila', in Weizsäcker, Ernst-Ulrich, Young, Oran R. and Finger, Matthias: *Limits to Privatization. How to Avoid Too Much of a Good Thing.* London.

Berry, Thomas (1999): *The Great Work. Our Way into the Future.* New York.

Bevilacqua, Piero (2000): 'Il concetto di risorsa: significati e prospettive', *Meridiana. Rivista di storia e scienze sociali*, No. 37: 13–31.

Bhalla, Surrit S. (2002): *Imagine There's No Country: Poverty, Inequality and Growth in the Era of Globalization*. Washington.

Biermann, Frank (1999): *Internationale Umweltverträge im Welthandelsrecht.* WZB-Wissenschaftszentrum Berlin für Sozialforschung. Discussion Paper FS II 99–403. Berlin.

Birdsall, Nancy (1998), 'Life is Unfair: Inequality in the World', in *Foreign Policy*, Summer 1998.

BMU (Bundesumweltministerium) (2002): *Vereinte Nationen – Bericht des Weltgipfels für nachhaltige Entwicklung, 26 August– 4 September 2002*. Johannesburg, http://www.bmu.de/files/johannesburg_declaration.pdf.

BMU (1992): *Umweltpolitik. Konferenz der Vereinten Nationen für Umwelt und Entwicklung im Juni 1992 in Rio de Janeiro. Dokumente. Klimakonvention, Konvention über biologische Vielfalt, Rio-Deklaration, Walderklärung*. Bonn.

BMWi (Bundesministerium für Wirtschaft) (2002): *Energie-Daten 2002*. Berlin.

Bourguignon, François et al. (2002): *Making Sense of Globalization: a Guide to the Economic Issues*. CEPR Policy Paper No. 8. London.

Brassel, Frank and Windfuhr, Michael (1995): *Welthandel und Menschenrechte*, Bonn.

Braungart, Michael and McDonough, William (2003): *Einfach intelligent produzieren*. Berlin.

Braunmühl, Claudia von, and Winterfeld, Uta von: 'Sustainable Governance or Reclaiming of the Political Sphere. Reflections on Sustainability, Globalisation and Democracy.' Wuppertal Paper No. 135e. Wuppertal.

Bringezu, Stefan (2004): *Erdlandung – Navigationen zu den Ressourcen der Zukunft*. Stuttgart, Leipzig.

Bringezu, Stefan and Schütz, Helmut (1995): 'Wie misst man die ökologische Zukunftsfähigkeit einer Volkswirtschaft? Ein Beitrag der Stoffstrombilanzierung am Beispiel der Bundesrepublik Deutschland', in Bringezu, Stefan (ed.), *Neue Ansätze der Umweltstatistik*. Berlin, Basle, Boston, pp. 26–54.

Bringezu, Stefan, Schütz, Helmut and Moll, Stephan (2003): 'Rationale for and Interpretation of Economy-Wide Material Flow Analysis and Derived Indicators', *Journal of Industrial Ecology*, 2, 7: 42–64.

British Geological Survey (2003): *European Mineral Statistics 1997–2001*. Keyworth, Nottingham.

Brouns, Bernd (2004): 'Was ist gerecht? Nutzungsrechte an natürlichen Ressourcen in der Klima und Biodiversitätspolitik'. Wuppertal Paper No. 146. Wuppertal.

Brown Weiss, Elizabeth (1992): 'Intergenerational Equity: a Legal Framework for Global Environmental Change', in Brown Weiss, E. (ed.), *Environmental Change in International Law*, Tokyo, pp. 385–412.

Buck, Matthias, Helmchen, Constanze and Moltke, Konrad von (2002): 'From Rio to Johannesburg – a Business Perspective'. Background Paper to the 7th International Business Forum, 20–22 August. Johannesburg.

Buck, Matthias and Verheyen, Roda (2001): *International Trade and Climate Change*

– *A Positive Way Forward*. FES-Analyse Ökologische Marktwirtschaft.

BUND/Misereor (eds.) (1996): *Zukunftsfähiges Deutschland. Eine Studie des Wuppertal Instituts*. Basle.

BWA (Bundesamt für Wirtschaft und Ausfuhrkontrolle) (2003): *Mineralöldaten für die Bundesrepublik Deutschland*.

Caruso, Emily, Cokhester, Marcus, MacKay, Fergus, Hildyard, Nick and Nettleton, Geoff (2003): *Extracting Promises: Indigenous People, Extractive Industries and the World Bank*. Synthesis Report. Baguio City.

Cassel, Amanda and Patel, Raj (2003): *Agricultural Trade Liberalization and Brazil's Rural Poor: Consolidating Inequality*. Institute for Food and Development Policy. Policy Brief No. 8. Oakland.

CEAS (Centre for European Agricultural Studies) (2000): *Study on the Relationship between the Agreement on TRIPS and Biodiversity-Related Issues*. Final report. EU Commission. Brussels.

CEPR (Center for Economic and Policy Research) (2001): *The Scorecard on Globalisation 1980–2000: Twenty Years of Diminished Progress*. Washington.

Chandrasekar, K. and Gujar, G. T. (2004): *Bt Cotton Benefits Short-lived: Study*. Indian Agricultural Research Institute, published in *Financial Express* (India), 11 February 2004.

Chang, Ha-Joon (2002): *Kicking Away the Ladder. Development Strategy in Historical Perspective*. London.

Charnovitz, Steve (2003): 'Trade and Climate: Potential Conflicts and Synergies', in Pew Center on Global Climate Change (ed.), *Beyond Kyoto. Advancing the International Effort against Climate Change*. Arlington.

China Ministry of Water Resources (2004): *Basic Readiness of Preparation Work for South to North Water Transfer Project. 14 November 2000*. www.nsbd.mwr.gov.cn/nsbd/news/j20011120.htm (30 September 2004).

Colombo, Umberto (2002): 'Technological Leapfrogging: the Lure and the Limits'. Paper presented at Delhi Sustainable Development Summit 2002. Ensuring Sustainable Livelihoods: Challenges for Governments, Corporates, and Civil Society at Rio+10, 8–11 February 2002, New Delhi.

Cornia, Giovanni Andrea and Court, Julius (2001): *Inequality, Growth and Poverty in the Era of Liberalization and Globalization*. World Institute for Development Economics Research. Policy Brief No. 4.

CUTS (Consumer Unity and Trust Society) (2003): *State of Play*. Issue Paper No. 2. Jaipur.

Dalkmann, Holger et al. (2004): *Wege von der nachholenden zur nachhaltigen entwicklung. Infrastruktur und deren Transfer im Zeitalter der Globalisierung*. Wuppertal Paper No. 140. Wuppertal.

Daly, Herman E. (1996): *Beyond Growth. The Economics of Sustainable Development*. Boston.

Daly, Herman E. (1996): 'The Perils of Free Trade. Economics routinely ignore its hidden costs to the environment and the community', *Scientific America*, 11, pp. 50–7.

Davidson, Carlos (2000): 'Economic Growth and the Environment: Alternatives to the Limits Paradigm', *Bio-Scene*, 50: 433–40.

Deaton, Angus and Drèze, Jean (2002): 'Poverty and Inequality in India. A Re-Examination', *Economic and Political Weekly*, 37, 36: 3729–45.

Deckwirth, Christina (2004): *Sprudelnde Gewinne? Transnationale Konzerne im Wassersektor und die Rolle des GATS*. Bonn.

Diefenbacher, Hans (2001): *Gerechtigkeit und Nachhaltigkeit. Zum Verhältnis von Ethik und Ökonomie*. Darmstadt.

DLR/ifeu/WI (Deutsches Zentrum für Luft- und Raumfahrt, Institut für Energie und Umweltforschung and Wuppertal Institut) (2004): *Ökologisch optimierter Ausbau der Nutzung erneuerbarer Energien in Deutschland. Forschungsvorhaben im Auftrag des Bundesministeriums für Umwelt, Naturschutz und Reaktorsicherheit*. Berlin.

DNR (Deutscher Naturschutzring e.V.) (2003): *Die Zukunft der Europäischen Union. Weltweite Regeln für globale Unternehmen*. EU-Rundschreiben, Sonderteil 06.03, 12/06. Berlin.

Duncan, Richard C. and Youngquist, Walter (1998): *The World Petroleum Life Cycle*. Unpublished manuscript. Los Angeles. http://www.dieoff. org/page133. htm.

Earth Charter Initiative (n.d.): www.earth-charter.org (30.9.2004).

Economist (2003): 'Damming Evidence', at Economist.com, 17 July.

EEA (European Energy Agency) (2003): *Europe's Environment: the Third Assessment*. Environmental Assessment Report No 10. Copenhagen.

EEB (European Environmental Bureau) (2004): *Green Eight Review of the EU Sustainable Development Strategy*. Brussels.

EFTA (European Fair Trade Association) (2002): *EFTA Yearbook: Challenges of Fair Trade 2001–2003*.

Eglin, Richard (1998): 'Trade and Environment', in Bhagwati, Jagdish and Hirsch, Mathias (eds.), *The Uruguay Round and Beyond. Essays in Honour of Arthur Dunkel*. Berlin, pp. 251–63.

Ehring, Lothar (2002): 'De Facto Discrimination in World Trade Law. National and Most-Favoured-Nation Treatment – or Equal Treatment?', *Journal of World Trade* 36, 5: 921–77.

EIA (Energy Information Administration) (2004a): *Country Analysis Brief Kazakhstan*. www.eia.doe.gov/emeu/cabs/kazak.html (30 September 2004).

EIA (2004b): *International Energy Outlook 2004*. www.eia.doe.gov/oiaf/ ieo/index.html (30 September 2004).

EIA (2000): *Long Term World Oil Supply. A Resource Base/Production Path Analysis*. Paris.

EIR (Extractive Industries Review) (2003): *Striking a Better Balance. The Final Report of the Extractive Industries Review*, vol. 1 (January) and vol. 2 (December). Washington/Jakarta.

Elliesen, Tillmann (2004): 'Trübe Aussichten für UN-Kodex', *E+Z* 4/2004, http://www.inwent.org/E+Z/content/heft-ger/an_art1.html.

Enquete-Kommission (2002): *Schlussbericht der Enquete-Kommission Globalisierung der Weltwirtschaft – Herausforderungen und Antworten*. Bundestags Drucksache

14/9200. Berlin.

European Commission (2003): *Entwicklung einer thematischen Strategie für die nachhaltige Nutzung der natürlichen Ressourcen*. KOM (2003) 572 onwards. Brussels.

European Commission (2001a): *Promoting a European Framework for Corporate Social Responsibility*. Green Paper. COM (2001) 366 onwards. Brussels.

European Commission (2001b): *Mitteilung der Kommission – Nachhaltige Entwicklung in Europa für eine bessere Welt: Strategie der Europäischen Union für die nachhaltige Entwicklung*. KOM(200i) 264 onwards. Brussels.

European Parliament (1998): 'Resolution on Climate Change in the Run-Up to the Conference in Buenos Aires (17 September 1998)', in *Global Equity and Climate Change*. Brussels.

Eurosolar (2001): *Memorandum für die Errichtung einer Internationalen Agentur für Erneuerbare Energien (IRENA)*, www.eurosolar.org (30 September 2004).

Eurostep et al. (2004): *New ACP–EU Trade Arrangements: New Barriers to Eradicating Poverty?* Brussels.

ExxonMobil (2004): *Long-Term Energy Outlook. An ExxonMobil Analysis*. (No place of publication mentioned.)

Fachverband Deutscher Floristen (2004): *Globale Wirtschaftsstrukturen: Schnittblumenproduktion und Handel weltweit*. www.fdf.de/meldung. htm?6o.

FAO (Food and Agriculture Organization of the United Nations) (2002): *World Agriculture:Towards 2015/2030*. Rome.

FAO (2001a): *FAO Statistical Databases* (CD-ROM). Rome.

FAO (2001b): 'Mobilising Resources to Fight Hunger', CFS: 2001/lnf7. Rome.

FAO (2001c): *Global Forest Assessment 2000*. Rome.

FAO (2000): *The State of World Fisheries and Aquaculture*. Rome.

FAO (1999): *Experience with the Implementation of the Uruguay Round Agreement on Agriculture – Developing Country Experiences (Based on Case Studies). FAO Symposium on Agriculture, Trade and Food Security: Issues and Options in the Forthcoming WTO Negotiations from the Perspective of Developing Countries*. 23–24 September 1999. Geneva.

FIAN (FoodFirst Informations- and Aktions-Netzwerk) (2004): 'Gewaltsame Vertreibung von 35 Adivasi-Familien aus ihrem Dorf Kinari'. www.fian.de (30 September 2004).

Fischedick, Manfred, Lanmiss, Ote and Nitsch, Joachim (2000): *Nach dem Ausstieg. Zukunftskurs Erneuerbare Energien*. Stuttgart.

Fischer Weltalmanach (2005): *Zahlen, Daten, Fakten*. Frankfurt/Main.

Fischer Weltalmanach (2003): *Zahlen, Daten, Fakten*. Frankfurt/Main.

FoEI (Friends of the Earth International) (2002): *Towards Binding Corporate Accountability*. FoEI position paper for the WSSD. Summary. http://www.foei.org/corporates/towards.html.

Folke, Carl et al. (2002): *Resilience and Sustainable Development: Building Adaptive Capacity in a World of Transformation*. Stockholm.

Forsythe, David P. (2000): *Human Rights and International Relations*. Cambridge.

Fraser, Nancy and Honneth, Axel (1998): *Redistribution or Recognition? A Political-Philosophical Exchange*. London.

Fritsche, Uwe R. and Matthes, Felix Christian (2003): *Changing Course. A Contribution to a Global Energy Strategy*. World Summit Paper of the Heinrich Böll Stiftung, No. 22. Berlin.

Fussler, Claude (1997): *Driving Eco-Innovation*. London.

Gabel, Landis H. and Sinclair-Desgagné, Bernard (2001): 'The Firm, Its Producers and Win-win Environmental Regulations', in Folmer, Frank (ed.), *Frontiers of Environmental Economics*. Cheltenham.

Gadgil, Madhav and Guha, Ramachandra (1995): *Ecology and Equity. The Use and Abuse of Nature in Contemporary India*. London.

Gardner, Gary, Assadourian, Erik and Sarin, Radhia (2004): 'Zum gegenwärtigen Stand des Konsums', in Worldwatch Institute (ed.), *Zur Lage der Welt 2004. Die Welt des Konsums*. Münster, pp. 39–68.

George, Susan (2003): *Another World Is Possible, If....* London.

Georges, Karl Ernst (1880): *Lateinisch-deutsches und Deutsch-lateinisches Handwörterbuch*. Leipzig.

Georgescu-Roegen, Nicholas (1971): *The Entropy Law and the Economic Process*. Cambridge.

Germanwatch (in collaboration with BUND and Friends of the Earth Netherlands) (2003): *Anwendung der OECD-Leitsätze für Multinationale Unternehmen*. *Handbuch für NGOs*. Berlin, Amsterdam.

Giljum, Stefan and Eisenmenger, Nina (2003): *North–South Trade and the Distribution of Environmental Goods and Burdens. A Biophysical Perspective*. SERI Working Paper No. 2, June. Vienna.

Gleich, Arnim von (ed.) (2001): *Bionik. Ökologische Technik nach dem Vorbild der Natur?* Wiesbaden.

Global Compact (2004): http://www.unglobalcompact.org.

Goldemberg, José (2003): 'Leapfrogging Technology', in Munn, Ted (ed.), *Encyclopedia of Global Environmental Change*, vol. 4. Chippenham.

Goldemberg, José (ed.) (2000): *World Energy Assessment: Energy and the Challenge of Sustainability*. New York.

Goldemberg, José and Johansson, Thomas B. (1995): *Energy as an Instrument for Socio-Economic Development*. New York.

Görg, Christoph (1998): 'Die Regulation der biologischen Vielfalt', in Flitner, Michael, Görg, Christoph and Heins, Voker (eds.), *Konfliktfeld Natur. Biologische Ressourcen und globale Politik*. Opladen, pp. 39–62.

GRAIN (2004): 'The Disease of the Day. Acute Treatytis. The Myths and Consequences of Free Trade Agreements with the US'. www.grain.org/briefings/?id=183 (30 September 2004).

GRAIN (2003): 'TRIPS-plus Must Stop: the European Union Caught in Blatant Contradictions. www.grain.org/briefings/?id=119 (30 September 2004).

Gray, Kevin R. (2003): *Right to Food Principles* vis-à-vis *Rules Governing International Trade*. British Institute of International and Comparative Law. London.

Grefe, Christiane (2003): 'Wie das Wasser nach Happyland kam', *Die Zeit*, 35.

Grim, John (ed.) (2001): *Indigenous Traditions and Ecology: the Interbeing of Cosmology and Community*. Cambridge.

Groombridge, Brian and Jenkins, Martin D. (2002): *World Atlas of Biodiversity. Earth's Living Resources in the 21st Century.* Prepared by the UNEP World Conservation Monitoring Centre. Berkeley.

Grossman, Richard L. and Adams, Frank T. (1993): *Taking Care of Business: Citizenship and the Charter of Incorporation.* Cambridge.

Grubb, Michael (1995): 'Seeking Fair Weather: Ethics and the International Debate on Climate Change', *International Affairs* 71, 3: 463–96.

GTZ (Deutsche Gesellschaft für Technische Zusammenarbeit) and Kaltheier, Ralf M. (2001): *Städtischer Personenverkehr und Armut in Entwicklungsländern.* GTZ Arbeitsfeld 4432, Transport und Mobilität. Eschborn.

Guruswamy, Lakshman D. (1998): 'Should UNCLOS or GATT/WTO Decide Trade and Environment Disputes?', *Minnesota Journal of Global Trade* 7, 287: 289–328.

Habermas, Jürgen (2004): 'Wege aus der Weltunordnung. Interview', *Blätter für deutsche und internationale Politik* 1: 27–45.

Haggart, Kelly and Chongqing, Yang (2003): 'Reservoirs of Repression: Part One', in *Three Gorges Probe,* 16 April 2003. www.threegorgesprobe. org/tgp/print.cfm?ContentlD=7007 (30 September 2004).

Haller, Tobias et al. (2000): *Fossile Ressourcen, Erdölkonzerne und indigene Völker.* Giessen.

Hamm, Brigitte (2002): 'Der Global Compact. Eine Bestandaufnahme', in Hamm, Brigitte (ed.), *Public Private Partnership und der Global Compact der Vereinten Nationen.* INEF Report, No. 62: 17–39.

Hamm, Brigitte, Hippler, Jochen, Messner, Dirk and Weiler, Christoph (2002): *Weltpolitik am Scheideweg. Der 11. September 2001 und seine Folgen.* SEF-Policy Paper 19. Bonn.

Hare, William (2003): *Assessment of Knowledge on Impacts of Climate Change – Contribution to the Specification of Art. 2 of the UNFCCC.* Externe Expertise für das WBGU-Sondergutachten 'Welt im Wandel: Über Kyoto hinausdenken. Klimaschutzstrategien für das 21. Jahrhundert'. Berlin.

Hargreaves-Allen, Venetia (2003): 'Cut Flowers', *The Ecologist* 33, 8: 34–5.

Hawken, Paul, Lovins, Amory B. and Lovins, Hunter L. (1999): *Natural Capitalism: Creating the Next Industrial Capitalism.* Boston.

Heerings, Hans and Zeldenrust, Ineke (1995): *Elusive Saviours. Transnational Corporations and Sustainable Development.* Utrecht.

Held, David (2004): 'Globalisation: the Dangers and the Answers'. www. openDemocracy.net (30 September 2004).

Held, David (2003): 'From Executive to Cosmopolitan Multilateralism', in Held, David and Koenig-Archibugi, Mathias: *Taming Globalization. Frontiers of Governance.* Cambridge, pp. 160–86.

Helm, Carsten (1995): *Sind Freihandel und Umweltschutz vereinbar? Ökologischer Reformbedarf des GATT/WTO-Regimes.* Berlin.

Henne, Gudrun (1998): *Genetische Vielfalt als Ressource: Die Regelung ihrer Nutzung.* Baden-Baden.

Hennicke, Peter and Müller, Michael (2005): *Weltmacht Energie.* Stuttgart.

Hennicke, Peter and Seifried, Dieter (2000): *Das Einsparkraftwerk*. Basle, Berlin.

Hillemanns, Carolin F. (2003): 'UN Norms on the Responsibility of Transnational Corporations and other Business Enterprises with regard to Human Rights', *German Law Journal* 4, 10: 1065–80.

Hindu Business Line (2003): 'Sterlite to Set Up Bauxite Mining Project in Orissa'. 9. June.

Hines, Colin (2004): *A Global Look to the Local. Replacing Economic Globalisation with Democratic Localisation*. London.

Hoekstra, Arjen Y. (2003): 'Virtual Water Trade between Nations: a Global Mechanism Affecting Regional Water Systems'. *IGBP Global Change Newsletter*, No. 54.

Höffe, Ottfried (1989): *Politische Gerechtigkeit*. Frankfurt/Main.

Hoffmann, Johannes and Gerhard Scherhorn (2002): *Saubere Gewinne*. Freiburg.

Höring, Uwe (2003): *Enttäuschte Hoffnungen: Privatisierungserfahrungen in Manila*. Brot für die Welt. Stuttgart.

Hornborg, Alf (2001): *The Power of the Machine: Global Inequalities of Economy, Technology, and Environment*. Lanham.

Howard, Patricia (2003): 'The Major Importance of "Minor" Resources: Women and Plant Diversity', Gatekeeper Series No. 112. London.

Human Rights Research and Education Centre (n.d.): *Declaration of Human Duties and Responsibilities*. Adopted by a High-Level Group Chaired by Richard J. Goldstone under the Auspices of the City of Valencia and UNESCO, www.cdp-hrc.uottawa.ca/publicat/valencia/ valenc23.html (30.9.2004).

Hummer, Waldemar (2000): 'Internationale nichtstaatliche Organisationen im Zeitalter der Globalisierung-Abgrenzung, Handlungsbefugnisse, Rechtsnatur', in Deutsche Gesellschaft für Völkerrecht: *Völkerrecht und Internationales Privatrecht in einem Sich globalisierenden internationalen System: Auswirkungen der Entstaatlichung transnationaler Rechtsbeziehungen*. Berichte der Deutschen Gesellschaft für Völkerrecht, vol. 26. Heidelberg, pp. 45–199.

Humphreys, Ian (2003): 'Organizational and Growth Trends in Air Transport', in Upham, Paul, Maughan, Janet, Raper, David and Thomas, Callum (eds.), *Towards Sustainable Aviation*. London, pp. 19–35.

Huq, Saleemul (2002): 'The Bonn-Marrakech Agreements on Funding', *Climate Policy* 2, 2–3: 243–6.

IATP (Institute for Agriculture and Trade Policy) (2003): *World Trade Agreement on Agriculture Basics*. Minneapolis/MN: Institute for Agriculture and Trade Policy. WTO Cancun Series, Paper No. 2.

ICAO (International Civil Aviation Organization) (1975–2001): *Civil Aviation Statistics of the World*. *ICAO Statistical Yearbook*. Montreal.

IEA (International Energy Agency) (2006). 'CO_2 Emissions from fuel Combustion. 1971–2004.' Paris

IEA (2004a): *World Energy Outlook 2004*. Paris.

IEA (2004b): *Analysis of the Impact of High Oil Prices on the Global Economy*. Paris.

IEA (2004c): 'On-line Data Services', http://data.iea.org/ieastore/default. asp (30 September 2004).

IEA (2003): *Key World Energy Statistics 2003*. Paris.

IEA (2002): *World Energy Outlook*. Paris.

IEA (1997): CO_2 *Emissions from Fuel Combustion. A New Basis for Computing Emissions of a Major Greenhouse Gas. 1972–1995*. Paris.

IFG (International Forum on Globalization) (ed.) (2002): *Alternatives to Economic Globalization. A Better World Is Possible*. San Francisco.

IFG (2001): *Does Globalization Help the Poor?* San Francisco.

Ignatieff, Michael (2001): *Human Rights as Politics and Idolatry*. Princeton.

IISD (International Institute for Sustainable Development) (2003): 'Special and Differential Treatment', *Trade and Development* Brief No. 2, Canada.

Illich, Ivan (1976): *Limits to Medicine. Medical Nemesis: the Expropriation of Health*, new edn., London.

Ingram, Gregory K. and Liu, Zhi (1997): *Motorization and the Provision of Roads in Countries and Cities*. Policy Research Working Paper 1842, International Bank for Reconstruction and Development. Washington.

International Iron and Steel Institute (2002): *World Steel in Figures 2002*. Brussels.

International Rivers Network (2003): *Human Rights Dammed Off at Three Gorges. An Investigation of Resettlement and Human Rights Problems in the Three Gorges Dam Project*. Berkeley.

IPCC (Intergovernmental Panel on Climate Change) (ed.) (2001a): *Climate Change 2001: the Scientific Basis. Contribution of Working Group I to the Third Assessment Report of the IPCC*. Cambridge.

IPCC (ed.) (2001b): *Climate Change 2001: Impacts, Adaptation and Vulnerability. Contribution of Working Group II to the Third Assessment Report of the IPCC*. Cambridge.

IPCC (1999): *Aviation and the Global Atmosphere*. Cambridge.

James, Clive (2002): *Global Review of Commercialized Transgenic Crops: 2001 Feature: Bt Cotton*. International Service for the Acquisition of Agri-Biotech Applications, ISAAA. Brief No. 26. Philippines.

Jawara, Fatouma and Kwa, Aileen (2003): *Behind the Scenes at the WTO: the Real World of International Trade Negotiations*. London, New York.

Jenner, Gero (2004): 'Und der Haifisch, der hat Zähne ... Die neue deutsche Privilegienpolitik'. Unpublished manuscript.

Jenner, Gero (1997): *Die arbeitsose Gesellschaft. Gefährdet Globalisierung den Wohlstand?* Frankfurt/Main.

Jochem, Eberhardt (2003): 'Energie rationeller nutzen: Zwischen Wissen und Handeln', *Gaia* 1 (2003): 9–14.

Kaiser, Karl, Weizsäcker, Ernst Ulrich von, Bleischwitz, Raimund and Comes, Stefan (1991): *Internationale Klimapolitik. Eine Zwischenbilanz und ein Vorschlag zum Abschluss einer Klimakonvention*. Bonn.

Kapstein, Ethan B. (1999): 'Distributive Justice as an International Public Good: a Historical Perspective', in Kaul, Inge et al. (eds.), *Global Public Goods. International Cooperation in the 21st Century*. New York, pp. 88–115.

Kenworthy, Jeffrey R. (2003): 'Transport Energy Use and Greenhouse Gases in Urban Passenger Transport Systems: a Study of 84 Global Cities'. Paper presented to the Third International Conference of the Regional Government Network for Sustainable Development. Murdoch WA.

Kesselring, Thomas (2003): *Ethik der Entwicklungspolitik. Gerechtigkeit im Zeitalter der Globalisierung*. Munich.

Khor, Martin (2003): *The WTO Agriculture Agreement: Features, Effects, Negotiations, and Suggested Changes*. Penang.

Khosla, Ashok (2003): 'Technological Leapfrogging', *Development Alternatives Newsletter*, 13, 3.

Klare, Michael T. (2000): *Resource Wars. The New Landscape of Global Conflict*, New York.

Knox, Paul, Agnew, John and McCarthy, Linda (2003): *The Geography of the World Economy*, fourth edition. London

Kothari, Ashish et al. (ed.) (1998): *Community and Conservation: Natural Resource Management in South and Central Asia*. New Delhi.

Kothari, Rajni (1993): *Growing Amnesia. An Essay on Poverty and Human Consciousness*. Delhi.

Kozul-Wright, Richard and Rayment, Paul (2004): *Globalization Reloaded: an UNCTAD Perspective*. UNCTAD Discussion Paper No. 167. New York.

KPMG (2002): *KPMG International Survey of Corporate Sustainability Reporting 2002*. De Meern.

Krebs, Angelika (2002): *Arbeit und Liebe. Die philosophischen Grundlagen sozialer Gerechtigkeit*. Frankfurt/Main.

Kuhndt, Michael, Tunçer, Burcu, Andersen, Kristian Snorre and Liedtke, Christa (2003): *Responsible Corporate Governance. An Overview of Trends, Initiatives and State-of-the-Art Elements*. Wuppertal Paper No. 139. Wuppertal.

Kuppe, René (2002): 'Indigene Völker, Ressourcen und traditionelles Wissen', in Brand, Ulrich and Kalcsics, Monika (eds.), *Wem gehört die Natur? Konflikte um genetische Ressourcen in Lateinamerika*. Frankfurt/Main, pp. 112–33.

Kürschner-Pelkmann, Frank (2003): *Flaschenwasser – der Markt boomt!* Stuttgart.

La Rovere, Emilio L., de Macedo, Laura V. and Baumert, Kevin A. (2002): 'The Brazilian Proposal on Relative Responsibility for Global Warming', in Baumert, Kevin, Blanchard, Odile, Llosa, S. and Perkaus, J. F. (eds.), *Building on the Kyoto Protocol: Options for Protecting the Climate*. Washington, pp. 157–74.

Lammi, Harri and Tynkkynen, Oras (2001): *The Whole Climate. Climate Equity and its Implications for the North*. Turku.

Landes, David S. (1998): *The Wealth and Poverty of Nations*. London.

Lane, Robert E. (2000): *The Loss of Happiness in Market Democracies*. New Haven.

Larrain, Sara (2001): *The Dignity Line as an Indicator of Socioenvironmental Sustainability: Advances from the Concept of Minimum Life towards the Concept of a Dignified Life*. Instituto de Política Ecológica. Santiago.

Lasén Díaz, Carolina (2005): *Intellectual Property Rights and Biological Resources: an Overview of Key Issues and Current Debates*. Wuppertal Paper No. 151. Wuppertal.

Latouche, Serge (2004): *Die Unvernunft der ökonomischen Vernunft*. Zurich, Berlin.

Le Monde Diplomatique (2003): *Atlas der Globalisierung*. Berlin.

Linz, Manfred (2004): *Weder Mangel noch Übermass. Über Suffizienz und Suffizienz-forschung.* Wuppertal Paper No. 145. Wuppertal.

Llorente, Marie and Zerah, Marie Helene (2003): 'The Urban Water Sector: Formal versus Informal Suppliers in India', *Urban India* 12, 1. New Delhi.

Lovins, Amory and Hennicke, Peter (1999): *Voller Energie.* Frankfurt/Main.

Lutzenhiser, Loren and Hackett, Bruce (1993): 'Social Stratification and Environmental Degradation: Understanding Household CO_2 Production', in Special Issue on the Environment, *Social Problems* 40, 1: 50–73.

Madeley, John (2001): *Crops and Robbers.* ActionAid.

Madeley, John (2000): *Hungry for Trade.* London.

Mani, Muthukumara and Wheeler, David (1997): *In Search of Pollution Havens? Dirty Industry in the World Economy, 1960–1995.* World Bank Research Working Papers: Poverty, Environment and Growth, No. 16. Washington.

Martens, Jens (2004): *Precarious Partnerships: Six Problems of the Global Compact between Business and the UN.* New York.

Martinez-Alier, Juan (2002): *The Environmentalism of the Poor: a Study of Ecological Conflicts and Valuation.* Cheltenham.

Martinez-Alier, Juan, Simms, Andrew and Rjinhout, Leida (2003): 'Poverty, Development and Ecological Debt', in *Deuda Ecológica.* www.deudaecologica.org/a_poverty.html (30 September 2004).

Mason, Melanie (1997): 'A Look behind Trend Data in Industrialization: the Role of Transnational Corporations and Environmental Impacts', *Global Environmental Change* 7: 113–27.

Mayer, Claudia, Frein, Michael and Reichert, Tobias (2002): *Globale Handelspolitik – Motor oder Bremse nachhaltiger Entwicklung?* Bonn.

Mazhar, Farhad and Akhter, Farida (2000): *Uncultivated Food.* Dhaka: UBINING.

McAfee, Kathrin (1998): 'Rettung oder Ausverkauf der Natur. Biologische Vielfalt oder grüne Modernisierung', in Flitner, Michael et al. (eds.), *Konfliktfeld Natur: Biologische Ressourcen und globale Politik.* Opladen, pp. 119–42.

McNeill, John (2003): *Blue Planet. Die Geschichte der Umwelt im 20. Jahrhundert.* Frankfurt/Main.

Meadows, Donella H., Meadows, Dennis L., Zahn, Erich K. O. and Milling, Peter (1972): *Limits to Growth: a Report for the Club of Rome's Project on the Predicament of Mankind.* New York.

Mehta, Lyla and Winiwarter, Verena (1996): *Stoffwechsel in einem indischen Dorf. Fallstudie Merkar.* Interuniversitäres Institut für Interdisziplinäre Forschung und Fortbildung – Abteilung Soziale ökologie. Vienna.

Menzel, Ulrich (1998): *Globalisierung versus Fragmentierung.* Frankfurt/Main.

Messner, Dirk (2001): 'Kooperative Weltmacht. Die Zukunft der Europäischen Union in der neuen Weltpolitik', *Politik und Gesellschaft* 1: 23–39.

Messner, Dirk and Nuscheler, Franz (eds.) (1996): *Weltkonferenzen und Weltberichte. Ein Wegweiser durch die internationale Diskussion.* Institut für Entwicklung und Frieden. Bonn.

Meyer, Aubrey (2000): *Contraction and Convergence. A Global Solution to Climate Change.* Totnes.

Meyer, William H. (2003): 'Activism and Research on TNCs and Human Rights: Building a New International Normative Regime', in Frynas, George and Pegg, Scott: *Transnational Corporations and Human Rights*. Basingstoke, New York.

Meyer, William H. (1998): *Human Rights and International Political Economy in Third World Nations: Multinational Corporations, Foreign Aid and Repression*. Westport.

Meyer-Abich, Klaus Michael (1991): *Wege zum Frieden mit der Natur. Praktische Naturphilosophie für die Umweltpolitik*. Munich.

Meyer-Ladewig, Jens (2003): *EMRK: Konvention zum Schutz der Menschenrechte und der Grundfreiheiten*. Baden-Baden.

MHR (2003): *Beef Meat: World Consumption per Head and per Country 1994–2002*. www.mhr-viandes.com/en/docu/docu/d0000358.htm (30 September 2004).

Milanovic, Branko (2003): 'The Two Faces of Globalization: against Globalization as We Know It', *World Development* 31, 4: 667–83.

Milanovic, Branko (2002): *Worlds Apart: International and World Inequality 1950–2000*. Washington.

Miller, David (2004): 'National Responsibility and International Justice', in Chatterjee, D. (ed.), *The Ethics of Assistance: Morality and the Distant Needy*. Cambridge.

Mitchell, Lawrence E. (2002): *Corporate Irresponsibility: America's Newest Export*. New Haven.

Mohan, Dinesh and Tiwari, Geetam (2000): *Sustainable Transport Systems: Linkages between Environmental Issues, Public Transport, Non-Motorised Transport and Safety*. Transportation Research and Injury Prevention Programme, Indian Institute of Technology. Delhi.

Moll, Stephan (1996): 'Ernährungsbilanz privater Haushalte und deren Verknüpfung mit physischen Input-Output-Tabellen. Abschlussbericht eines Werkvertrages für das Statistische Bundesamt'. Wiesbaden.

Monbiot, George (2003): *The Age of Consent. Manifesto for a New World Order*. London.

Moser, Michael, Prentice, Crawford and Frazier, Scott (1996): 'A Global Overview of Wetland Loss and Degradation', in *Proceedings of the 6th Meeting of the Conference of Contracting Parties of the Ramsar Convention*, vol. 10, March.

Müller-Plantenberg, Urs (2002): 'Rawls weltweit', in Gabbert, K., Gabbert, W., Goedeking, U. et al. (eds.), *Jahrbuch Lateinamerika. Analysen und Berichte*. Münster.

Muradian, Roldan, O'Connor, Martin and Martinez-Alier, Joan (2002): 'Embodied Pollution in Trade: Estimating the Environmental Load Displacement of Industrialised Countries', *Ecological Economics* 41: 51–67.

MWV (Mineralölwirtschaftsverband) (2004): Personal communication with Dr Mayer Bukow, MWV, Hamburg. 19 February 2004.

Myers, Norman and Kent, Jennifer (2004): *The New Consumers. The Influence of Affluence on the Environment*. Washington.

Myers, Norman and Kent, Jennifer (2003): 'New Consumers: the Influence of Affluence on the Environment', *PNAS* 8, 100: 4963–8.

Narain, Sunita (2003): Editorial in *Down to Earth*, 15 December.

NATO (1999): *The Alliance's Strategic Concept*. Brussels.

Natural Resources Canada (2002): *World Non-Ferrous Metal Statistics*, 22 November. www.nrcan.gc.ca/mms/efab/mmsd/wnf/wnfstats.htm (30 September 2004).

Neumann, Jan (2001): *Die Koordination des WTO-Rechts mit anderen völkerrechtlichen Ordnungen. Konflikte des Materiellen Rechts und Konkurrenzen der Streitbeilegung*. Berlin.

Neumayer, Eric (1999): *Weak versus Strong Sustainability. Exploring the Limits of Two Opposing Paradigms*. Cheltenham.

Nickel, Herbert J. (1973): *Unterentwicklung und Marginalität in Lateinamerika. Einführung und Bibliographie zu einem Lateinamerikanischen Thema*. Munich.

Nima Hunter Inc. (2003): *The Business of Business – Managing Corporate Social Responsibility: What Business Leaders Are Saying and Doing 2002–2007. Executive Overview*. Nima Hunter Inc. and Ethical Corporation Magazine. London.

Normand, Roger (2000): *Separate and Unequal: Trade and Human Rights Regimes. Background Paper for the Human Development Report 2000*. New York.

Nun, José et al. (1968): La marginalidad en América Latina. Buenos Aires.

Nuscheler, Franz (2001): *Multilateralismus vs. Unilateralismus. Kooperation vs. Hegemonie in den transatlantischen Beziehungen*. Stiftung Entwicklung und Frieden, Policy Paper 16. Bonn.

Nussbaum, Martha C. (1996): *For Love of Country: Debating the Limits of Patriotism*. Boston.

OAU (Organization of African Unity) (2000): *African Model Legislation for the Protection of the Rights of Local Communities, Farmers and Breeders, and for the Regulation of Access to Biological Resources*. Lagos. http://www.grain.org/docs/oua-modellaw-2000-en.pdf.

Oberthür, Sebastian and Ott, Hermann E. (1999): 'The Kyoto Protocol', *International Climate Policy for the 21st Century*. Berlin.

OECD (Organization for Economic Cooperation and Development) (2004): *OECD Guidelines for Multinational Enterprises: Frequently Asked Questions*. http://www.oecd.org.

Öko-Institut (2004): *Gentechnik-Nachrichten* No. 49. Berlin.

Öko-Institut (2002): *Gentechnik-Nachrichten* Nos 33/34. Berlin.

Oliviera, Luciana Correa (1998): *Energias Não-convençionais no Brasil e a Agenda am Biental do Banco Mundial*. Monografia de graducão em Ciencias Economicas. No place.

O'Neill, Onora (2000): *Bounds of Justice*. Cambridge.

Orlitzky, Marc, Schmidt, Frank L. and Rynes, Sara L. (2003): *Corporate Social and Financial Performance: a Meta-analysis*. London.

Ott, Hermann E., Winkler, Harald, Brouns, Bernd et al. (2004): *South–North Dialogue on Equity in the Greenhouse. A Proposal for an Adequate and Equitable Global Climate Agreement*. Eschborn. http://www.wuperinst.org/download/io85_proposal.pdf.

Pabst, Sabine, Mankame, Ashwini and Purohit, Preeti (eds.) (2004): *Investigating some Alleged Violations of the Human Right to Water in India.* Heidelberg.

Parikh, Jyoti (2003): 'Consumption Patterns: Economic and Demographic Change', in Munn, Ted and Douglas, Ian (eds.), *Encyclopedia of Global Environmental Change*, vol. 3. Chippenham, Wiltshire.

Parnreiter, Christoph (1999): 'Migration: Symbol, Folge und Triebkraft von globaler Integration. Erfahrungen aus Zentralamerika', in Parnreiter, Christoph et al. (eds.), *Globalisierung und Peripherie. Umstrukturierung in Lateinamerika, Afrika und Asien.* Frankfurt/Main, pp. 129–49.

Parry, Martin et al. (2001): 'Millions at Risk: Defining Critical Climate Change Threats and Targets', *Global Environmental Change* 11: 181–3.

Patnaik, Utsa (2003): *Global Capitalism, Deflation and Agrarian Crisis in Developing Countries.* Social Policy and Development Programme Paper 15. Geneva.

Pauli, Gunter (1999): *UpCycling. Wirtschaften nach dem Vorbild der Natur für mehr Arbeitsplätze und eine saubere Umwelt.* Munich.

Paulitsch, Katharina, Burdick, Bernhard and Baedeker, Carolin (2004): *Am Beispiel Baumwolle: Flachennutzungskonkurrenz durch exportorientierte Landwirtschaft.* Wuppertal Paper No. 148. Wuppertal.

Perna, Tonino (1998): *Fair Trade. Lasfida etica al mercato mondiale.* Turin.

Pernice, Ingolf (2003): 'Begründung und Konsolidierung der Europäischen Gemeinschaft als Rechtsgemeinschaft', in Zuleeg, Manfred (ed.), *Der Beitrag Walter Hallsteins zur Zukunft Europas, Referate zu Ehren von Walter Hallstein.* Baden-Baden, pp. 56–70.

Petersen, Rudolf and Schallaböck, Karl-Otto (1995): *Mobilität für morgen. Chancen einer zukunftsfähigen Verkehrspolitik.* Basle, Berlin.

Petersmann, Ernst-Ulrich (2003): *Theories of Justice, Human Rights and the Constitution of International Markets.* European University Institute Working Paper, Law, No. 2003/17. Florence.

Pingali, Prabhu and Traxler, Greg (2002): 'Changing Focus of Agricultural Research: Will the Poor Benefit from Biotechnology and Privatization Trends?', *Food Policy* 27.

Pogge, Thomas (2003): 'Ein Dollar pro Tag. Von den Schwierigkeiten, die Weltarmut zu Berechnen', *Neue Züricher Zeitung* 41.

Pogge, Thomas (2002): *World Poverty and Human Rights.* Cambridge.

Polanyi, Karl (1968): *Primitive, Modern and Archaic Economies: Essays of Karl Polanyi*, ed. by George Dalton. Boston.

Pomeranz, Kenneth (2002): 'Continuities and Discontinuities in Global Development. Lessons from the New East/West Comparisons', *World Economics* 3, 4: 73–86.

Pomeranz, Kenneth (2000): *The Great Divergence: China, Europe, and the Making of the Modern World Economy.* Princeton.

Porter, Gareth (1999): 'Trade Competition and Pollution Standards: "Race to the Bottom" or "Stuck at the Bottom"', *Journal of Environment and Development* 8, 2: 133–51.

Posey, Darrel Addison (1999): 'Introduction: Culture and Nature – The Inextricable Link', in UNEP (ed.), *Cultural and Spiritual Values of Biodiversity. A*

Complementary Contribution to the Global Biodiversity Assessment. Nairobi, pp. 3–18.

Postel, Sandra, Daily, Gretchen and Ehrlich, Paul (1996): 'Human Appropriation of Renewable Freshwater', *Science* 271: 785–8.

Pretty, Jules and Hine, Rachel (2001): 'Reducing Food Poverty with Sustainable Agriculture: a Summary of New Evidence', in Brot für die Welt and Greenpeace (eds.), *Ernährung sichern: Nachhaltige Landwirtschaft – eine Perspektive aus dem Süden.* Frankfurt/Main.

Preuss, Ulrich K. (1998): 'Citizenship in the European Union: a Paradigm for Transnational Democracy?', in Archibugi, Daniele, Held, David and Kähler, Martin (eds.), *Re-imagining Political Community: Studies in Cosmopolitan Democracy,* Cambridge, pp. 138–51.

Quiroz, Consuelo (1994): 'Biodiversity, Indigenous Knowledge, Gender and Intellectual Property Rights', *Indigenous Knowledge and Development Monitor.* The Hague.

Radermacher, Franz Josef (2002): *Balance oder Zerstörung. Ökosoziale Marktwirtschaft als Schlüssel zu einer weitweiten nachhaltigen Entwicklung.* Vienna.

Radermacher, Franz Josef et al. (2004): *Global Marshall Plan: a Planetary Contract.* Hamburg.

Radkau, Joachim (2000): *Natur und Macht. Eine Weltgeschichte der Umwelt.* Munich.

Raina, Vinod et al. (1999): *The Dispossessed: Victims of Development in Asia.* Hong Kong.

Ravallion, Martin (2003): *The Debate on Globalization, Poverty and Inequality: Why Measurement Matters.* World Bank Development Research Group Working Paper 3038.

Ravallion, Martin and Chen, Shaohua (2004): *How Have the World's Poorest Fared since the Early 1980s?* Washington.

Rawls, John (1999): *The Law of Peoples.* Cambridge.

Rawls, John (1972): *A Theory of Justice,* Oxford.

Reddy, Amulya K. N. (2000): 'Energy and Social Issues', in UNDP 2000, *World Energy Assessments. Energy and the Challenge of Sustainability.* New York.

Reinicke, Wolfgang H., Deng, Francis, Witte, Jan Martin and Benner, Thorsten (2000): *Critical Choices: the United Nations, Networks, and the Future of Global Governance.* Ottawa.

Ribeiro, Silvia (2002): 'Biopiraterie und geistiges Eigentum – Zur Privatisierung von gemeinschaftlichen Bereichen', in Görg, Christoph and Brand, Ulrich: *Mythen globalen Umweltmanagements: Rio+10 und die Sackgassen nachhaltiger Entwicklung.* Münster.

Richter, Judith (2002): *Codes in Context: TNC Regulation in an Era of Dialogues and Partnership.* The Corner House, Briefing 26. Dorset.

Rifkin, Jeremy (2004): *European Dream: How Europe's Vision of the Future Is Quietly Eclipsing the American Dream.* New York.

Rist, Gilbert (1996): *The History of Development: from Western Origins to Global Faith.* London.

Ritsert, Jürgen (1997): *Gerechtigkeit und Gleichheit.* Münster.

Ritter, Wigand (1994): *Welthandel: Geographische Strukturen und Umbrüche im internationalen Warenaustausch*. Darmstadt.

Rodrik, Dani (2001): *The Global Governance of Trade as if Development Really Mattered*. Background Paper to the UNDP Trade and Human Development Project. New York.

Roozen, Nico and van der Hoff, Frans (2003): *Max Havelaar. L'avventura del commercio equo e solidale*. Milan.

Roy, Arundathi (1999): 'The Greater Common Good'. http://www. narmada. org.

Sachs, Wolfgang (2003): *Environment and Human Rights*. Wuppertal Paper No. 137. Wuppertal.

Sachs, Wolfgang (1998): *Planet Dialectics: Explorations in Environment and Development*. London.

Sachs, Wolfgang (1992): *The Development Dictionary: a Guide to Knowledge as Power*. London.

Sachs, Wolfgang et al. (2002): *The Jo'burg Memo. Fairness in a Fragile World. Memorandum for the World Summit on Sustainable Development*. Published by the Heinrich Böll Stiftung. Berlin. (www.joburgmemo.org)

Sahai, Suman and Rahman, Shakeelur (2003): 'Performance of Bt Cotton – Data from First Commercial Crop', *Economic and Political Weekly* 38.

Sala-I-Martin, Xavier (2002): *The World Distribution of Income (estimated from individual country estimations)*. Cambridge.

Salameh, Mamdouh G. (2004): 'How Realistic are Opec's Proven Oil Reserves?', *Petroleum Review*, August: 26–29.

Santarius, Tilman, Dalkmann, Holger, Steigenberger, Markus and Vogelpohl, Karin (2003): *Balancing Trade and Environment. An Ecological Reform of the WTO as a Challenge in Sustainable Global Governance*. Wuppertal Paper No. 133e. Wuppertal.

Sassen, Saskia (1998): *Globalization and Its Discontents*. New York.

Sassen, Saskia (1996): *Losing Control? Sovereignty in an Age of Globalization*. New York.

Schäfer, Christine, Gutiérrez, Martha, Klemp, Ludgera, Henne, Gudrun and Müller, Alice (2002): *The Convention on Biological Diversity: Ensuring Gender-Sensitive Implementation*. Eschborn. http://www.gtz.de/biodiv/download/gender_bro.pdf.

Schaik, L. van and Egenhofer, C. (2003): *Reform of the EU Institutions: Implications for the EU's Performance in Climate Negotiations*. CEPS Policy Brief No. 40. Brussels.

Scheer, Hermann (2003): 'IRENA – Ein Weltprojekt im Spannungsfeld zwischen Uni- und Multilateralismus', *Solarzeitalter* 15, 2: 2–4.

Scheer, Hermann (1999): *Solar Economy: Renewable Energy for a Sustainable Global Future*. London.

Scheffler, Samuel (2001): *Boundaries and Allegiances: Problems of Justice and Responsibility in Liberal Thought*. Oxford.

Schindler, Jörg and Zittel, Werner (2000a): *Fossile Energiereserven (nur Erdöl und*

Erdgas) und mögliche Versorgungsengpasse aus Europäischer Perspektive. Endbericht der Vorstudie im Auftrag des Deutschen Bundestages, des Ausschusses für Bildung, Technik und Technikfolgenabschätzung. Vorgelegt dem Büro für Technikfolgenabschätzung (TAB).

Schindler, Jörg and Zittel, Werner (2000b): *Weltweite Entwicklung der Energienachfrage und der Ressourcenverfügbarkeit. Schriftliche Stellungnahme zur öffentlichen Anhörung von Sachverständigen durch die Enquete Kommission des Dt. Bundestages 'Nachhaltige Energieversorgung unter den Bedingungen der Globalisierung und der Liberalisierung'.* Ottobrunn.

Schmid, Wilhelm (1998): *Philosophie der Lebenskunst: eine Grundlegung.* Frankfurt/ Main.

Schmidt-Bleek, Friedrich (1998): *Das MIPS-Konzept: weniger Naturverbrauch – mehr Lebensqualität durch Faktor 10.* Munich.

Schmidt-Bleek, Friedrich (1993): *Wieviel Umwelt braucht der Mensch? MIPS – das Mass für ökologisches Wirtschaften.* Berlin, Basle, Boston.

Scholz, Fred (2003): *Ein neues Entwicklungsparadigma für die globalisierte Welt? Positionspapier für den Workshop des Beirates der Stiftung Entwicklung und Frieden am 24/25.1.* Zentrum für Entwicklungsländerforschung, FU Berlin.

Scholz, Fred (2002): 'Die Theorie der "fragmentierten Entwicklung"', *Geographische Rundschau,* 54, 10: 6–11.

Schütz, Helmut, Moll, Stephan and Bringezu, Stefan (2003): *Globalization and the Shifting Environmental Burden Material Trade Flows of the European Union.* Wuppertal Paper No. 134e. Wuppertal.

Schweizer, Gerhard (2004): *Metropole Moloch Mythos. Eine Reise durch die Megastädte Indiens.* Stuttgart.

Schweizer, Gerhard (1987): *Zeitbombe Stadt.* Stuttgart.

Segal, Jerome M. (1999): *Graceful Simplicity: Towards a Philosophy and Politics of Simple Living.* New York.

Sen, Amartya (1999): *Development as Freedom.* New York.

Senti, Richard (2001): *Die WTO auf dem Weg nach Katar. Anstehende Probleme – neue Herausforderungen.* HWWA Discussion Paper No. 135. Hamburg.

Sharma, Devindar (2003): 'Politics of Diversity and Food Security', in Kothari, Smitu, Ahmad, Imtiaz and Reifeld, Helmut (eds.), *The Value of Nature. Ecological Politics in India.* Delhi, pp. 170–90.

Shiva, Vandana (2002): *Biopiraterie. Kolonialismus des 21. Jahrhunderts. Eine Einführung.* Münster.

Shiva, Vandana (1992): 'Resources', in Sachs, Wolfgang (ed.), *The Development Dictionary: a Guide to Knowledge as Power.* London.

Shue, Henry (1999): 'Global Environment and International Inequality', *International Affairs* 75, 3: 531–45.

Shue, Henry (1980): *Basic Rights. Subsistence, Affluence and US Foreign Policy.* Princeton.

Siddiqi, Toufiq A. (1995): 'Energy Inequities within Developing Countries: an Important Concern in the Global Environmental Change Debate', *Global Environmental Change* 5, 5: 447–54.

Slaughter, Anne-Marie (2004): *A New World Order*. Princeton.

Smil, Vaclav and Mao, Yushi (1998): *The Economic Costs of China's Environmental Degradation*. Cambridge.

Smith, Jackie, Bolyard, Melissa and Ippolito, Anna (1999): 'Human Rights and the Global Economy: a Response to Meyer', *Human Rights Quarterly* 21, 1: 207–19.

Spar, Debora L. (1998a): 'Multinational Cooperations and Human Rights: a Case of Strange Bedfellows', *Human Rights Interest Group Newsletter*, American Society of International Law 8, 1: 13–16.

Spar, Debora L. (1998b): 'The Spotlight and the Bottom Line: How Multinationals Export Human Rights', *Foreign Affairs* 77, 2: 7–12.

Sprenger, Rolf-Ulrich (1997): 'Globalisation, Employment, and Environment', in *OECD Proceedings, Globalisation, and Environment*, OECD, Paris, pp. 315–66.

SRU (Der Rat von Sachverständigen für Umweltfragen) (1994): *Umweltgutachten 1994 – für eine dauerhaft-umweltgerechte Entwicklung*. Bundestags-Drucksache 12/6995. Bonn.

Statistics Finland (2006), World in figures. www.stat.fi/tup/maanum/index_en.html.

Steffen, Will et al. (2004): *Global Change and the Earth System: a Planet under Pressure*. Berlin.

Steger, Sören (2005): *Der Flächenrucksack des europäischen Aussenhandels mit Agrargütern*. Wuppertal Paper No. 152. Wuppertal.

Steinberg, Richard H. (2002): 'In the Shadow of Law or Power? Consensus-based Bargaining and Outcomes in the GATT/WTO', *International Organization* 6, 2: 339–74.

Steiner, Henry J. and Alston, Philip (eds.) (1996): *International Human Rights in Context: Law, Politics, Morals*. Oxford.

Stevens, Christopher (2003): *From Doha to Cancun: Special and Differential Treatment*. Institute of Development Studies.

Stiftung Entwicklung und Frieden (2001): *Globale Trends 2002*. Frankfurt/Main.

Stiglitz, Joseph E. (2002): *The Roaring Nineties. Why We're Paying the Price for the Greediest Decade in History*, New York.

Streck, Charlotte (2002): 'Global Public Policy Networks as Coalitions for Change', in Esty, Ivanova (ed.), *Global Environmental Governance. Options and Opportunities*. New Haven.

Tarasofsky, Richard G. (1999): 'The WTO Committee on Trade and Environment: Is It Making a Difference?', in *Max Planck Yearbook of United Nations Law*, vol. 3: 471–88.

Taylor, Charles (1992): *Multiculturalism and the 'Politics of Recognition'*. Princeton.

Taylor, Peter J. (2003): 'The State as Container: Territoriality in the Modern World-System', in Brenner, Neil et al. (eds.), *State/Space: A Reader*. Oxford, pp. 101–13.

Thomas, Frieder and Vögel, Rudolf (1993): *Gute Argumente. Ökologische Landwirtschaft*. Munich.

Thrupp, Lori Ann (1995): *Bittersweet Harvest for Global Supermarkets. Challenges in Latin America's Agricultural Export Boom*. Washington.

Tripathi, Ruchi (2001): 'Food Patenting – a Threat to Food Security'. Paper presented at the Regional Programme on Farmers' Rights to Livelihood. ActionAid, Kathmandu, 12–13 July.

Turnbull, Shann (2002): *A New Way to Govern – Organisations and Society after Enron*. New Economics Foundation.

US Department of the Interior/US Geological Survey (2004): *Mineral Commodity Summaries 2004*. Washington. http://minerals.usgs.gov/minerals/pubs/mcs/ 2004/mcs 2004.pdf (30 September 2004).

UNCED (United Nations Conference on Environment and Development) (1992): 'Rio-Erklärung über Umwelt und Entwicklung'. www.un.org/ Depts/german/conf/agenda21/rio.pdf (30 September 2004).

UNCTAD (United Nations Conference on Trade and Development) (2003): *World Investment Report 2003. FDI Policies for Development: National and International Perspectives*. New York.

UNCTAD (1997): *Trade and Development Report, 1997. Globalization, Distribution and Growth*. New York, Geneva.

UNDP (United Nations Development Programme) (2005), Human Development Report 2005. International cooperation at a crossroads. Aid, trade and security in an unequal world. New York.

UNDP (2004): *Human Development Report 2004. Cultural Liberty in Today's Diverse World*. New York.

UNDP (2003): *Making Global Trade Work for People*. London.

UNDP (2000): *Human Development Report*. New York.

UNDP/TCDC (United Nations Development Programme/Technical Cooperation Among Developing Countries) (2001): *Sharing Innovative Experiences*, vol. 5, *Examples of Successful Initiatives in Agriculture and Rural Development in the South*. Rome.

UNDSD (United Nations Department of Economic and Social Affairs: Division for Sustainable Development) (2002): *Johannesburg Declaration on Sustainable Development*.

UNECE (United Nations Economic Commission for Europe) (2003): *State of Europe's Forests 2003*. Vienna.

UNECE (1998): *Convention on Access to Information, Public Participation in Decision-Making and Access to Justice in Environmental Matters done at Aarhus, Denmark, on 25 June 1998*. http://www.unece.org/env/pp/documents/cep43e.pdf.

UNEP (United Nations Environment Programme) (2002): *Global Environmental Outlook 3*. London.

UNEP (2000): *Global Environment Outlook 2000*. Nairobi.

UNEP (1999): *Cultural and Spiritual Values of Biodiversity. A Complementary Contribution to the Global Biodiversity Assessment*. Nairobi.

UNESCO (United Nations Educational, Scientific and Cultural Organization) (2003): *Water for People, Water for Life. The United Nations World Water Development Report*. Barcelona.

UNFCCC (United Nations Framework Convention on Climate Change) (2001): *Report of the Conference of the Parties on Its Seventh Session. Held at Marrakesh from*

264   *Fair Future*

29 October to 10 November 2001. Addendum. Part Two: Action Taken by the Conference of the Parties. FCCC/CP/200l/13/Add.2. Bonn.

UNFCCC (1998): *Kyoto Protocol to the United Nations Framework Convention on Climate Change.* FCCC/CP/1997/7/Add.1. Bonn.

UNFCCC (1997): *Proposed Elements of a Protocol to the UN FCCC. Presented by Brazil in Response to the Berlin Mandate.* FCCC/AGBM/1997/MISC.1/Add.3. Bonn.

UNHCHR (United Nations High Commissioner on Human Rights) (2001): *United Nations Guide for Indigenous People.* Geneva. http://www.unhchr.ch/html/racism/oo-indigenousguide.html.

United Nations Population Division (2002): *World Population Prospects: the 2002 Revision.* New York.

USGS (United States Geological Survey) (2000): *World Petroleum Assessment 2000.* Denver.

USGS (1995): *Results of Groundwater, Surfacewater, and Waterquality Monitoring. Black Mesa Area. Northeastern Arizona 1992–93.* Water Resources Investigations Report 95–4156. Tucson.

Vajpayee, Shri Atal Bihari (2002): *Speech at the High Level Segment of the Eighth Session of Conference of the Parties to the UN Framework Convention on Climate Change. 30 October 2002.* Manuscript. New Delhi.

VDA (Verband der Deutschen Automobilindustrie) (several years): *Tatsachen und Zahlen aus der Verkehrswirtschaft. Mehrere Jahrgänge.* Frankfurt/Main.

Venetoulis, Jason, Chazan, Dahlia and Gaudet, Christopher (2004): *Ecological Footprint of Nations 2004.* Oakland.

Vogel, David (2000): 'Environmental Regulation and Economic Integration', *Journal of International Economic Law*, pp. 265–79.

Wackernagel, Mathis et al. (2002): 'Tracking the Ecological Overshoot of the Human Economy', in *Proceedings of the National Academy of Sciences* 99: 9266–71.

Wackernagel, Mathis and Rees, William (1997): *Unser ökologischer Fussabdruck: Wie der Mensch Einfluss auf die Umwelt nimmt.* Basle.

Waddell, Steve (2003): *The Climate Action Network: Civil Society Tackling Global Negotiations.* www.gan-net.net/about/examples.html (30 September 2004).

Wade, Robert Hunter (2003): 'The Disturbing Rise in Poverty and Inequality: Is It All a Big Lie?', in Held, David and Koenig-Archibugi, Mathias (eds.), *Taming Globalization. Frontiers of Governance.* Padstow.

Wal-Mart (2002): *Annual Report 2002.* http://www.walmartstores.com/Files/2002_annualreport.pdf.

Walk, Heike and Brunnengräber, Achim (2000): *Die Globalisierungswächter. NGOs und Ihre Transnationalen Netze im Konfliktfeld Klima.* Münster.

Walzer, Michael (1983): *Spheres of Justice. A Defence of Pluralism and Equality.* Oxford.

WBGU (Wissenschaftlicher Beirat der Bundesregierung globale Umweltveränderungen) (2004): *Renewable Energies for Sustainable Development. Impulses for Renewables 2004.* Berlin.

WBGU (2003a): *Sondergutachten 2003: Über Kyoto hinaus denken – Klimaschutz-*

strategien für das 21 Jahrhundert. Berlin.

WBGU (2003b): *Hauptgutachten 2003: Welt im Wandel: Energiewende zur Nachhaltigkeit*. Berlin.

WBGU (2002): *Nutzungsentgelte für globale Gemeinschaftsgüter*. Policy Paper 2. Berlin.

WCD (World Commission on Dams) (2000): *Dams and Development*. London.

WCED (World Commission on Environment and Development) (1987) *Our Common Future*. Oxford.

WCSDG (World Commission on the Social Dimension of Globalization) (2004): *A Fair Globalization: Creating Opportunities for All*. Geneva.

Weber, Christoph and Perrels, Adriaan (2000): 'Modelling Lifestyle Effects on Energy Demand and Related Emissions', *Energy Policy* 28: 549–66.

WEF (World Economic Forum) (2002): *Responding to the Leadership Challenges: Findings of a CEO Survey on Global Corporate Citizenship*.

Weiss, Norman (2002): 'Transnationale Unternehmen – Weltweite Standards? Eine Zwischenbilanz des Global Compact', *MenschenRechtsMagazin (MRM)* 2: 86–9.

Weizsäcker, Ernst Ulrich von, Lovins, Amory and Lovins, Hunter (1997): *Factor Four: Doubling Wealth, Halving Resource Use. The New Report to the Club of Rome*. London.

Werner, Helmut (1989): *Latein. Lexikon der lateinischen Sprache. Lateinisch–Deutsch*. Darmstadt.

Whalley, John (1999): *Special and Differential Treatment in the Millennium Round*. CSGR Working Paper No. 30. Warwick.

Whitelegg, John (2003): 'The Case for "No Growth"', in Upham, Paul, Maughan, Janet, Raper, David and Thomas, Callum (eds.), *Towards Sustainable Aviation*. London, pp. 19–35.

Whitelegg, John and Haq, Gary (eds.) (2003): *The Earthscan Reader on World Transport Policy and Practice*. London.

Whiteley, Peter and Masayesva, Vernon (1998): 'The Use and Abuse of Aquifers. Can the Hopi Indians Survive Multinational Mining?', in Donahue, John M., Johnston, Barbara Rose (eds.), *Water, Culture and Power. Local Struggles in a Global Context*. Washington, pp. 9–35.

Wichterich, Christa (2000): *The Globalized Woman. Report from a Future of Inequality*. Reinbek.

Windfuhr, Michael (2003): *Das WTO-Agrarabkommen und das Recht auf Nahrung. Zusammenhänge, Konflikte, Menschenrechtsverletzungen*. FoodFirst Informations- und Aktionsnetzwerk, factsheet series 'Ernährung sichern – Handel und Menschenrechte'. Heidelberg.

Windfuhr, Michael (1993): 'Transnationale Unternehmen in der Dritten Welt: Entwicklungshemmnis oder Entwicklungshelfer?', *Nord–Süd Aktuell* (third quarter): 492–6.

Woodroffe, Jessica (1999): 'Regulating Multinational Corporations in a World of Nation States', in Addo, Michael K. (ed.), *Human Rights Standards and the Responsibility of Transnational Corporations*. The Hague.

World Bank (2006), World Development Indicator Data Query. http://devdata.worldbank.org/data-query.

World Bank (2004): *Global Economic Prospects 2004. Realizing the Development Promise of the Doha Agenda.* Washington.

World Bank (2003): *World Development Indicators 2003.* Washington.

World Bank (2002a): *Globalization, Growth, and Poverty. Building an Inclusive World Economy.* A World Bank Policy Research Report. Washington.

World Bank (2002b): *Global Economic Prospects.* www.worldbank.org/prospects/gep2002 (30 September 2004).

World Bank (2001): *China: Water, Air, and Land.* Washington.

World Energy Council (2001): *Survey of Energy Resources 2001.* London. www.worldenergy.org/wec-geis/publications/reports/ser/overview.asp (30 September 2004).

Wörner, Manfred (1990): *The Future of the Atlantic Alliance.* Speech at the National Defence Institute in Lisbon, 5 November.

WRI (World Resources Institute) (2003): *World Resources 2002–2004. Decisions for the Earth: Balance, Voice, and Power.* Washington.

WRI (2000): *World Resources 2000–2001. People and Ecosystems: the Fraying Web of Life.* Washington.

WRI et al. (2001): *A Watershed in Global Governance?: An Independent Assessment of the World Commission on Dams.* Washington.

WTO (World Trade Organization) (2003): *World Trade Statistics 2003.* Geneva.

WTO (2002a): *Discussion Paper on the Environmental Effects of Services Trade Liberalization. Note by the Secretariat.* WT/CTE/W/218. Geneva.

WTO (2002b): *The Relationship between the TRIPs Agreement and the Convention on Biological Diversity.* IP/C/W/368. Geneva.

WWF (Worldwide Fund for Nature) (2006), Living Planet Report 2006. Gland.

WWF (2004): *Living Planet Report,* Gland.

Wynberg, Rachel (2002): 'Sharing the Crumbs with the San'. http://www.biowatch.org.za/csir-san.htm.

Young, Oran R. and Osherenko, Gail (1995): 'Testing Theories of Regime Formation: Findings from a Large Collaborative Research Project', in Rittberger, Volker (ed.), *Regime Theory and International Relations.* Oxford, pp. 223–51.

Zimmermann, Clovis (2002): 'Das Stadtplanungsmodell von Curitiba', TÓPICOS 2: 26–8.

Index